On Behavior

Also by Karen Pryor

Karen Pryor On Behavior

ESSAYS
&
RESEARCH

Sunshine Books, Inc., North Bend, Washington 98045

Photo Credits

Lizzie Brown, back cover
Jon Lindbergh 334, 350, 368, front cover
National Marine Fisheries Service 134, 144, 299
Omaha Symphony p. 68
Karen Pryor 144, 147, 148, 160, 161, 162, 164, 179, 180, 264, 324
Sea Life Park 2, 30, 52, 106
Ralph Silva, Jr. 297
Bernt Würsig 252
United States Navy 122
United States Tuna Foundation 142

Sunshine Books, 44811 South East 166th St., North Bend, Washington 98045.
Phone (206) 888-3737. FAX (206) 888-9836.

Permission to reprint previously published material will be found in the first footnote for each reprinted chapter.

First edition
First printing. April, 1995

Book design by Typesetter Plus.
Library of Congress Catalog Card Number: 94-67130
ISBN number 0-9624017-1-4

To Jon

Contents

Part One: Hawaii 1963-1972

Part Two: New York 1976-1981

Part Three North Bend, Washington: Riverbend 1981-1985

Part Four North Bend:
Mountain View 1985 to now

Part Five New Worlds 1992 to...

Acknowledgments

Many people had a part in the creation of this book and, of course, in the events here described. My thanks go first to my dear husband, Jon Lindbergh. His support and encouragement made this work possible. I am grateful too for his sound counsel, for our travels, for his photographs, including the cover shot and interior photographs, and also for multiple proofreadings and the creation of the index.

My friend from Hawaii days, Anna Blackwell, was the copy editor. Cal Ebens proofread the galleys. Charlene and Larry Woodward, of Direct Book Service, sparked the idea for this project. Howard Frank and designer Melody Greeves, at Typesetters Plus, worked with us with patience and skill. Our printer, Jeff Wise of Snohomish Publishing, is also our well-named advisor on the mechanics and economics of publishing.

I am thankful to all the publications that permitted the reprinting of previously published essays and articles in *On Behavior*, and also to my collaborators who permitted the republishing of joint efforts: Gale Pryor, Kenneth Norris, Ingrid Shallenberger, and Jon Krueger. Ellie Reese's generous offer to write the foreword was an honor and the result is a pleasure.

Finally, the success of our *Don't Shoot the Dog!* seminars and videos has made many things possible, including this book; and for that we owe thanks to our fellow trainers and entrepreneurs, Gary and Michele Wilkes.

Foreword

By Ellen P. Reese

We had *Skinner for the Classroom*, (Epstein, 1982) and now we have Pryor for the classroom, and the zoo and aquarium, the obedience class and show ring; for parents, preschool teachers, graduate school teachers, veterinarians, health-care practitioners—for just about all of us who want to help others or who need help ourselves. Surely no one writes with more humor or felicity than Karen Pryor. She is one savvy animal trainer and she has enormous respect for both the learner and for her subject matter—a neatly integrated view of both applied behavior analysis and behavioral biology.

On Behavior is a collection of essays and articles about understanding the meaning, or function, of behavior, together with analysis of the events and procedures that change behavior. As she did in her best-selling book, *Don't Shoot the Dog!*, Pryor amplifies the principles of behavior analysis as well as their manifold applications. That is why those academics among us can honorably assign this as a textbook (rather than, say, as enrichment) even as animal trainers will adopt it as their bible, and students will rip off copies from the library, or use this book to reinforce the completion of other readings that may be assigned.

There are 23 chapters, each with an introductory note and a postscript that describes the results of publication; plus an index and a bibliography. The featured players in half of the chapters are whales and dolphins. Four of these chapters (Ch. 1, 9, 16,

18) focus on the physical characteristics, sensory capacities, learning abilities, or social behavior of various species of cetaceans. The import and impact of the other chapters, however, extend well beyond the particular characteristics of these species. Chapter 2, for example, is about the shaping of creative behavior. A companion piece (Ch. 4) analyses the behavior of orchestra conductors who, Pryor contends, would make good dolphin trainers. This estimate is based on the skill with which they establish and maintain stimulus control (the technical name of the procedure that guarantees that the players will both understand and obey the conductor's signals.)

Four of the "dolphin" chapters (3, 7, 19, 21) together with Ch. 22, include descriptions of the misunderstanding and inadvertent mismanagement of behavioral procedures by the public and behavior analysts alike. A familiar example is the ease with which we shape up whining or even temper tantrums in our children. We put polite requests on extinction—perhaps we are busy with Important Matters—and only when the whining or screaming becomes increasingly aversive do we attend to the request. The behavior we don't want to see is established and maintained by positive reinforcement when we finally accede to the demand. Our behavior of giving in is maintained by negative reinforcement, or escape, from the aversive behavior we established in the first place. Pryor provides many examples of these kinds of problems; and she tells us how to prevent them and how to correct them once we recognize the contingencies that are actually in effect.

As a trainer, Pryor has also developed or refined a number of procedures that many academics overlook or never knew: the importance of a conditioned reinforcer; "targeting" the learner's attention; the messages that can be conveyed by the judicious use of mini- and maxi- (jackpot) reinforcers; the subtleties of establishing and then using stimulus control; and a marvelous procedure called "Pony's Choice," in which the learner is sometimes given a signal that he or she, rather than the trainer, gets to decide how to proceed.

Throughout the book, but most specifically in three of the chapters on training, Pryor stresses the power of praise (Ch. 11) and the perils of punishment (Chs. 12, 21). Dolphins differ from most pets and family members in that, no matter how angry or frustrated we get, one *can't* use punishment. One can't strike an animal that just swims away, and, we are told, you can't even yell at them because they don't *care*. Other chapters on training include the contributions of behavioral procedures to the welfare of animals in zoos (Ch. 6) and domestic animals (Chs. 22, 23). Chapter 8 is informative on a number of accounts. It describes the (eventually) successful teaching of Pryor's father, the author Philip Wylie, to dance. We learn that Wylie was "a really rotten dancer" who needed 10 private lessons at the Arthur Murray Dance Studio to learn to tap his foot in time to the music and a further 80 lessons before he was allowed to join the other students and their teachers on the main dance floor. But the story has a happy, conjugal ending, which I shall not reveal.

The remaining chapters address a broad range of topics. Three (Ch. 14, 19, 22) describe interspecies communication and are discussed below as important contributions to the literature on animal cognition. Chapter 20 describes a human-dolphin cooperative fishing system in Brazil in which the dolphins tell the fishermen where and when to cast their nets. Chapter 10 is about observing behavior, but, in this case, the animals are observing the behavior of a person. Chapter 5 is an amusing dissertation on the weather conditions generated by city architecture (and about the behavior of people who live in large cities.) Chapter 15 describes Pryor's service on the Marine Mammal Commission. This is where you learn why you don't want to work for the Federal Government even if you haven't hired an illegal alien.

An astonishing contribution (Ch. 17) comes from the updated version of Karen's and her daughter Gale's book, *Nursing Your Baby*. This chapter describes the interactions between nursing mothers and their infants, including the development of appropriate mothering behavior. What is astonishing to this reader is the reported neglect in both the medical and psychological literatures of the importance of breastfeeding to our understanding of attachment behavior or bonding. Pryor says that a recent (and presumably authoritative) monograph,

Growing Points of Attachment Theory and Research, includes not a single reference on breastfeeding. Pryor states that, contrary to current medical opinion, breastfeeding is a *cause,* rather than a *result,* of a mother's feelings of nurturance, and she will document this position if asked. I am inclined to suggest that breastfeeding and nurturing behavior may be a joint result of a series of biobehavioral interactions; but this discussion aside, how are we to evaluate a literature that doesn't even consider breastfeeding as a variable? I would also note that this chapter discusses father-infant bonding and reviews a body of relevant animal research.

In my view, Chapter 14, *Reinforcement as Interspecies Communication,* and, to a lesser extent, Chapter 22, *If I could Talk to the Animals,* are major contributions to the literature on animal cognition. Pryor does, of course, "talk" to the animals, and they "talk" back. What is more important is that she and the animals also listen, or otherwise attend, to what the other is communicating. Her approach to animal cognition or, more precisely, animal conceptual behavior, is functional. She carefully describes the behavior, including its context, that allows her to draw inferences about what a particular animal is feeling or thinking when it engages in a particular activity at a particular time. Chapter 14 contains many examples of animals' checking out the rules, or contingencies, of a training task, usually by making a graded series of errors, and of animals delivering unanticipated social or tangible reinforcers to their trainers, presumably as a way of saying, "Thank you."

What is notable about Pryor's observations of animals' creative, insightful, and sometimes downright manipulative behavior is that the behavior takes place in the open view of an empirical world. No nonphysical internal states, processes, or structures need be inferred or invoked. The actions she describes are replicable and, given sensitive observers who are knowledgeable about the species, they are undoubtedly predictable. What remains, at least for a radical behaviorist, is whether or not these kinds of behavior can be controlled in the sense of being produced on demand. I don't see why not. Pryor has long since produced and documented creative, or novel, behavior in dolphins (Ch. 2). The performance of novel behavior, defined as something that has never before been reinforced, is now sufficiently predictable and controllable that it is a standard procedure for dolphin training and enrichment in many aquaria and oceanaria. I am also willing to bet that Pryor knows enough about the contingencies that prompt an animal to test the rules of training, to put the trainer on Time Out, and the various other games that animals play (see Chapter 19) so that she and some of her students and colleagues could produce these activities with some reliability.

Still, on the subject of animal conceptual behavior, I understand that Pryor has been charged with anthropomorphism for maintaining that at least some animals think and have feelings, and that these are appropriate topics for scientific study. I would suggest that, when we consider the possible function of some activity or interaction, a little cautious anthropomorphism is far more likely to advance our understanding of animal behavior than is a rigid adherence to the anthropocentrism that so often muddies our vision.

A final word to instructors. If you don't plan to assign the whole book, don't deprive yourself or your students of the following chapters: Ch. 6, *The Rhino Likes Violets*: I assign this in my first class to introduce the power and possibilities of operant procedures; Ch. 7, *Why Porpoise Trainers are not Dolphin Lovers*: Terrible title, but important message; Ch. 14, *Reinforcement Training as ...Communication*: A gem, and give a copy to any cognitive ethologist you know; Ch. 19, *The Dreadful Dowager Dolphin*: Required reading for all of us who think we know something about shaping and then ignore the fact that it is an interactive process. *The Dreadful Dowager* is a poignant chronicle; it is also Pryor at her wittiest and most perceptive.

Ellen P Reese
South Hadley, Massachusetts, March 3, 1995.

References
Epstein, R., Ed., 1982. *Skinner for the Classroom*. Research Press, Champaign, IL.

Preface

I have always had two principal lines of work: writing, and science. The science that interests me is natural history, and more particularly, the natural history of behavior: what living creatures do, and why, and how they do it.

In college, like many young women in the '50s, I was discouraged when I looked into majoring in science. For example, ornithology was a favorite subject and I thought of choosing it for a major, but the professor flatly told me he didn't take girls in his program because there was no place in the woods for them to go to the bathroom. So I majored in English, took every natural history course I could get into, read widely, and became a devotee of the works of the German scientist, Konrad Lorenz, who pioneered the field of ethology, the study of the behavior of animals in their natural setting.

My first book, *Nursing Your Baby*, a book for mothers about breastfeeding, was researched and written while I was raising my own babies and doing graduate work in marine zoology at the University of Hawaii. My publishers regarded *Nursing Your Baby* as a medical book, but to me it was a book about behavior—the natural behavior of mothers and babies, and how our medical system often manages to hash it up.

During the years that I was writing that book, my husband, Tap Pryor, created and developed an oceanarium, Sea Life Park, in Hawaii. Kenneth Norris, Ph.D., who was a marine mammal researcher, a professor at the University of California, and the ex-curator of a pioneering oceanarium, Marineland of the Pacific, was our scientific advisor. Ken decreed that our dolphin shows would be of a new sort: scientific, educational, and tasteful—no pilot whales in funny hats; no demeaning jokes about the animals. He also decreed that training would not be done by old-fashioned circus methods, waving fish and shouting commands, but by a new system called operant conditioning.

Ken provided our trainers with a manual, written by a student of B.F. Skinner's, on training dolphins with operant conditioning. The manual, however, was difficult reading. About three months before Sea Life Park was due to open, it became apparent that the dolphins had trained the trainers to give them fish for nothing.

I was the only person at Sea Life Park with any training experience: I had trained one dog and one pony. On Ken's recommendation, nevertheless, I was hired as Sea Life Park's head dolphin trainer, an experience I have described in my second book, *Lads Before the Wind.*

Working with dolphins and scientists involved me in research projects and scientific publications about dolphins, and also in a consuming new interest, the principles of operant conditioning and positive reinforcement by which dolphins are trained. At Sea Life Park's research facility, the Oceanic Institute, I could pick the brains of specialists in Skinner's brand of behaviorism. Skinner himself came to visit our dolphins, as did Konrad Lorenz, and from then on I could pick the brains of those original thinkers, too.

In 1972 Tap Pryor and I were divorced, Sea Life Park was sold, and I turned to writing as a way of supporting myself and my children. The science had a funny way of intruding, however. Without ever joining a faculty or taking a formal 9-5 job in science I went on to make a career partly by writing and lecturing, and partly by study, research, and consulting, all on the topic of behavior.

Our culture separates scientists from non-scientists. It's almost as if there were a law that if you do anything BUT science, then you are not legally a scientist. To write a popular article on joking, for example, (an important and interesting behavior, I think) is to prove that you are not a "real" scientist. Worse yet, working at a professional level in one field of science almost forbids one to show an interest in some other. This is especially unfortunate if you're interested in behavior because, alas, we seem to have developed two kinds of behavioral science.

One kind stems from biology, and focuses on innate or genetically-based behavior. This is Konrad Lorenz's area of interest, called ethology or behavioral ecology. Such concepts as the alpha animal, submissive displays, dominance hierarchies, social and solitary species, and predator-prey relationships come from behavioral biology. The other kind of behavioral science is the branch of psychology that deals with learned or acquired behavior. B.F. Skinner and his followers largely defined this science, which is presently called behavior analysis. Such concepts as positive and negative reinforcement, successive approximation, and conditioned reinforcers come from behavioral psychology.

What is baffling to me is that specialists in these two branches of science by and large ignore each other. It was true thirty years ago and it's true now. They do not know each other's terminology. They do not recognize or understand the "other" kind of behavior when they see it. They do not realize that you need to consider both kinds of behavior—learned and innate—to really understand what an animal is doing.

Worse yet, behavioral scientists mostly do not realize the enormous usefulness of each approach to the other. I have personally used my understanding of training with reinforcement as a window into the meaning of an animal's natural behavior, not just once, but often. Conversely I can use an animal's natural behavior to turn a training situation into real—not sentimental but real—two-way communication with this member of another species.

So, in my maverick career, I have written, talked, and labored, often and in many ways, to build a bridge between the two kinds of behavioral thinking. This book contains selections from the writing I have done about behavior. Sometimes my intended audience members are biologists. Sometimes they are psychologists. Often they are people who are not scientists at all. In some cases I am wearing a biologist's hat; in some, my psychology vestments. In some cases, such as the piece about the behavior of the wind, my hat has blown away altogether.

Some of the articles which follow are scientific papers, published in the peer-reviewed literature, which you may find both technical and dry. There are good reasons, however, for the constraints of scientific writing. Here's how my graduate-school zoology professor once put it: "Imagine that an Ethiopian graduate student a hundred years from now has just come across your paper in the library, and finds that it is absolutely crucial to his research. Imagine that his English is not good. Don't make jokes he won't understand; don't be long-winded; and don't get fancy and use 'red' in one place and 'scarlet' in another so you send the poor fellow to the dictionary twice." Good advice.

In addition, in a scientific paper, you must include the data necessary to defend your findings against foreseen and unforeseen arguments raised by others in your field; this usually entails statistics and graphs. If plowing through this stuff doesn't interest you, just skip it. Lots of other pieces are full of fun, or so I hope.

On the other hand, if you are comfortable with scientific writing, but skeptical of the popular press, take note that I don't drop my scientific standards just because the style is light; one can learn something, I hope, from any piece here. As the philosopher Gregory Bateson liked to point out, we are never so serious as when we are joking.

The chapters are arranged more or less in the order in which the events therein occurred. I've included a note at the start of each piece as to why or how I came to write it, and a note at the end about what happened as a result of the piece—sometimes absolutely nothing, of course, but sometimes rather startling events which I could never have anticipated.

The reader may note some inconsistencies of style from chapter to chapter in this book. Journals and editors differ in their demands for specific usage. I have usually retained the style as it was originally published. Thus, for example, you will find "bottlenosed" dolphins, with a final "d," in some chapters, but "bottlenose," with no final "d," in others. Reference forms and requirements also differ considerably from journal to journal. In those chapters which contain citations I have attempted to make the reference sections at least similar in format.

Sometimes the passage of time dictated changes. For example, in the 1960s the word "porpoise" was favored by many American scientists as the generic term for any small cetacean. By the 1980s the preference had tipped toward the word "dolphin" as the generic term. I followed custom in this matter. As another example, my second-in-command at Sea Life Park, Ingrid Kang, remarried in the early 1980s. Thus she became Ingrid Shallenberger in papers published after that time. Some articles have been abridged slightly to avoid unnecessary repetition. Beyond these circumstantial variations, any errors, inconsistencies, or oversights are mine.

A lot of this writing, directly or indirectly, is about training. When I started out with the dolphins, the people who best understood the interweaving of biology and psychology in behavior were my fellow trainers. Today I am finding it is still the trainers who most enthusiastically get the whole picture, whether they are music teachers or dog obedience instructors, professors or horsewomen. It's for you trainers that I put this book together, and at your request. Thanks for asking, and I hope it is useful.

Karen Pryor

Part One

Hawaii
1963-1972

Karen Pryor, head trainer at Sea Life Park, and a favorite spinner dolphin, Haole. Note the spinner's long, slender rostrum, or beak, and the delicate color pattern, very different in appearance from the more familiar bottlenose dolphin (page 52).

Discovering dolphins....

This was the first scientific paper I published completely on my own. Actually it was a hand-me-down from Ken Norris, our scientific advisor. From the day we opened, in 1963, Ken Norris, the researcher, and I as his trainer, were doing innovative things with dolphins, such as training them to accompany us in the open ocean to show us how deep they could dive and how fast they could swim. Also Sea Life Park was catching all kinds of strange animals in the ocean around Hawaii. We kept several species of dolphins and small whales in our tanks that had never been seen alive by scientists before. I knew we were discovering facts about marine mammal behavior that both the public and the scientific community were unaware of. I was itching to find a way to put these observations into print.

When the German nature journal, *Naturwissenschaften*, invited Ken to write a summary article on the behavior of cetaceans, he was loaded with other commitments and suggested that I do it instead. The editors not only accepted me as a substitute, they published the piece with very little in the way of correction, even though I had included all kinds of observations that were not the sort of thing one usually finds in a biology journal.

Take, for example, the account of Malia, a rough-toothed dolphin, forgiving me with a social gesture for making a stupid training mistake (p 21). I thought, and still think, that that was one of the most unusual pieces of behavior — one of the most intelligent pieces of behavior — that I ever observed in an animal. Apparently the editors liked it too; they set it off in smaller type, to show that it was a bit of a digression, but they didn't delete it.

A paper of this sort is not a report of completed research, but a "review" paper. In such a paper, the references at the end are very important to other scientists. Ken struggled with me for weeks to get my reference section up to par; he opened his own library and card files to me, and in essence supervised my education in this particular matter in a way for which I was to be grateful again and again in future years.

CHAPTER ONE

Behavior and Learning
in Porpoises and Whales

Karen W. Pryor[1]

Abstract:

Based on observations of nine species of cetaceans at Hawaii's Sea Life Park, the author describes behavior comparable to that of other highly social animals, inter- and intra-specifically, and as directed toward man. Forms of signaling include sound, posture, gesture, and movement. Sound is also used for echo-location. A brief discussion is given of gross physical characteristics and capabilities, of training systems, and of cetacean intelligence. Examples are given of species differences in temperament and responses, and of aggression toward humans. Porpoises are being used as domestic animals working at liberty in the open sea, with increasing success. Porpoise and whale stocks in the wild represent a major resource which is in danger of depletion.

The *Delphinidae* as a group

Porpoises have interested artists and poets for centuries, and in the last thirty years, since becoming relatively common in

[1]Reprinted with permission from *Naturwissenschaften* 60, 412-420 (1973), Springer-Verlag.

captivity, they have uniquely captured the public's fancy. They seem uncannily docile and friendly to man; they are among the most intelligent animals; they are easily tamed and trained, often playful and affectionate, and attractive in appearance. The speculations of John Lilly have led to a widespread hope that dolphins are as intelligent as man, or even more intelligent, and that they might be able to communicate with man or each other on an abstract level comparable to human language (Lilly 1962).

As a result of these public fancies, a mystique of dolphin lore has arisen to which even scientific investigators are vulnerable. The staff of Sea Life Park and the Oceanic Institute at the Makapuu Oceanic Center have completed eight years of working closely with species of the family *Delphinidae,* and of coordination with the staffs of other oceanaria and research organizations. Our formal and informal observations lead us to believe that while the delphinids are a very interesting animal group, with many remarkable physical and behavioral specializations, many of the activities of porpoise and whales which seem marvelous and even humanoid can better be considered as comparable to the behavior of other highly social and intelligent large mammals. However, we are just beginning to realize the extensive potential of this group as pleasant companions and domestic animals useful to man.

The Odontoceti, or toothed whales, which include all the porpoises and most of the small whales, are apparently only distantly related to the Mysticeti, or whalebone whales, most of which are very large and feed on plankton. Almost all of the odontocetes live in social groups and have many physical and behavioral characteristics in common. Perhaps as a result the delphinids seem to interact interspecifically more commonly than some other taxonomic groups. In captivity, where groups of mixed species are frequently kept together, one often sees ordinarily intra-specific social behavior carried out between species as well as among members of the same species. Animals as different in appearance as a 1200-pound false killer whale *(Pseudorca crassidens)* and a 100-pound spinning porpoise *(Stenella longirostrus hawaiiensis)* may share in such activities as play, mimetic behavior, copulation, and care-giving behavior. The "distress call" of the Atlantic bottlenosed porpoise, *Tursiops truncatus,* taped and played underwater, was seen to evoke panic in a group of spinning porpoises at the Makapuu Oceanic Center. At Marine-land of the Pacific, Palos Verdes, California, a pilot whale *(Globicephala sp.)* was observed removing the placenta from a tiny Pacific whitesided porpoise *(Lagaenorhynchus obliquidens)* that was giving birth. In Hawaii a male killer whale *(Orcinus orca)* that escaped from a training pen in the ocean has been seen several times living in apparent amity with a school of Hawaiian spinning porpoises that might ordinarily form its prey. The live birth at the Makapuu Oceanic Center of a hybrid between a female rough-toothed porpoise, *Steno bredanensis,* and a male Atlantic bottlenosed porpoise on October 4, 1971, suggests that even species which are widely different in appearance and classed not only in different genera but in different families may not be as far apart genotypically as has been previously assumed.

In any case, most porpoises respond to human beings as if the human beings were porpoises of some kind too. A porpoise which is not fearful will offer to a human swimmer the same responses it might offer to another porpoise, such as soliciting stroking, swimming in unison, playing with objects, making sexual advances, and attempting to establish rank order by aggressive display. We think nothing of it when a dog, cat, or even a horse directs the social responses of its species towards a human; but we tend to react with undue and anthropocentric amazement at the opportunity to interact socially with something that looks so very much like a fish.

All of the delphinids, except perhaps the pygmy killer whale, *Feresa attenuata,* are apt to be docile upon capture (Pryor *et al.* 1965). This often causes amazement; we are so accustomed to a captured animal struggling with all its might that the cetacean docility seems to imply wisdom or insight on the part of the animal. However, the porpoise's defenses, primarily flight and ramming, are impossible once the animal is out of the water. Exhaustion and the impact of two totally new experiences, being held out of the water and being separated from others of its kind, probably contribute to the newly captured animal's tendency to lie motionless. Though nearly immobile, a newly captured porpoise or small whale is certainly frightened, and death from shock is not uncommon.

On introduction into the confinement of a tank, reactions may range from shock and withdrawal lasting for days or weeks to investigative behavior, normal activity, and prompt feeding. Absence of fear of humans, even in a completely naive individual, is neither the rule nor the exception in delphinids, whatever the species, but may occur anywhere along a scale from complete acceptance to panic. And if it occurs it is perhaps comparable to many recorded instances of large, wild mammals with, no previous experience of man (wolves, moose) exhibiting, on first meeting with a human, some curiosity and only moderate caution.

Empirically, we find that a juvenile of any species adapts most quickly. Large adults usually withdraw severely and neither swim nor feed, unless forced, for prolonged periods, but an occasional animal will adapt dramatically rapidly. We have seen two examples in eight years of collecting. A large, male Pacific bottlenosed porpoise *(Tursiops gilli)* was introduced into a tank containing another large male of the same species and a human swimmer who had his arm around the tame animal and was putting fish into its mouth. The new animal shortly put himself under the swimmer's other arm and accepted fish too. In another case, a large female rough-toothed porpoise was introduced into a tank containing another rough-toothed porpoise which was being conditioned to press a lever for a food reward. Within 24 hours the new animal was also pressing the lever and soliciting food from the trainer.

Communicative behavior

One area of cetacean behavior very apt to be misinterpreted is communication. Like all social animals porpoises spend a lot of their time interacting and have an extensive repertoire of social signals, including body postures, gestures, movement patterns, and sound. The ability of most of the delphinids to emit a wide variety of sounds has attracted much interest, particularly since it is possible to elicit, by training, sounds vaguely resembling human words. A porpoise, like dogs and many other animals, can be taught to recognize and respond to spoken human words, and to offer specifically conditioned sounds on cue, but there seems to be no good evidence of anything more than conditioned responses in this kind of behavior.

Porpoise sounds are generally considered to fall roughly into two groups, those used for echolocation or biosonar ("clicks")and those which probably constitute sign stimuli ("whistles") (Lilly and Miller 1961). There is some overlap both in the physical nature of the sounds and their use; for example, the Pacific spotted porpoise *(Stenella attenuata)* appears to use an extremely loud click train as a threat display. A single animal can emit both kinds of sound simultaneously (Busnel 1966; Evans 1967). Each animal seems to rely solely on its own sonar for sensing its environment. Echolocation sounds are directional and aimed in a narrow beam in front of the animal, while the whistle sounds seem omnidirectional (Norris 1963). Some investigators have recorded extensive "vocabularies" of whistles, both in captivity and in the wild, and indicate that certain whistles are duplicated in different species (Dreher 1966), while others feel that the apparent classifications of whistles are of unknown significance and that each animal emits only its own "signature" call (Caldwell and Caldwell 1965). One investigator maintains that what sounds like a single whistle may actually be made up of two or more parts each emitted by a different animal (Gregory Bateson, pers. comm.). As do other animals, porpoises quickly learn to distinguish between tape recordings of whistles and actual sounds of another animal and to respond only to the latter (Lang and Smith 1965). In caring for captive porpoises most trainers learn to respond to at least three separate porpoise sounds: a piercing, rising and falling whistle which, whatever the species, seems to signal serious distress (Lilly 1963), a plaintive repeated peeping which often occurs when an animal is unhappy but not frightened, for example, when abruptly isolated, and the "jaw clap" or "bark" emitted by the bottlenosed porpoise in threat (Tavolga 1966) .

Some sound signals are associated with breathing. Echolocation sounds are not normally accompanied by emission of air from the blowhole, but whistles frequently are, producing a stream of bubbles which is no doubt easily perceived by another porpoise, and which can be useful to the human observer whose hearing range may not extend into the upper frequencies favored by porpoises. Normal respiration rate increases with excitation, and alarmed animals tend to respire with a pronounced "chuff!" which is distinctly different from the exhalation sound of calm animals. Porpoises also produce sound by coming into contact with the water surface. All species we have observed can produce a remarkably loud crack by slapping the water surface with the tail. In the wild this signal is often followed by "sounding" or diving directly down; one such slap may send the whole school out of sight (Norris and Prescott 1961).

Gestural displays at the water surface are common and sometimes function communicatively. In training animals, we at the Makapuu Oceanic Center have come to regard several gestures as being related to frustration or anger, and these seem to occur in a graded scale, according to the degree of emotion being expressed. Mildest is a slap of the tail on the water, differing from the loud "alarm" crack only in intensity, and sometimes repeated. Next is a slap of the head or forward part of the body on the water surface; and finally, a twisting leap in the air called breaching (or broaching by whaling men) in which the animal comes down sidewise and slaps the water with body and dorsal fin. The rough-toothed porpoise varies this by leaping half out of the water with forward impetus, and cupping air between body and pectoral fins before failing back in, resulting in a loud cracking sound. The pygmy killer whale has been observed to pat the water with the pectoral fin, rhythmically, at a rate which increased when strangers approached.

Many species will also tap the water rhythmically with the tail while swimming upside down. This inverted, repetitive tail slapping has been observed in the wild as well as in captivity; its social function is not known but it does not appear to be related to the signals of frustration or anger described above.

One of the charms of the porpoise group is their predilection for lively and often spectacular aerial display. Simple leaping across the surface ("porpoising") is often a by-product of being in a hurry; but many other leaps occur and almost certainly serve a social function. Several species we have observed seem to have one leap which is conspicuous and peculiarly uniform to the species. We informally classify in this context a leap seen in the Pacific bottlenosed porpoise in which the animal comes head-first out of the water, arches six or more feet above the surface, and returns head-first, describing a tear-drop-shaped pattern of travel and re-entering the water "in the same hole it came out of," in the words of one trainer. The spinning porpoise is so called for the typical leap in which the animal rotates rapidly on its longitudinal axis while travelling several feet above the water, sometimes making five complete revolutions in a single jump. The Pacific spotted porpoise, a superficially very similar species, is inept at spinning even when conditioned, but in captivity and in the wild performs a dramatic leap in which the animal leaves the water straight up, arches the body in an S-curve, and travels horizontally in the air fifteen feet or more before falling back in. Both of these species of *Stenella* also perform a flip in which the body performs a 180° arc, tail over head, in the air.

In captivity, the species-typical leap may occur when a male animal is defeated in a social encounter. An animal will also leap or spin to rid itself of a physical encumbrance such as a piece of string. A spin can be elicited in a tame spinning porpoise by tickling it under the pectoral fin or by arousing it sexually. All of these behavior patterns are capable of being brought under stimulus control and can be developed as conditioned responses.

Underwater gestures are, of course, more difficult to observe and much remains to be done in understanding them. All porpoises seem to enjoy being touched by people or other porpoises and animals often stroke each other, while swimming, with tail flukes or pectoral fins. They may also strike blows with flukes or fins. Pairs frequently "hold hands," swimming with pectoral fins overlapping and in contact even during rapid and complex maneuvers. A conspicuous behavior labeled "beak-genital propulsion" by Gregory Bateson consists of one animal physically propelling another forward or sidewise through the water by applying its beak to the other animal's genital area, and appears to be related to status. Porpoises, like most social animals, are concerned with status; the "pecking order" however is not strictly linear; also some animals appear to remain "outsiders" without, however, necessarily being of low status. Status is also established among porpoises by aggressive threats such as jaw-clapping and a threat posture in which the animal arches the head down while remaining stationary in the water, and by some fighting, including slaps and blows with the tail, pectorals, or even dorsal fin, and head-on ramming. An animal may register submission by prostrating itself across another animal's rostrum. Bateson has also observed in a captive school of spinning porpoises that while resting the animals take up a circular swimming course, and arrange themselves by pairs and trios in a vertical stack in which the dominant animals are on top and rise to breathe first, followed in order by animals which are beneath them both socially and physically.

Some physical attributes

While it is beyond the scope of this paper to survey what is known about porpoises physically and physiologically, it seems appropriate to mention some general physical attributes which affect the training of the animals and their maintenance in captivity.

Porpoises appear to be reasonably long-lived (fifteen years or more) and hardy, once acclimated to confinement. They are, however, subject to infection from many pathogens commonly found in and on human beings and are especially subject to pneumonia. They will reproduce in captivity. They can be held and transported out of water for considerable periods provided the skin is not allowed to dry out and cause the animal to overheat.

Porpoises are powerful animals and can develop skill at opening or breaking gates or barriers in their tanks, ranging from tearing up netting by holding a small piece in the teeth and shaking the head, much as a dog would do, to in one instance shearing the bolts which held a pipe barrier to the concrete by putting the tail flukes between pipe and wall and prying. The motive behind such actions is almost always a desire to relieve boredom rather than a desire to escape captivity.

Some species of porpoises in the wild have been radio-tracked diving frequently to depths of 600 feet (Evans 1971). At least one domesticated individual, an Atlantic bottlenosed porpoise, has been trained to dive to 1000 feet on command. Porpoises normally respire two or three times a minute but the rate may increase after a dive. The species with which we are familiar rarely submerge longer than five minutes and most dives are shorter in duration.

Porpoises have been credited with the ability to swim at physically improbable high speeds, largely because they can often be seen accompanying ships at sea which are moving at speeds upwards of thirty knots. Probably the comfortable "cruising speed" varies from one species to another, as does the maximum attainable speed. In experiments to determine maximum swimming speeds of various species, and in working with trained individuals of various species at sea, it would seem that the Pacific bottlenosed porpoise can comfortably sustain a speed of 11 or 12 knots for long periods of time but has to work hard to go 15 knots (Norris 1965). Two Pacific spotted porpoises were trained to follow a lure the speed of which could be predetermined and increased. Maximum obtainable speeds were in the neighborhood of 21.5 knots for brief times and distances only (Lang and Pryor 1966).

The higher speeds observed at sea are almost certainly due to the skill of porpoises in riding on the pressure waves caused by a ship's passage, and thus coasting as fast as the ship itself is going. Porpoises perform this feat of riding a ship's bow-wave in all the oceans of the world, almost certainly purely for sport. They do not overtake the ship but intercept it on a tangent. Porpoises can "surf" similarly in almost any kind of wave from storm surf to the "bow-wave" of a water-skier's skis.

Empirical evidence suggests that porpoises have a well-developed kinesthetic awareness and a skin sensitive to touch all over the body. Porpoises almost never collide with each other or any solid object by accident; they maneuver unharmed within inches of fast-moving ships and even propellers. The outer epidermis is thin, ticklish, and easily damaged; one can draw blood with a fingernail.

Porpoises appear to use their eyes, and to see well, both in and out of the water (except for those fresh-water species which are almost or totally blind). They can learn to see upwards through the air-water interface, for example to locate a jump target, probably much as some human fishermen learn to discriminate what they are seeing looking down through the same interface. Little detail is known of porpoises' visual acuity at long and short distances or above and below water. We do not know if they perceive colors. While their field of vision is bilateral, like a horse, looking sideways, the eyes are so situated that the porpoise cannot see upwards at all, without tilting his body, but has binocular vision downwards, and in the case of at least the pygmy killer whale, backwards; if you swim underneath a porpoise and look up you will find him looking down at you with both eyes. There is a blind spot directly in front of the animal as well as overhead; the porpoise literally cannot see what is in front of its nose, and presumably uses echolocation for close inspection of anything in that area.

Porpoises, although they have adequate vision, are not as responsive to visual signals as are some other animals (seals and birds for example) and are much more likely to notice auditory stimuli. One investigator who was using a lightbulb as a conditioned stimulus found that his porpoise subject was listening to the lightbulb going on and off rather than looking at it, and it responded just as well when the bulb was hidden by black plastic (Louis Herman pers. comm.).

Porpoises hear much more acutely than humans and over a much wider range. They can hear in the air but possibly less distinctly than underwater. Sound travels poorly through the air-water interface and a signal must be loud and clear if it is to be emitted in the air but discriminated by a porpoise underwater. It is necessary in working with porpoises to take into account that the animal's sensory world is vastly different from ours. If it is difficult for the human trainer and experimenter to extrapolate the responses of an animal which relies on hearing more than vision, how much more difficult it becomes when we realize that the porpoise's most acute sense may well be echolocation. By echolocation alone, porpoises can discriminate the size, shape, distance, texture and even the internal structure of an object

(Norris 1968). They can choose a preferred species of fish over another of the same size and shape, or locate an object as small as five millimeters in diameter on a tank floor (Kellogg 1961). One can postulate that to a newly captured cetacean the ricochet of acoustical signals from the tank walls is as disconcerting as being surrounded by searchlights would be to a human being. One can also postulate that when an animal perceives for example a diver underwater he "sees" not the human outline or black diver's suit we might see first but the airspaces inside the diver's head or body (Mackay 1966).

Porpoises are interested in sound and, as reported by the ancient Greeks, sometimes like to hear people sing. We have noticed animals approaching and lying with one side or all of the head above the surface whenever someone happens to be working around the tanks and singing. We have never observed any continued interest in recorded music however.

Training

Porpoise training is presently accomplished by standard techniques of operant conditioning. A stimulus is paired with food as a reinforcement, and used to mark desirable actions. The sound of a whistle is often used; it can be emitted rapidly by a human and perceived both above and below water by a porpoise. Leaps and other freely occurring behavior can be conditioned and brought under stimulus control in a matter of days. Artificial or "shaped" behaviors such as ball-playing, retrieving objects, or locating targets by echolocation while blind-folded are trained by the psychology laboratory technique known as successive approximation, in which the trainer selectively rewards behavior while gradually raising and modifying his criteria until the desired response is obtained (Reynolds 1968).

Unison behavior such as a simultaneous leap by several animals is easily accomplished by rewarding a single animal for the behavior; others will, in due course, mimic his action and are then rewarded also.

Porpoises appear to enjoy training if only because it breaks the monotony of a captive existence, provided the trainer is consistent and does not frustrate the animal by poor technique.

It is seldom necessary to food-deprive porpoises to provide adequate motivation for learning. They are usually willing to work for their entire food ration, unless the required task is exhausting or painful, or the learning situation is improperly presented and thus frustrating.

Reinforcements other than food can be used, such as access to sight, sound, or presence of other animals, access to a favorite toy, or stroking. These can interfere with training, as when an animal would rather go without food than give up its toy. Stroking can be useful in the training of wearing harness or blindfolds, in the initial stages of which the animal may be alarmed and consequently inappetant. Negative reinforcement is not easily available to the porpoise trainer; a mild negative reinforcement is the "time out," in which the trainer signals displeasure by abruptly taking the food away and leaving the animal alone during a training session.

Preliminary experiments at the Oceanic Institute, Hawaii, indicate that porpoises may be trained by restraint and coercion on a harness and a leash, as dogs and horses are trained, and that in skilled hands this method can achieve very rapid results. In Hawaii, where the water is warm, we customarily habituate every animal to human handling and to tolerating swimmers without exhibiting fear or aggression, but this is not necessary to successful training.

Once a response has been conditioned and shaped to meet the desired set of criteria it is usually brought under stimulus control. The animal is taught to respond "on cue" by being rewarded for responses in or following the presence of a chosen stimulus and not in its absence. Porpoise trainers often use hand motions as conditioned stimuli. At the Makapuu Oceanic Center we also make extensive use of sounds, usually electronically generated tones or tone combinations, which are amplified underwater through a hydrophone and can be controlled by the trainer. For convenience we use sounds which can easily be distinguished and discriminated by the human ear.

It is our experience that human words are not discriminated clearly by porpoise at a distance or through the air-water interface, so we do not use them as signals. However, porpoises, like dogs, horses and many other animals, sometimes do learn to associate meaning with human words and phrases, and also to interpret tone of voice correctly. After much exposure to humans, shy porpoises can be coaxed by voice and a misbehaving porpoise will sometimes correct himself if yelled at.

While hand signals and underwater sounds are the most commonly used methods of signaling conditioned responses, they are by no means the only methods. Anything that the animal is capable of perceiving may be used as a conditioned stimulus; we have conditioned behavior to such stimuli as flags, blowing bubbles under water, touching or pushing the animal, visual patterns (i.e., numbers or words on large cards), and presentation of equipment. Animals may also be conditioned (often accidentally) to perform at very specific time intervals, for example 17 seconds *after* a given event occurs. Also once an animal has been conditioned the stimulus can be gradually decreased until it is all but imperceptible, without loss of strength of response. A wave of the arm can dwindle to a lift of the finger and produce the same response. Psychologists call this "disappearing the stimulus;" it is a technique much used by circus trainers.

A porpoise may be trained in one long daily session or several shorter ones, the pattern being governed by practicalities such as available working time and by the common-sense customs of all animal trainers. If learning is to be accomplished with all possible speed, it is wise, for example, to stop a training session before the animal becomes bored or fatigued. In practical training the goal of a given session is progress, no matter how small, rather than the achievement of a predesignated end-point. The best indication of good training technique is a confident and zestful animal.

Porpoises easily discriminate one human from another and may or may not become attached to their trainer. Sometimes the attachment is social; more often it is a reflection of the trainer's skill: associating with him is interesting and rewarding and the animal responds with affection. Likewise porpoises can take a dislike to individuals; at Sea Life Park a SCUBA diver who had secretly been in the habit of teasing a young false killer whale he was required to work with found himself harmlessly but terrifyingly pinned to the bottom of the tank one day. Fortunately the diver had an ample air supply; the whale held him down for several minutes before responding to its trainer's call.

While the intelligence and disposition of individual animals no doubt varies, the tasks demanded of porpoises whether for public entertainment or research are seldom of a nature to tax a given porpoise's intelligence noticeably. Of far more importance to successful learning are the animal's physical well-being, and his position in the status structure if he is a member of a group, Sick animals, of course perform poorly, and low-status animals are often afraid to compete for food.

All porpoises, like other intelligent mammals such as elephants and chimpanzees, seem to be capable of higher-order learning. Examples of phenomena generally considered to be associated with high levels of intelligence are:

Learning by observation. A dramatic case occurred at Sea Life Park in the summer of 1969, involving two female rough-toothed porpoises. One had been trained to perform a number of serial behaviors in response to sound cues, including jumping through a hoop held high above the water. This animal had been taught to wear blindfolds but had never performed work while doing so. The other had been trained to wear blindfolds and while doing so to retrieve rings on its rostrum and to negotiate barriers by echolocation. Both animals had ample previous opportunity to watch each others' performances through barred gates. During a public demonstration, the trainers inadvertently switched the animals; both animals performed each other's tasks with such fidelity that the trainers were unaware of the switch until after the performance, noting only an unusually high level of excitability during the work period.

Single-trial learning. Acoustical discrimination experiments by L. Herman of the University of Hawaii routinely require a Pacific bottlenosed porpoise to make a correct choice after a single exposure to a new stimulus, a task the animal performs without difficulty. K. Norris reports similar occurrences.

Set learning or the learning of generalized rules. To teach a porpoise to offer a conditioned response in the presence of a given stimulus but not in its absence may take many training sessions the first time it is done. However, the animal that has learned to jump when it hears a buzzing sound, and to lie on the bottom when it hears a bell ring, and has now learned that slapping the water with its tail will be rewarded by food, can learn to associate the third response with a third sound within a day. It has presumably generalized the concept that sounds are "cues" and different sounds signal different responses.

Understanding of general rules can easily be acquired by porpoises, which greatly facilitates their training. Quite complex rules can be taught. At the Makapuu Oceanic Center we succeeded in establishing in two animals the rule that "in each training session, reinforcement will occur only for a response that has never been reinforced previously" (Pryor *et al.* 1967).

When the animals began to respond at the level of the generalized rule they offered actions not only never before reinforced but never before seen to occur spontaneously by any of the experimenters such as leaping upside-down and backwards, coming out of the water and lying at the trainer's feet on the cement, and spitting water into the air.

Delayed responses. Delays of one minute between presentation of a discriminative stimulus and opportunities to make a response have been successfully established. Longer delays seem possible. A porpoise which was inadvertently kicked by a swimmer who was leaving the tank one evening delivered a single blow of similar intensity to the same swimmer at the first opportunity the following morning. The trainer who was involved considered this typical porpoise politesse.

Competency motivation. In addition to working (offering responses) for positive reinforcements such as food or relief from boredom, porpoises sometimes appear to work out of interest in the task. A rough-toothed porpoise was being trained by the author to choose a visual pattern which matched a sample. In the training session in which the animal first made consistent correct responses it showed evidence of excitement, continued responding until it had earned its normal day's ration of fish, and then still continued responding, accepting fish but not eating them, until it had earned and dropped on the floor of the tank another 50 percent of its usual daily food intake.

Cooperative Behavior. Mutual assistance, such as support of an injured animal at the surface or attempts by one animal to remove a rope or other impediment from another are sometimes seen both in captivity and in the wild. At Sea Life Park a young false killer whale and a young Pacific bottlenosed porpoise shared adjoining tanks and preferred to share the same tank. The porpoise developed the ability to jump over the partition into the less agile whale's tank and did so frequently. Since it was sometimes difficult to separate the animals, and necessary to do so for performances for the public, a barricade wide enough to deter jumping was placed over the partition. The whale, with his superior strength, shoved the barricade aside just enough for the porpoise to jump in; the cooperation continued at night and between shows, while the moved barricade was blamed on human intervention, until the whale's effort happened to be observed by a trainer. It is worth noting that for some time both animals considered the operation to be illicit and made no attempt to join each other unless there were no people around.

Temperament

While all porpoises exhibit intelligence, the species differ widely in temperament. Members of the genus *Stenella* are timid, easily panicked and shocked, fearful of objects, highly dependent on the presence of other porpoises for security, and react adversely to change. They mimic each other and easily learn to work in unison groups. They display confidence performing repetitive and familiar tasks. They are magnificent aerial acrobats and can be trained far more easily to jump and leap than to touch or carry an object or press a lever. A group of spinning porpoises make delightful shy and gentle swimming companions and will harmlessly play with a human swimmer for half an hour at a time, drifting into the swimmer's arms, swirling around him, and pacing every human movement with their own in a kind of interspecific water ballet.

The bottlenosed porpoises, both Atlantic and Pacific, are most widely kept in captivity and seem well-suited to it. They are investigative, bold, curious, enjoy variety, and adapt readily to new conditions. The Atlantic bottlenosed porpoise has a very mobile head and can catch and throw objects with great accuracy from its jaws. Bottlenosed porpoises are not fearful of objects, and can easily be trained to wear or manipulate equipment. They are, however, easily bored and if required to perform unchallenging, monotonous work may rebel or institute their own variations. Bottlenosed porpoises seem to enjoy a human swimming companion but are large animals and sometimes play too roughly for human safety.

The rough-toothed porpoise is even bolder and more investigative than the bottlenosed porpoise, has a long attention span, "loves a puzzle," and is the trainer's choice for complex and prolonged tasks. However, they are potentially dangerous swimming companions as they are hot-tempered. Rough-toothed porpoises might be said to be unforgiving; trainer error, such as confusion or contradiction in the presentation of reinforcement, may produce strong emotional response.

> A trainer was reinforcing a rough-toothed porpoise for leaping, and the animal was offering the response readily. In the course of work the animal happened to make an interesting noise which the trainer also reinforced. The animal repeated the noise several times, and the trainer became more interested and stopped reinforcing leaps to reinforce the sound.
>
> That was an error. This animal had not yet had any experience of failing to be reinforced for something it had learned to offer in expectation of reward. After several unreinforced leaps the animal exhibited anger, refused to come to the trainer for fish, went to the far side of the tank and stayed there. It refused all food for the next two days. Physical examination showed no sign of illness. On the third day it volunteered a leap and accepted food. The trainer reinforced subsequent leaps and then established a stimulus control that leaping would be reinforced only when the trainer's hand was lifted. The animal began to show response to this new criterion, leaping when the hand was raised and waiting when it was lowered, and in one of these waiting periods it made the noise. The trainer immediately reinforced the noise and then raised the hand, elicited a jump, and reinforced that. Possibly the porpoise recognized this sequence as clarifying the rules governing when leaping would be reinforced as opposed to noise-making. It approached the trainer and stroked the trainer's arm gently and repeatedly with its pectoral fin, a gesture very frequent between porpoises but extremely rare from porpoise to human, and in the next ten minutes not only demonstrated correct response to the "leap"

stimulus but acquired some reliability of response to a different hand signal for "make noise."

The small whales also differ from each other and from the porpoises in temperament. Pilot whales are placid and sometimes lethargic and stubborn. They change fixed habits slowly. Large males have been known to sulk and to have what certainly seem to be temper tantrums. They are clumsy and relatively slow-moving. The false killer whale is fast, agile, volatile, emotional. It learns rapidly, forms intense attachments to other cetaceans and to people, and is excitable and sometimes aggressive. A common threat display consists of swimming full speed as if to ram the offending object or person and then halting abruptly a few inches from contact.

Aggression

Aggressiveness towards the trainer is a factor which must be taken into consideration in all species in circumstances which require the trainer to be in or near the water. Aggression usually occurs in animals which have been in captivity long enough to lose all fear of humans. A newly caught animal lies docile out of water, but an animal that has been in captivity four or five years may, with thrashing tail and snapping jaws, chase the veterinary across the floor of an empty tank. Even timid spinning porpoises do not necessarily regard the human as a social superior, and if annoyed may threaten or actually cuff or strike a swimmer with fins, tail or rostrum. One defense (not recommended here) is to strike back; another is the previously described "time-out."

Porpoises rarely close their jaws on either humans or each other aggressively. Raking one another with the teeth with jaws held open is common and is probably a form of sexual play or dominance sparring but biting almost always seems to be feeding behavior rather than aggressive behavior. There have been several instances of humans being bitten by captive whales (*Globicephala, Pseudorca, Orcinus orca*), but it is our impression that these are accidental results of an attempt by the whale to manipulate the person in play or to pull the person away from a cherished object, rather than biting *per se*. An interaction between a killer whale and a girl swimmer, at Sea World in San Diego, California, appears to be a case in point. The girl was riding the whale, wearing a bathing suit rather than the diver's rubber suit the whale was accustomed to. The whale grabbed her by the leg, and its teeth punctured the leg in many places. It didn't shake or rend her as if she were being treated like food, and it seems likely that if the motive had been social aggression the whale would not have mouthed her but would have rammed her.

Something as innocuous as splashing can be used aggressively. bottlenosed porpoises and rough-toothed porpoises when aroused to anger in a frustrating situation may drench their trainer with water by breaching or jumping and falling sideways, directly in front of the person. They are capable of selecting the intended recipient of this display from among a group of people at tank-side. While some splashing of bystanders by active animals is accidental when a specific person is soaked four or five times in as many minutes by a specific animal and both are moving about freely it does seem deliberate. Interestingly this kind of display sometimes seems to be precipitated by a situation in which the animal wants help; it wants to be fed, or it has been isolated from its porpoise neighbors and wants an intervening gate opened; and it often splashes the human with whom it is most familiar, who one might surmise, "*should* be helping and isn't." Possibly some aggressive behavior between porpoises is similarly motivated: a female Pacific spotted porpoise which was customarily reinforced with fish along with a male of the same species when the male jumped through a hoop, could be heard and seen making a loud chattering sound and chasing him about the tank whenever he failed to make the jump correctly.

We have never seen a porpoise "go berserk" and attack a human with persistence as a dog or a horse may do. One gains the subjective impression that the porpoise is a firm, fair disciplinarian, exhibiting just as much aggression as will serve its purpose and no more. A female rough-toothed porpoise, mother of a hybrid calf, was kept in a tank alone with her calf and frequently solicited stroking from her trainer. The calf occasionally situated itself between mother and trainer while the mother was being stroked. When the calf was approximately a month old, the trainer in this situation one day stroked the calf. The mother swung her tail from the water, reached up and out, and struck the trainer a sharp but not damaging blow across the shoulders, and then with no further apparent fear or anger continued to solicit stroking for herself.

Open ocean training and the working animal

A recent development in use of cetaceans has been training of various species to perform useful work in the open sea. The first publicly announced successful releases of trained animals occurred in 1964, in parallel programs conducted by the Oceanic Institute in Hawaii and the Naval Undersea Center at Pt. Mugu, California. Since then, use of porpoises at sea has become frequent in the United States and other nations (Norris 1965).

In most programs, one or more animals are trained to return to a shoreline or floating pen in response to an underwater sound stimulus. Animals may also be conditioned to accompany a boat in return for occasional food rewards. The task to be performed at sea is conditioned in captivity. The animal is then released for periods of up to four hours daily, required to perform its learned tasks, and returned to the pen for rest.

Such an animal may be used for research purposes requiring more room than a tank affords, such as diving physiology studies (Norris *et al.* 1965), hydrodynamic studies (Norris 1965; Lang and Pryor 1966), or long-range echolocation investigation. Or it may be used for domesticated tasks; porpoises have been successfully used to locate mislaid or salvageable items on the sea floor; to locate "lost" divers; to carry messages, tools, and other small items from diver to diver or between diver and boat; to dive on command; and even to push a surfer and his surfboard back out to sea. Current programs in Hawaii and elsewhere are attempting to develop porpoise-trainer teams to warn against sharks, to herd fish, and to recover fish traps.

Although several species have been used in this work, so far the Atlantic and Pacific bottlēnosed porpoises have proved most reliable; individuals of other species may revert to their wild state and depart permanently, but bottlenosed porpoises seem to feel dependent on the trainer, rarely stray more than 200 yards away, and will retreat to the holding pen or the trainer's side if alarmed.

An animal may get out of his pen, but once the animal has effected a way out of his confinement he usually wishes to go back and forth at will. Sometimes it is easier to permit this than prevent it. At the Makapuu Oceanic Center some porpoises are kept in pens alongside a pier in the ocean. At the time of this writing, two such animals have for three months spent most of their time at liberty in the pier area but jump back into the pen if anything alarming occurs such as the arrival of an unfamiliar boat, or if instructed to do so by the trainer. The presence of small fish in the area does not interfere with training. Like many captive animals, once accustomed to a single kind of food, the bottlenosed porpoise is reluctant to change, and prefers the dead fish in the trainer's bucket to whatever live fish may be nearby. I have seen a bottlenosed porpoise, wild-caught as an adult and in captivity but a few months, soliciting dead smelt from the trainer while its head and body were almost obscured by a school of live fish of smelt-like size and shape.

A more serious distraction is passing boats. Porpoises enjoy the free ride they can get from a boat's bow waves, and may be seduced from the training area if another boat passes through. The passing of another porpoise school in the distance has not yet been seen to be a distraction. The appearance of sharks in the work area can cause flight or retreat to the pen.

Conclusion: Porpoises, Whales and Man

Porpoises and small whales represent a large and little-known group of mammals of particular interest to the physiologist, the ethologist, the psychologist, the acoustical physicist, and the lay public. Present techniques allow the keeping of most species of *Delphinidae* in captivity and it is reasonable to assume that these techniques will be extended to the great whales during the next ten years. Some species of porpoises seem to be well-suited to domestication, and are able to perform useful work for man in an alien environment comparable to the work done by the camel in the desert and the sled dog in the arctic.

Porpoises and whales represent an important potential and world-wide natural food resource, In the opinion of some ecologists the great whales constitute the most efficient way to harvest the plankton protein resources of the polar seas, which may some day become of vital importance on this crowded planet [36]. Present whale stocks are seriously depleted by insufficiently controlled hunting. Opportunity to study the behavior of the great whales is lacking; that such study might prove interesting is suggested by recently discovered elaborate "songs" of the Humpback Whale *(Megaptera nodosa);* a phenomenon for which at present no satisfactory explanation exists (Payne 1971).

Many ocean-going peoples regard the porpoise with superstitious affection and refrain from hunting it; nevertheless some porpoise populations are far from immune to human predation, and porpoises may be expected to be decimated like most other large mammals in the years ahead if precautions are not instituted. Porpoises are an important food or oil resource in some areas (Japan, New Hebrides, Peru, Okinawa, Labrador), where whole schools are driven ashore and slaughtered. New methods of fishing for tuna involve locating porpoise schools which live in association with tuna, surrounding both species with very large nets, and catching the tuna while letting the porpoises go. Despite some efforts of fishermen to save the porpoises, up to 50 percent of the school are drowned in the nets in each cast, or more than 200,000 animals a year in the eastern tropical Pacific alone; a predation rate which cannot long be tolerated by animals which reproduce at a rate of a single offspring but once every one or two years.

In addition to further investigations of porpoises and whales in captivity there is imperative need for world-wide studies leading to accurate population assessments, understanding of migration patterns, and management of this resource to prevent depletion.

References

Busnel, R.G., 1966. Information in the human whistled language and sea mammal whistling. In: *Whales, Dolphins, and Porpoises,* K.S. Norris, Ed., University of California Press, Berkeley.

Caldwell, M.C., and D.K. Caldwell, 1965. Individualized whistle contours in bottlenosed dolphins, *Tursiops truncatus*. *Nature* 207: 434.

Dreher, J.J., 1966. Cetacean communication: small-group experiment. In: *Whales, Dolphins, and Porpoises*, K.S. Norris, Ed., University of California Press, Berkeley.

Evans, W.E., 1967. Vocalization among marine mammals. In: *Marine Bio-Acoustics*, Vol. 2, W.N. Tavolga, Ed., Pergamon Press, New York.

Evans, W.E., 1971. Orientation behavior of delphinids: radio telemetric studies. *Ann. NY Acad. Sci.* 188: 142.

Kellogg, W.N., 1968. *Porpoises and Sonar*. University of Chicago Press.

Lang, T.G., and K.W. Pryor, 1966. Hydrodynamic performance of porpoises *(Stenella attenuata)*. *Science*, 152: 531.

Lang, T.G., and H.A.P. Smith, 1965. Communication between dolphins in separate tanks by way of an acoustic link. *Science* 150: 1839.

Lilly, J.C., 1963. Distress call of the bottlenose dolphin. *Science* 139: 116.

Lilly, J.C., 1962. Vocal behavior of the bottlenose dolphin. Proc. *Amer. Philos. Soc.*, 106: 520.

Lilly, J.C. and A.M. Miller, 1961. Sounds emitted by the bottlenose dolphin. *Science* 133.

Mackay, R.S., 1966. Telemetering physiological information from within cetaceans. In: *Whales, Dolphins, and Porpoises*, K.S. Norris, Ed., University of California Press, Berkeley.

Norris, K.S., 1963. Some problems of echolocation in cetaceans. In: *Marine Bio-Acoustics* Vol. 1, W.N. Tavolga, Ed., Pergamon Press, New York.

Norris, K.S., 1965. Trained porpoise released in the open sea. *Science* 147: 1048.

Norris, K.S., 1968. The echolocation of marine mammals In: *The Biology of Marine Mammals*, H.T. Anderson, Ed., Academic Press, New York.

Norris, K.S., H.A. Baldwin, and D.J. Samson, 1965. Open ocean diving test with a trained porpoise *(Steno bredanensis)*. *Deep-Sea Res.* 12: 505

Norris, K.S., and J.H. Prescott, 1961. Observations on Pacific cetaceans of Californian and Mexican waters. *Univ. Calif. Publ. Zool.*, 63: 291.

Payne, R., 1971. *Songs of the Humpback Whales*. CRM Records, Del Mar, Calif.

Pryor, K.W., Haag, R., and J. O'Reilly, 1967. The creative porpoise: training for novel behavior. *J. Exper. Anal. Behav.* 12, 653.

Pryor, T.A., Pryor, K.W., Norris, K.S., 1965. Observations on a pygmy killer whale *(Feresa attenuata* Gray) from Hawaii. *J. Mammal.* 46: 450.

Reynolds, G.S., 198. *A Primer of Operant Conditioning*. Scott-Foresman and Co. Glenview, IL.

Tavolga, M.C., 1966. Behavior of the bottlenose dolphin *(Tursiops trancatus):* Social interactions in a captive colony. In: *Whales, Dolphins, and Porpoises*, K.S. Norris, Ed., University of California Press, Berkeley.

Two decades later...

When this paper was written, we at Sea Life Park called our small cetaceans "porpoises;" nowadays, along with most scientists, I would call all the animals here "dolphins," and restrict the word porpoise to one particular subgroup of cetaceans found in colder waters. Otherwise I see little, twenty years later, that has changed, except perhaps my optimism for the future of dolphins as working domestic animals in the open sea.

I still think there are marvelous possibilities, both in scientific work and in sheer adventure, for using dolphins as working partners in their natural habitat. However the Marine Mammal Protection Act has ringed dolphin researchers around with so many rules and regulations that it is no longer possible to take one's research animals out of their cages in the casual way we so often did. I'm a champion of that legislation, but in this case I think it restricts the scientific imagination most unwisely; I'm glad we got to do as much experimental work at sea as we did. It was just about the most fun I've ever had in my life, too.

Hou, a rough-toothed dolphin, spits water at trainer Ingrid Kang, a behavior Hou invented during the "Creative Porpoise" experiment at the Ocean Science Theatre at Sea Life Park.

Reaching into an animal's mind...

This piece of research began more or less by accident, as you will see in the report. Malia, the rough-toothed dolphin who had surprised me before, now surprised me again by catching onto the idea that we wanted her to think up new things to do. Gregory Bateson, the philosopher, who was resident guru at the Oceanic Institute, was fascinated with this event and its implications about the intelligence of dolphins. Gregory's enthusiasm convinced the Office of Naval Research to fund a repetition of the training process.

I functioned as chief investigator; Ingrid Kang, my second-in-command then, did the training, and two psychology graduate students from the University of Hawaii, Dick Haag and Joe O'Reilly, recorded the data and turned it into graphs, a hellish job for which there was no existing system (so we made one up). I wrote up the results in a Navy research report. The Navy also made a small film about the experiment, and *Psychology Today* published an article about it. None of those things however, constituted real scientific publication, which must take place in a "peer-reviewed" scientific journal. So I worked for some months on a paper that could be submitted to the scientific publication we'd settled on, *The Journal of Experimental Analysis of Behavior*. What excited me about the experiment was not the cleverness of the dolphin but the fact that we had hit on a way to use operant conditioning to tell the dolphin, "Show us how clever you can be." That was what I wanted the paper to demonstrate.

When you submit a manuscript to a scientific research journal, the editor sends it out to senior scientists in your field for anonymous review. Sometimes they shoot it down completely. Sometimes they offer suggestions. This manuscript came back from the *J.E.A.B.* editor to me with two reviews, each of them many pages long, criticizing and correcting and questioning nearly every sentence. Dick and Joe were appalled, but I was thrilled, because on close reading those two reviews told me exactly what I needed to know. First, these anonymous but distinguished reviewers had taken the time to tell me, almost line by line, how to make the paper publishable. Secondly at no point did they disagree with our methods or with my conclusions. Besides, one of the readers said that he thought they should do everything possible to try to publish "this elegant, natural science account." That reinforcement sustained me nicely through the revision period.

CHAPTER TWO

The Creative Porpoise: Training for Novel Behavior

Karen Pryor, Richard Haag, and Joseph O'Reilly[1,2]

Abstract:

Two rough-toothed porpoises (Steno bredanensis) were individually trained to emit novel responses, which were not developed by shaping and which were not previously known to occur in the species, by reinforcing a different response to the same set of stimuli in each of a

[1]Contribution No. 35, the Oceanic Institute, Makapuu Oceanic Center, Waimanalo, Hawaii. Carried out under Naval Ordnance Testing Station Contract #N60530-12292, NOTS, China Lake, California. A detailed account of this experiment, including the cumulative records for each session, has been published as NOTS Technical Publication. #4270 and may be obtained from the Clearing House for Federal Scientific and Technical Information, U.S. Department of Commerce, Washington, DC. A 16-mm film, "Dolphin Learning Studies," based on this experiment, has been prepared by the U.S. Navy. Persons wishing to view this film may inquire of the Motion Picture Production Branch, Naval Undersea Warfare Center, 201 Rosecrans Street, San Diego, California 92132. The authors wish to thank Gregory Bateson of the Oceanic Institute, Dr. William Weist of Reed College, Oregon, and Dr. Leonard Diamond of the University of Hawaii for their extensive and valuable assistance; also Dr. William McLean, Technical Director, Naval Undersea Research and Development Center, San Diego, California, for his interest and support.

[2]Reprinted with permission from *the Journal of the Experimental Analysis of Behavior*, 1969, 12, 653-661.

series of training sessions. A technique was developed for transcribing a complex series of behaviors on to a single cumulative record so that the training sessions of the second animal could be fully recorded. Cumulative records are presented for a session in which the criterion that only novel behaviors would be reinforced was abruptly met with four new types of responses, and for typical preceding and subsequent sessions. Some analogous techniques in the training of pigeons, horses, and humans are discussed.

The shaping of novel behavior, that is, behavior that does not occur or perhaps cannot occur, in an animal's normal activity, has been a preoccupation of animal trainers for centuries. The fox-terrier turning back somersaults, the elephant balancing on one front foot, or Ping-Pong playing pigeons (Skinner, 1962) are produced by techniques of successive approximation, or shaping. However, novel or original behavior that is not apparently produced by shaping or differential reinforcement is occasionally seen in animals. Originality is a fundamental aspect of behavior but one that is rather difficult to induce in the laboratory.

In the fall of 1965, at Sea Life Park at the Makapuu Oceanic Center in Hawaii, the senior author introduced into the five daily public performances at the Ocean Science Theater a demonstration of reinforcement of previously unconditioned behavior. The subject animal was a female rough-toothed porpoise, *Steno bredanensis*, named Malia. Since behavior that had been reinforced previously could no longer be used to demonstrate this first step in conditioning, it was necessary to select a new behavior for reinforcement in each demonstration session. Within a few days, Malia began emitting an unprecedented range of behaviors, including aerial flips, gliding with the tail out of the water, and "skidding" over the tank floor, some of which were as complex as responses normally produced by shaping techniques, and many of which were quite unlike anything seen in Malia or any other porpoise by Sea Life Park staff. It appeared that the trainer's criterion, "only those actions will be reinforced which have not been reinforced previously," was met by Malia with the presentation of complete patterns of gross body movement in which novelty was an intrinsic factor. Furthermore, the trainers could not imagine shaped behaviors as unusual as some emitted spontaneously by the porpoise.

To see if the training situation used with Malia could again produce a "creative" animal, the authors repeated Malia's training, as far as possible, with another animal, one that was not being used for public demonstrations or any other work at the time. A technique of record keeping was developed to pinpoint if possible the events leading up to repeated emissions of novel behaviors.

Method

A porpoise named Hou, of the same species and sex as Malia, was chosen. Hou had been trained to wear harness and instruments and to participate in physiological experiments in the open sea (Norris, 1965). This individual had a large repertoire of shaped responses but its "spontaneous activity" had never been reinforced. Hou was considered by Sea Life Park trainers to be a docile, timid individual with little initiative.

Training sessions were arranged to simulate as nearly as possible Malia's five brief daily sessions. Two to four sessions were held daily, lasting from 5 to 20 min each, with rest periods of about half an hour between sessions. Hou was given normal rations; it is not generally necessary to reduce food intake or body weight in cetaceans to make food effective as a reinforcer. Any food not earned in training sessions was given freely to the animal at the end of the day, and it was fed normal rations, without being required to work, on weekends. During the experimental period, no work was required of Hou other than that in the experiment itself. A bell was rung at the beginning and end of sessions to serve as a context marker. The appearance and positioning of the trainers served as an additional stimulus that the opportunity for reinforcement was now present.

To record the events of each session, the trainer and two observers, one above water and one watching the underwater area through the glass tank walls, wore microphones and made a verbal commentary; earphones allowed the experimenters to hear each other. The three commentaries, and the sound of the conditioned reinforcer, the whistle, were recorded on a single tape. A typed transcript was made of each tape; then, by comparing transcript to tape, the transcript was marked at 15-sec intervals. Each response of the animal was then graphed on a cumulative record, with a separate curve to indicate each type of response in a given session (Fig. 2 to 6).

It was necessary to make a relatively arbitrary decision about what constituted a reinforceable or recordable act. In general, a reinforceable act consisted of any movement that was not part of the normal swimming action of the animal, and which was sufficiently extended through space and time to be reported by two or more observers. Such behavior as eye-rolling, inaudible whistling, and gradual changes in direction may have occurred, but they could not be distinguished by the trainers and therefore could not be reinforced, except coincidentally. This unavoidable contingency probably had the effect of increasing the incidence of gross motor responses. Position and sequence of responses were not considered. An additional criterion, which had been a contingency in much of Hou's previous training, was that only one type of response would be reinforced per session.

The experimental plan of reinforcing a new type of response in each session was not fully met. Sometimes a previously reinforced response was again chosen for reinforcement, to strengthen the response, to increase the general level of responding, or to film a given behavior. Whether the "reviewing" of responses was helpful or detrimental to the animal's progress is open to speculation.

Inter-observer reliability was judged from the transcripts of the taped sessions, in which a new behavior was generally recognized in concert by the observers. Furthermore, each new behavior chosen for reinforcement was later diagrammed in a series of position sketches. At no time did any of the three observers fail to agree that the drawings represented the behaviors witnessed. These behavior diagrams were matched, at the end of the experiment, with film of each behavior, and were found to represent adequately the topography of those behaviors that had been reinforced (see Fig. 1).

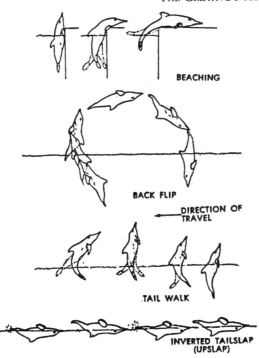

Fig. 1. Diagrams of four reinforced novel behaviors, includng one shaped behavior, the tailwalk.

After 32 training sessions, the topography of Hou's aerial behaviors became so complex that, while undoubtedly novel, the behaviors exceeded the powers of the observers to discriminate and describe them. This breakdown in observer reliability was one factor in the termination of the experiment.

Steno bredanensis, the species of which Hou and Malia are members, has not been kept in captivity in the United States except at Sea Life Park. Therefore, data pertaining to normal behavior, plentiful for more common species such as *Tursiops truncatus,* are lacking. To corroborate the experimenters' observation that certain of Hou's responses were not in the normal repertoire of the species, and constituted genuine novelties, the diagrams of each reinforced behavior were shown or sent to the 12 past and present staff members who had had occasion to work with animals of this species. Each trainer was asked to rank the 16 behaviors in order of frequency of occurrence in a free-swimming untrained animal. The sketches were mounted on index cards and presented in random fashion to each rater separately. A coefficient of concordance (W) of 0.598 was found for agreement between trainers on the ranking of various behaviors; this value is significant at the 0.001 level, indicating a high degree of agreement (Siegel, 1956).

To test the possibility that the trainers were judging complexity rather than novelty in ranking, another questionnaire was prepared requesting ranking according to relative degree of complexity of action. Because some of the original group of 12 trainers were unavailable for retesting, the questionnaire was presented to a group of 49 naive students. The coefficient of concordance (W) for agreement between students was +0.295, significant at the 0.001 level. When the rankings for complexity and frequency were contrasted for each behavior, it was found that some agreement existed between the scores given by the two rating groups, Spearman Rank Correlation (RHO) +0.54, significant at the 0.05 level.

Thus, there seems to be some agreement between complexity and frequency, which should be expected, since complex behaviors require more muscle expenditure than simple ones. Furthermore, analysis was biased by the fact that the experienced group was asked to rate all behaviors serially, and had no way other than complexity to rate the several behaviors which many of them stated they had never seen. However, the agreement between complexity and frequency was not as large between groups as it was within groups; allowing for the fact that the use of two rating groups makes it impossible to generalize the rating comparisons in a strict sense, the low frequency assigned to some non-complex behaviors by the experienced group suggests that complexity and novelty are not necessarily positively correlated.

Results

Sessions 1 to 14

In the first session, Hou was admitted into the experimental tank and, when given no commands, breached. Breaching, or jumping into the air and coming down sideways, is a normal action in a porpoise. This response was reinforced, and the animal began to repeat it on an average of four times a minute for 8 min. Toward the end of the 9-min session it porpoised, or leaped smoothly out of the water and in, once or twice. It continued to breach in the absence of the trainer, during a half-hour break. In the second session porpoising was reinforced and was repeated several times.

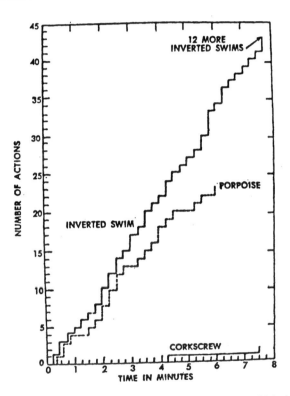

Fig. 2. Cumulative record of Session 7, a typical early session, in which the porpoise began by emitting the previously reinforced response. This response gradually extinguished when another response was reinforced.

Hou began the third session by porpoising; when this behavior was not reinforced, the animal rapidly developed a behavior pattern of porpoising in front of the trainer, entering the water in an inverted position, turning right side up, swimming in a large circle, and returning to porpoise in front of the trainer again.

It did this 25 times without interruption over a period of 12.5 min. Finally, it stopped and laid its head against the pool edge at the trainer's feet. This behavior, nicknamed "beaching," was reinforced and repeated (Fig. 2).

Sessions 5, 6, and 7 followed the same pattern. Hou began each session with the behavior that had been reinforced in the previous session. Occasionally this behavior was chosen for reinforcement when the trainer felt it had not been strongly established in the previous session. If the first response was not reinforced, Hou ran through its repertoire of responses reinforced in previous sessions: breaching, porpoising, beaching, and swimming upside-down. If no reinforcement was forthcoming, it took up the rigid pattern of porpoising, inverting, circling.

The trainers decided to shape specific responses in order to interrupt Hou's unvarying repetition of a limited repertoire. Session 8 was devoted to shaping a "tail walk," or the behavior of balancing vertically half out of the water. The tail walk was reinforced in Session 9, and Sessions 10 and 11 were tie-voted to shaping a "tail wave," the response of lifting the tail from the water. The tail wave was emitted and reinforced in Session 12.

While this represented a departure from the primary goal of conditioning novel behavior, the experimenters realized that Malia, the show animal, had experienced some training sessions in which, no new spontaneous action being emitted, some specific response was shaped. It was not known whether or not the shaping sessions had contributed to Malia's ability to emit novel responses. Therefore, the inclusion of shaping in Hou's training seemed permissible. It also seemed desirable to prevent a low level of reinforcement from leading to extinction of all responses.

At the end of Session 10, Hou slapped its tail twice, which was reinforced but not repeated. At the end of Session 12, Hou departed from the stereotyped pattern to the extent of inverting, turning right-side up, and then inverting again while circling. The experimenters observed and reinforced this underwriter revolution from a distance, while leaving the experimental area.

Although a weekend then intervened, Hou began Session 13 by swimming in the inverted position, then right-side-up, then inverted again. This behavior, dubbed a "corkscrew," was reinforced, and by means of an increasing variable ratio, was extended to five complete revolutions per reinforcement. In Session 14, the experimenters rotated their positions, and reinforced any descent by the animal toward the bottom of the tank, in a further effort not only to expand Hou's repertoire but also to interrupt the persistent circling behavior.

Sessions 15 and 16

The next morning, as the experimenters set up their equipment, Hou was unusually active in the holding tank. It slapped its tail twice, and this was so unusual that the trainer reinforced the response in the holding tank. When Session 15 began, Hou emitted the response reinforced in the previous session, of swimming near the bottom, and then the response previous to that of the corkscrew, and then fell into the habitual circling and porpoising, with, however, the addition of a tail-slap on re-entering the water. This slap was reinforced, and the animal then combined slapping with breaching, and then began slapping disassociated from jumping; for the first time it emitted responses in all parts of the tank, rather than right in front of the trainer. The 10-min session ended when 17 tailslaps had been reinforced, and other non-reinforced responses had dropped out.

Session 16 began after a 10-min break. Hou became extremely active when the trainer appeared and immediately offered twisting breaches, landing on its belly and its back. It also began somersaulting on its long axis in mid-air. The trainer began reinforcing the last, a "flip," common in the genus *Stenella* but not normally seen in *Steno*, and Hou became very active, swimming in figure eights (unprecedented) and leaping repeatedly. The flip occurred 44 times, intermingled with some of the previously reinforced responses and with three other responses that had not been seen before: an upside-down tailslap, a sideswipe with the tail, and an aerial spin on the short axis of the body (see Fig. 3).

The previous maximum number of types of responses offered in a single session was five. The average number of types was

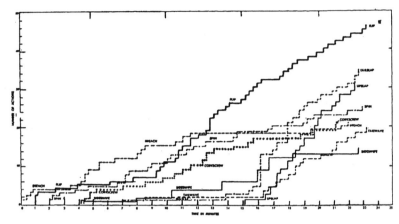

Fig.3. Cumulative record of Session 16, in which the porpoise emitted eight different types of responses, four of which were novel (flip, spin, sideswipe, and upslap.)

less than two per session. At no time before Session 16 was more than one new behavior seen, and in all but three cases— breaching, beaching, and porpoising—the new behavior was at least partly developed by the trainer. In Session 16, Hou emitted a total of eight behaviors, each one many times, including four completely new, unreinforced behaviors, two of which, the spin and the flip, were elaborately performed from the beginning.

This session also differed from previous ones in that once the flip had become established, the other behaviors did not tend to drop out. After 24 min, the varied activity—tailslaps, breaches, sideswipes with the tail, and the new behavior of spinning in the air—occurred more rather than less frequently, until the session was brought to a close by the trainer. The previous maximum number of responses in a given session was 110 (in Session 9, a 31-min session). In Session 16, Hou emitted 192 responses in a 23-min session, an average of 8.3 per min compared to a previous maximum average of 3.6 per min.

By Session 16, the experimenters had apparently been successful in establishing a class of responses characterized by the description, "only new kinds of responses will be reinforced," and consequently the porpoise was emitting an extensive variety of new responses. The differences between Session 16 and previous sessions may be seen by comparing the cumulative record for Session 16 (Fig. 3) with that of Session 7, a typical earlier session (Fig. 2).

Sessions 17 to 27

In Sessions 17 to 27, the new types of responses emitted in Session 16 were selected, one by one, for reinforcement, and some old responses were reinforced again so that they could be photographed. Other new responses, such as unclassifiable twisting jumps, and sinking head downwards, occurred sporadically. The average rate of response and the numbers of types of responses per session remained more than twice as high as pre-Session 16 levels.

Hou's general activity changed in two other ways after Session 16. First, if no reinforcement occurred in a period of several minutes, the rate and level of activity declined but the animal did not necessarily resume a stereotyped behavior pattern. Secondly, the animal's activity now included much behavior typically associated in cetaceans with situations producing frustration or aggressiveness, such as slapping the water with head, tail, pectoral fin, or whole body (Burgess, 1968).

Sessions 28 to 33

In all of the final sessions, the criterion that the behavior must be a new one was enforced. A new behavior that had been seen but not reinforced previously, the inverted tailslap, had been reinforced in Session 27. Session 28 began with a variety of responses, including another that had been seen but not reinforced before, a sideswipe at water surface with the tail, which was reinforced. In Session 29, Hou's activity included an inverted leap that fulfilled the criterion (Fig. 4). In Session 30, Hou offered 60 responses over a period of 15 min, none of which were considered new, and were not therefore reinforced.

In Sessions 31, 32, and 33, held the next day, Hou's behavior was more completely controlled by the criteria that only new types of responses were reinforced and that only one type of

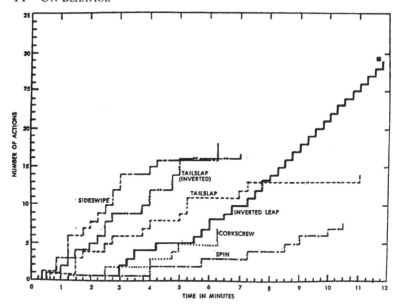

Fig. 4. Cumulative record of Session 29, in which the porpoise emitted the three most recently reinforced responses initially, but soon emitted a novel response. When this response was reinforced the others extinguished.

response was reinforced per session. In Session 31, Hou entered the tank and, after a preliminary jump, stood on its tail and clapped its jaws at the trainer, who, taken by surprise, failed to reinforce the maneuver. Hou then emitted a brief series of leaps and then executed a backwards aerial flip that was reinforced and immediately repeated 14 times without intervening responses of other types. In Session 32, after one porpoise and one flip, Hou executed an upside-down porpoise, and, after it was reinforced, repeated this new response 10 times, again without other responses (Figs. 5, 6).

In the third session of the day, Hou did not initially emit a response judged new by the observers. After 10 min and 72 responses of variable types, the rate of response declined to 1 per min and then gradually rose again to seven responses per minute after 19 min. No reinforcements occurred during this period. At the end of 19 min, Hou stood on its tail and clapped its jaws,

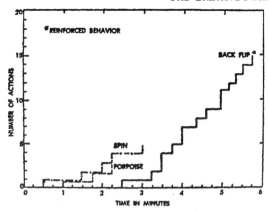

Fig. 5. Cumulative record of Session 31. The porpoise emitted a novel response early in the session, and other responses extinguished immediately when the novel response was reinforced.

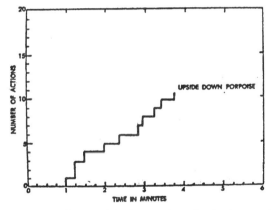

Fig. 6. Cumulative record of Session 32. The porpoise emitted only a novel response in this session.

spitting water towards the trainer; this time the action was reinforced, and was repeated five times.

Hou had now produced a new behavior in six out of seven consecutive sessions. In Sessions 31 and 32, Hou furthermore began each session with a new response and emitted no unreinforceable responses once reinforcement was presented. This establishment of a series of new types of responses was considered to be the conclusion of the experiment.

Discussion

Over a period of 4 yr since Sea Life Park and the neighboring Oceanic Institute were opened, the training staff has observed and trained over 50 cetaceans of seven different species. Of the 16 behaviors reinforced in this experiment, five (breaching, porpoising, inverted swimming, tail slap, sideswipe) have been observed to occur spontaneously in every species; four (beaching, tailwalk, inverted tail slap, spitting) have been developed by shaping in various animals but very rarely occur spontaneously in any; three (spinning, back porpoise, forward flip) occur spontaneously only in one species of *Stenella* and have never been observed at Sea Life Park in other species; and four (corkscrew, back flip, tailwave, inverted leap) have never been observed to occur spontaneously. While this does not imply that these behaviors do not sometimes occur spontaneously, whatever the species, it does serve to indicate that a single animal, in emitting these 16 types of responses, would be engaging in behavior well outside the species norm.

A technique of reinforcing a series of different, normally occurring actions, in a series of training sessions, did therefore serve, in the case of Hou, as with Malia, to establish in the animal a highly increased probability that new types of behavior would be emitted.

This ability to emit an unusual response need not be regarded as an example of cleverness peculiar to the porpoise. It is possible that the same technique could be used to achieve a similar result with pigeons. If a different, normally occurring action in a pigeon is reinforced each day for a series of days, until the normal repertoire (turning, pecking, flapping wings, etc.) is exhausted, the pigeon may come to emit novel responses difficult to produce even by shaping.

A similar process may be involved in one traditional system of the training of five-gaited show horses, which perform at three natural gaits, the walk, trot, and canter, and two artificial gaits, the slow-gait and the rack. The trainer first reinforces the performance of the natural gaits and brings this performance under stimulus control. The discriminative stimuli, which control not only the gait, but also speed, direction, and position of the horse while executing the gait, consist of pressure and release from the rider's legs, pressures on the reins and consequently the bit, shifting of weight in the saddle, and sometimes signals with whip and voice. To elicit the artificial gait, the trainer next presents the animal with a new group of stimuli, shaking the bit back and forth in the horse's mouth and vibrating the legs against the horse's sides, while preventing the animal from terminating the stimuli (negative reinforcement) by means of the previously reinforced responses of walking, trotting, or cantering. The animal will emit a variety of responses that eventually may include the pattern of stepping, novel to the horse though familiar to the trainer, called the rack (Hildebrand, 1965). The pattern, however brief, is reinforced, and once established is extended in duration and brought under stimulus control. (The slow-gait is derived from the rack by shaping.)

Upon conclusion of this experiment, Hou was returned to the care of Sea Life Park trainers and introduced as a performer in five daily shows six days a week until the time of writing (April 1969). Hou performs a number of behaviors under stimulus control, some of which first appeared during this experiment. Spitting, for example, is now offered in response to the discriminative stimulus of a hand signal, and, as is the case for all conditioned behaviors used for performance, has been successfully extinguished in the absence of the stimulus. The trend towards the emission of novel behavior has, in the case of both Hou and Malia, been reversed during normal training and performance; they respond to learned stimuli correctly, with no more than normal unconditioned activity, and a single new response can be reinforced and shaped with no great increase occurring in types of responses offered. However, both animals can be stimulated to a high rate of activity, including novel behavior, if the trainer leaves the normal demonstration training platform and takes up a position across the tank in the station used during the experiment. Thus, a session of reinforcing novel behavior can be introduced occasionally into a show without interfering with the normal presentation of behaviors under stimulus control. This occurs perhaps once a month. At least one behavior—flapping the last third of the body in the air, while hanging head down in the water—has been first reinforced, later to be brought under stimulus control, during such a session.

Comparison may be made here between this work and that of Maltzman (1960). Working in the formidably rich matrix of human subjects and verbal behavior, Maltzman described a successful procedure for eliciting original responses, consisting of reinforcing different responses to the same stimuli, essentially the same procedure followed with Hou and Malia. It is interesting to note that behavior considered by the authors to indicate anger in the porpoise was observed under similar circumstances in human subjects by Maltzman: "An impression gained from observing Ss [subjects] in the experimental situation is that repeated evocation of different responses to the same stimuli becomes quite frustrating; Ss are disturbed by what quickly becomes a surprisingly difficult task. This disturbed behavior indicates that the procedure may not be trivial and does approximate a non-laboratory situation involving originality or inventiveness, with its frequent concomitant frustration."

Maltzman also found that eliciting and reinforcing original behavior in one set of circumstances increased the tendency for original responses in other kinds of situations, which seems likewise to be true for Hou and Malia. Hou continues to exhibit a marked increase in general level of activity. Hou has learned to leap tank partitions to gain access to other porpoises, a skill very seldom developed by a captive porpoise. When a trainer was occupied at an adjoining porpoise tank Malia jumped from the water, skidded across 6 ft of wet pavement, and tapped the trainer on the ankle with its rostrum or snout, a truly bizarre act for an entirely aquatic animal.

Maltzman also observed that under some conditions originality may be increased by evoking a relatively large number of different responses to different stimuli. The confirmation of this hypothesis is suggested by our informal observations of performing cetaceans, at least some of which develop a tendency to original behavior after a year or two of reinforcement with respect to many different kinds of stimuli and responses. We do not observe this "sophistication" developing in animals that are trained with respect to one group of responses and stimuli and then continue in the same pattern, however complex, for months or years.

Individual differences in the ability to create unorthodox responses no doubt exist; Malia's novel responses, judged *in toto,* are more spectacular and "imaginative" than Hou's. However, by using the technique of training for novelty described herein, it should be possible to induce a tendency towards spontaneity and creative or unorthodox response in most individuals of a broad range of species.

References

Burgess, K. The behavior and training of a killer whale at San Diego Sea World. *International Zoo Yearbook,* 1968, 8, 202-205.

Hildebrand, M. Symmetrical gaits of horses. *Science,* 1965, 150, 701-708.

Maltzman, I. On the training of originality. *Psychological Review,* 1960, 67, 229-242.

Norris. K. S. Open ocean diving test with a trained porpoise *(Steno bredanensis). Deep Sea Research,* 1965, 12, 505-509.

Siegel, S. *Nonparametric Statistics for the Behavioral Sciences.* New York: McGraw-Hill, 1956.

Skinner, B. F. Two synthetic social relations. *Journal of the Experimental Analysis of Behavior.* 1962, 5, 531-533.

Surprise, surprise...

At first when this paper came out people kept asking me when I was going to continue with this experiment. Continue how? The creative rabbit? We had already demonstrated what we meant to, it seemed to me.

I gave the matter no further thought; but gradually, outside of Hawaii, and to my astonishment, this maverick paper became rather famous. It was anthologized in several textbooks. It became standard teaching fodder in psychology courses all over the country. Other dolphin trainers adapted the techniques to make life more interesting for their dolphins. Dog trainers tried it out, to the great enjoyment of their dogs. The study of variability in behavior, as opposed to repeatability, is now respectable, and the people doing it cite this paper.

Malia lived long and happy years at Sea Life Park, working with trainers who loved her, challenged her, and kept her interested with new projects (three times Malia's amazing stunts won the dolphin training association's Behavior of the Year trophy). Long after I left Sea Life Park I went back to visit Malia now and then. I don't know if she remembered me personally but she always greeted me courteously (by looking at me straight on and allowing me to touch her) and that was honor enough.

Early days of blindfold training. Karen practices on Kane, Makua's tankmate. "I am touching Kane's forehead with the suction cup. Kane is suspicious; he's making me reach for him, and his nearest eye (under shadow of wrist) is squinted shut."

"A nice book about dolphins....."

About ten years after Sea Life Park had opened, my life took a new direction. Tap and I were divorced. The Park was sold and the original management dispersed. I was out of a job. I moved into a small house in the suburbs with my three children, who were now in high school.

I did not miss the dolphins; I knew I had done all I wanted to do with them. I had worked with many animals and many species. One more new animal, one more new behavior held no challenge. I had taught other trainers and they were carrying on the work, often much better than I could.

I was still fascinated, however, with operant conditioning, the magically effective training principles we used. I knew these principles applied to a lot more than dolphins — to raising children, to learning skills, to running companies, for that matter. I wanted to write about operant conditioning.

Clare Booth Luce, a family friend (the widow of the man who started the *Time/Life* publishing empire), was living in Hawaii. She asked me to dinner.

"Now that you are on your own," she said, "what are you going to do?" I told her I wanted to write a book about training.

"Who wants to read that? I certainly don't," she said. I had no clear answer.

"Write a nice book about your dolphins," Clare said. "TIME magazine will review it and everyone will read it and you can stick your training business in somewhere if you feel you have to."

I was furious; I wanted to write a serious book. On the drive home, however, I realized that there was a certain merit to Clare's view. I had a family to support. The world might be in need of a serious book about training, but "a nice book about dolphins" would certainly be easier to sell.

My agents in New York sent the outline for my dolphin book to Harper and Row, who had published *Nursing Your Baby*. They bought it for $5000, which enabled me and my kids to eat, buy gas, and pay rent for the year it took me to write the book.

The publishers and I had a struggle over the title: they wanted to call it *Porpoise Lady*. I wanted a poetic title, and chose a quote from Herman Melville, describing dolphins: "These are the lads that live before the wind..."

We were both wrong, of course. *Porpoise Lady* was crass and would soon have been out of date. *Lads Before the Wind* on the other hand didn't tell you what the book was about. Also it was hard to remember and impossible to say clearly aloud, a great handicap in promoting the book on radio talk shows.

I wrote the book. Konrad Lorenz, with whom I was corresponding, wrote a marvelous foreword. I managed to absolutely cram the book with descriptive information about operant conditioning and how to apply it, using my own experiences as examples. The excerpt that follows describes how I learned to understand and use two of the most confusing concepts in applied behavior analysis: 1) stimulus control as a means of extinguishing unwanted behavior, and 2) the building of behavior chains.

CHAPTER THREE

From *Lads Before the Wind,* Chapter III, "Signaling."

Makua's blindfold training

...Everything was going well except for the blindfold training of Makua [a large male bottlenosed dolphin]. He would have to be blindfolded to exhibit his underwater sonar or echo-location ability. On Ken Norris's recommendation we were using rubber suction cups that stuck over the animal's eyes. We went through a lot of design changes. We tried using purchased suction cups designed to hold ski or surfboard racks onto the roof of a car. We tried using those suction cups but modifying them by grinding them thinner so the suction wouldn't be so strong. We tried casting suction cups out of silicone rubber. We tried making a fiberglass blinker that would cover the animal's eye without touching it; the blinker was held in place with suction cups that went on the animal's head, not directly over his eye.

No matter: Makua was having none of it. As soon as he saw the suction cup in Chris's or Gary's hand, he got ugly and began threatening with his teeth and striking with his rostrum. He was menacing, and the trainers were justifiably unnerved.

As head trainer, I had to cope with whatever was stumping Chris and Gary. I gave them Hoku and Kiko, who were making good progress on several behaviors now, and went to work myself on the bottlenoses....

I decided to practice blindfold training on crippled old Kane, who would never be a show animal. I separated him from Makua for the first sessions. First I tried shaping him to sit still right in front of me and allow me to cover his eyes with my hands, one eye and then the other and then both. No problem. In addition to a whistle and fish reward, I rewarded him with stroking, which he loved. I deliberately refused to stroke him in the normal course of events, but I patted him vigorously after every whistle and before tossing the fish.

Then I rewarded him for allowing me to touch his body with one of the rubber suction cups. I showed it to him, I touched it here and there on his body, I rewarded him from time to time as I did so, until he was completely used to it—horse-training methods. Psychologists call it "habituation." Finally I stuck the suction cup on Kane's back. Catastrophe! Kane broke away and went crashing and leaping all over the tank, trying to dislodge this nasty thing clinging to him. In due course he did dislodge it, and I retrieved it with a net. Then he would not come near the suction cup again.

So I revamped the shaping recipe. Now I trained Kane to press his rostrum against my right hand for prolonged periods, no matter what I was doing with my left hand. I counted the seconds, shaping a ten-second press, a twenty-second press, while I touched, tugged, and poked him here and there with my free hand. When the pressing behavior was well established (we called it "stationing," and learned to use it for all kinds of things) I used my free hand to stick and instantly unstick the suction cup from his back. Since he had learned to "stand still no matter what" he stood for it. From there we rapidly progressed to putting the suction cup anywhere on his body (not his head) and to Kane swimming away with it and bringing it back for me to take off. He had learned that the sticky little thing was harmless, and that I could be trusted to take it off for him.

It just took patience then to get him to tolerate its presence over an eye; and when we'd reached that stage, I switched to Makua.

As soon as Makua saw the suction cup in my hand, he put on his show, rapping my arms and swinging his jaws about. But I had learned something from Gus the dog and Echo the pony stallion, after all; they had both been bold, aggressive animals too. The first time Makua rapped my hand, I was frightened and angry, and I rapped him right back on the rostrum. I couldn't possibly hit him hard enough to hurt, but my intent was clear, and to make it clearer I yelled "No!" and slapped the water with both hands.

Makua sank down about 3 feet and emitted a huge bubble of air underwater. This, I think, is something a porpoise does when it is surprised, though not frightened, by some unexpected turn of events. I have often seen an animal do it when it first notices some change in a prop, or when it suddenly "catches on" to a training idea that has been puzzling it. I was once on a ship that nearly bumped a large whale. When the whale noticed the ship, suddenly so close, it emitted a huge bubble of air as it startled and dove. The behavior always reminds me of a cartoon character with a balloon over its head and a bunch of question marks and exclamation points in the balloon.

Makua gave up trying to strike me after I hit him back, but he still swung his head about with his jaws open; so the next time he did that I grabbed my fish bucket and walked away, giving him a time out for that performance. When I returned, Makua was lolling about with a "Gee, what did I do?" air. He soon gave up all his threatening behavior.

Makua's training then followed Kane's. Soon I could put the blindfolds over both eyes while he stationed in front of me; and I was looking forward to being able to ask him to do things with the blindfolds in place.

He still did not *enjoy* the necessity of having his eyes covered, whether by suction cups or by blinders. One morning when Makua was being particularly sulky and recalcitrant, he suddenly let out his breath and sank to the bottom of the tank, where he lay motionless. A half-minute passed, and then a minute. I became most alarmed. Had he died? It certainly looked like it. I rushed off to find Chris to help me get Makua up again. When Chris looked in the tank, he laughed. "Makua's just sulking. Look at him—he's watching us." Sure enough, through the water surface I could make out Makua's little eye, regarding us wickedly.

Playing possum, Chris told me, was something he had seen several times when a bottlenose was displeased. The first time he saw it he too thought the animal was dying. He jumped in and pulled it up, only to have it take a breath and sink right to the bottom again, more displeased than ever at being hauled about so. He pulled it to the top five times before it became clear to him that the animal was sinking on purpose.

I can't imagine what earthly value this behavior pattern is to a Pacific bottlenose porpoise which spends most of its life in water about 3 miles deep and could hardly sink immobile to lie on the bottom every time it felt miffed. But they sure did it in our tanks.

Once Makua was down there, there was not much I could do. Time outs had no effect; indeed, by sinking, he was giving *me* a time out. There was no way to punish him. Oh, I could have got a long stick, perhaps, and poked him until he came up, but the trouble with that approach is that it makes the subject mad, he gets more resistant, you have to increase the vigor of your punishment to get a reaction, and pretty soon you are resorting to cruel and unusual means, or to violence. That is the nasty trap built into negative reinforcement which we can see operating around us all the time, from treatment of criminals to escalation of bombings. I wasn't about to get involved in that chain of events.

So I dipped into Ron Turner's manual and read and reread the sections on extinction. How do you get rid of a behavior you don't want?

You can punish the undesired behavior; that was out.

You can let it die away by itself for lack of reinforcement; but that wouldn't work this time. As long as Makua persisted in this behavior when I brought out the blindfolds, he was getting reinforced. He was postponing blindfold training, which was what he wanted. Besides, he could and did stay down for five minutes at a time, and one could lose an awful lot of valuable training time waiting for him to come up.

You can interpose some incompatible behavior, training the animal to do something else that can't be done while lying on the bottom; but that is what I was trying to do anyway.

The word "extinction" cropped up quite a lot in the business of bringing behavior under stimulus control; when the behavior is occurring on cue, it is extinguishing off cue. There was the answer! I would train Makua to lie on the bottom on purpose, in response to a sound cue. Then I would extinguish the behavior off cue. Then when I *didn't* want him to play possum, I wouldn't give him the cue.

The next time Makua sank himself, I blew the whistle and threw him a handful of fish. He emitted his large, astonished bubble, and surfaced and ate the fish. We went back to blindfold work. By and by he got mad and sank himself again. I reinforced it again. By the next day he was sinking over and over, and I began requiring a certain length of sinking time and giving him a time out if he came up too soon. Soon I had the sinking behavior stretched to a reliable thirty seconds, and I introduced a sound cue. Makua rapidly learned this, having already assimilated two other sound cues, one for ringing the bell and one for breaching.

At last spontaneous sinking disappeared. Makua sank on command a few times at the end of each session, and he buckled down and wore his blindfolds like a gentleman when asked.

The submerging turned out to be an amusing performance behavior. It was corny, but it was funny. In our glass tank the audience could see Makua above and below water. As he stuck his head out at the training platform, the narrator might explain that the trainer had asked Makua to do something, but forgot to say "please;" and then the cue would go on, quietly, and down Makua would go to the bottom, sinking tail first and lying there, the picture of hurt pride, until the trainer "repaired the error," and turned the cue off. Makua bounced happily to the surface, and the trainer surreptitiously rewarded him with a fish....

Behavior chains

I still had in my mind's eye a vision of Hoku and Kiko [a pair of Pacific spotted dolphins] passing intricately through underwater hoops. A vertical arrangement was difficult to manage in our shallow training tanks, so I decided upon a sort of slalom, a chain of hoops through which the animals would pass, left to right, right to left, like children playing "Go in and out the windows." This would show off the suppleness and grace so characteristic of "kikos" [Hawaiian for spotted], and would also fill up the Ocean Science Theater tank visually in a satisfying way.

The stiff yet bendable plastic pipe used in landscape irrigation systems could be bent into splendid 5-foot-diameter hoops, lightweight, sturdy, and waterproof. We "liberated" some of this pipe from the Sea Life Park construction site and made up a bunch of hoops.

When I had the animals going through one hoop well, I added a second one, at an angle, and tried to get them to go through that one after the first. No luck. They carefully avoided the second hoop. I tried hanging it so close to the first hoop that they practically had to go through it, and yet they would weasel out of the gap, unless there was no gap at all, in which case both hoops looked like one, anyway.

If I gave them no fish unless they went through both hoops, they stopped swimming through hoops altogether, and the behavior extinguished. What was wrong? Surely they weren't afraid of the second hoop? Why couldn't they figure it out— why did they work so hard to *avoid* the second hoop?

I plunged back into the manual and finally even called Ron Turner long distance. It seemed that what we had was not a single behavior but a "behavior chain." A behavior chain is a series of behaviors, each one of which is rewarded by the opportunity to do the following one, until the end is reached. And a behavior chain, curiously, has to be trained backwards.

To train a slalom through several hoops, I had to train, first, the behavior of passing through a single hoop in a single direction, from left to right, and then *put that behavior on cue.* That hoop now became the last hoop in the chain: with my six-hoop plan, it would be hoop 6.

Now I put another hoop in the water, hoop 5, coaxed the animals through it, and rewarded them for swimming back and forth through it, until they were comfortable. Then, when they swam through hoop 5 from right to left, instead of giving them a fish, I turned on the "hoop" cue. They knew what that meant; swim through hoop 6 from left to right, and you'll get a fish.

Thus the cue for hoop 6, left to right, was the reward for hoop 5, right to left.

When they would go through both hoops easily, I started turning the cue on as they approached hoop 5, and leaving it on as they went through. If my timing was right, they went through hoop 5 and then turned and went through hoop 6. If my timing was wrong, they ducked around hoop 5 and went only through hoop 6, but when they did that I could correct them by turning the cue off before they finished the behavior. Soon I could hang both hoops in the tank side by side, put the cue on no matter where the animals were, and they would position themselves and take hoop 5 right to left and hoop 6 left to right, every time.

Now I could introduce hoop 4 in front of hoop 5, use the cue as a reward for passing through that new hoop, left to right, and so on, until we had a handsome slalom of six hoops, having backed all the way up the behavior chain to hoop 1.

The six-bar jump, which had already been accomplished, was of course also a behavior chain, one I had trained successfully through dumb luck. Just by accident, before I tried to get the animals to jump two bars in succession, I had already taught them to jump one bar on cue, and one bar in any part of the tank. It was not difficult for them, then, if they jumped a bar, and the cue was still on, and there was another bar in front of them, to go ahead and jump that one, too. The hoop chain, with its necessity of reversing direction each time, was not so obvious, and skipping the business of putting the behavior on cue first was fatal. Ron pointed out to me that if you start the chain from the front end, and then add the new thing, you are asking an animal to do something he knows, go unreinforced, and then try to get reinforced by doing something he doesn't know. You have to *end up* with the guaranteed sure thing...

...A curious thing happened to the chain of hoops behavior when we eventually got it into the shows. In the training tanks, which were shallow, there was not much water above or below the hoop chain. At Ocean Science Theater, which was 14 feet deep, we hung the chain through the middle of the water, with 5 or 6 feet of water under and over it. Hoku took to going down the chain underneath Kiko, instead of beside her. He paced her exactly, turn for turn, tail beat for tail beat, but under the hoops, not in them. One day, narrating a show, the solution to this problem suddenly occurred to me: I signaled the trainer and the assistant and said to the audience, "We'll lower the hoops to touch the bottom. Then Hoku can't possibly go under them." The assistant slacked the rope, the hoops sank 6 feet, the trainer turned on the cue, and as Kiko went through the hoops, Hoku neatly positioned himself and paced her down the chain, turn for turn, tail beat for tail beat —*over* the hoops. It was hilarious, and we kept it in the show, letting Hoku run under the hoops, lowering the hoops to the bottom and letting him run over them, in every show.

A training book, after all...

When *Lads Before the Wind* was done, I started job-hunting in earnest, leaning on my writing skills. After two months of interviews I landed a job as an advertising copywriter; meanwhile I also got a night job reviewing plays for the Honolulu newspaper. Both jobs were fun, I thought, and easy, compared to what I had been doing. Dry. Indoors. No fish scales under the fingernails. And twice the pay.

Lads was published, sold a few thousand copies, and went out of print. The publishers were mystified; they expected dolphin lovers to buy my book, but in fact, dolphin lovers didn't like this book. A leader in the "Save the Whales" movement finally explained that to me.

"I was so disappointed," she said. "I didn't like finding out that dolphins fight among themselves, and that they aren't always friendly and gentle to people." Konrad Lorenz had said, in his wonderful foreword to *Lads*, "The truth about an animal is far more exciting...and beautiful than all the myths woven about it." Not to everyone, I guess.

As Konrad had also written, however, *Lads* made a pretty good textbook on animal learning and operant conditioning. I began getting letters about it.

"Where can I get your book? I'll buy any old copies you have in the attic."

"Please republish *Lads*; I'm tired of photocopying the whole thing."

"I found a copy in a used-book store but they wanted $50."

This demand was sporadic but urgent. And it was coming, not from dolphin lovers, but from dog trainers, of all things. I couldn't interest any publisher, even a dog book publisher, in reissuing *Lads*, though I tried. Eventually, in 1987, I self-published a paperback edition of *Lads Before the Wind* and advertised it in dog training publications. It is now in its third printing, and increasing steadily in popularity. Its readers don't think of it as a nice book about dolphins but as a useful book about training: just what I'd hoped for all along.

A change of tune...

During the difficult time of transition, when I was in divorce proceedings and had left Sea Life Park, but had not started anything new, a friend asked me to join the chorus she sang in. I needed something to do. I went without even asking what kind of music they sang.

When I got there I found it was not hymns or barbershop we were preparing to sing, but the Mahler Resurrection Symphony with the Honolulu Symphony Orchestra. Wow! I had a little musical training, enough to bury myself in the alto section and learn from my betters. And it was fun; you cannot sing at the top of your lungs and feel sorry for yourself at the same time.

After we had rehearsed for some weeks under the choral master, the symphony conductor came to rehearse us himself. I was astonished. Here was the first example I'd seen—and a downright flamboyant example at that—of operant conditioning in the real world.

My press privileges, as well as my being in the chorus, gave me backstage access at the Honolulu concert hall. I began haunting rehearsals, watching visiting conductors teach their signals to the musicians, quizzing the conductors when I could. I didn't know what I was going to do with this information; I just was curious. One day I was chatting on the phone with a writer friend, Carol Tavris, who was then an editor of *Psychology Today*, and I happened to mention my thoughts about symphony conductors. "I'll buy that!" Carol said: bingo, I'd sold a magazine article.

Not all conductors are punishers. The late Maestro Joseph Levine, rehearsing the Omaha Symphony, reinforces a soloist with a grin while simultaneously raising volume in the strings with his left hand, and cuing an entrance in the woodwinds with his right. Photo kindness of Mary Levine.

CHAPTER FOUR

Orchestra Conductors Would Make Good Porpoise Trainers

by Karen Pryor[1]

At Lincoln Center's Julliard Theater, Erich Leinsdorf, guest conductor, is leading a rehearsal of the New York Philharmonic Orchestra.

The music is monumental, demanding. Leinsdorf turns to the cellos on his right. The baton, in his right hand, beats time. His left hand flies up in front of his face in a warning gesture, and he says, "Softly, softly," as the cellists begin a difficult passage. With his eyes and body still turned toward the cellos, he throws his left hand out almost behind him, fluttering his fingers to bring in the woodwinds, also softly. The cellists complete their passage. A fleeting look of satisfaction, almost a smile, crosses Leinsdorf's face as he turns to the whole orchestra, right hand marking the beat, left hand conveying, in a sweeping flow, the mood and flavor of the music.

Now he scowls at the violins; they play in gorgeous unity and the scowl fades. A solo horn enters, above the orchestra, in a virtuoso plume of melody. On the horn's last note, as Leinsdorf uses a swirl of the baton and a considerable amount of body English to bring the whole orchestra to a crescendo, he throws

---

[1]Reprinted with permission from *Psychology Today,* February, 1977.

the horn player a thumbs-up gesture with his left hand, glares at the violas and shouts, "No, no!" He drops his hands and brings the music to a tumbling halt. "*No*, it is not right. We are not together. You must not sit on that dotted quarter note. Again. Please."

In about 25 seconds of music Leinsdorf has given the orchestra perhaps a hundred signals. He has used at least nine different kinds of cues, ranging from spoken commands to a brief glance. He has clearly rewarded several actions, including the cello passage and the horn solo. He has used what psychologists call negative reinforcement by scowling at the violins until their sound was better; he has used punishment by scolding the violas and by stopping the music. His timing has been extremely effective. Every reward or punishment has occurred during the event it was meant to affect and not so much as a split second after.

Leinsdorf would make a great porpoise trainer.

Tricks of the trade

I first noticed the similarities between porpoise training and conducting when I, a porpoise trainer by trade, took up choral singing for a hobby. Our chorus was preparing to sing the Mahler Resurrection Symphony with the Honolulu Symphony Orchestra. One night the symphony's conductor, Robert LaMarchina, came to rehearse us. I had never seen a proper conductor from the front before, and I was so fascinated I couldn't sing. He was using every trick of the porpoise trainer's trade.

I train my porpoises with techniques of psychology called operant conditioning, or behavior modification, or reinforcement theory, the laws of learning first codified by Harvard psychologist B.F. Skinner and his followers. Here, with enormous rapidity and correct techniques, LaMarchina was establishing discriminative stimuli, fading and transferring stimuli, chaining behavior, using successive approximation to shape behavior, and so on. All my jargon fit. LaMarchina was using the same clear-cut rules I followed to get my porpoises to throw balls, wear blindfolds, and jump through hoops to turn 60 amateur voices into one responsive instrument. In an hour.

We knew the music, and now we were learning, almost entirely without verbal instruction, how he wanted it sung. I had to admire the enormous amount of training accomplished in 60 minutes.

Early in that first rehearsal, LaMarchina gave a fine example of the trainer's skill. Just as the men in the bass section were filling their lungs, preparing to make their usual booming entrance, the conductor crouched backwards, mimed an expression of wild alarm, and threw his hand, palm out, across his face as if to ward off a blow. This was something we'd never seen before in music—a neutral stimulus—but the meaning was clear: "It's urgent that you don't make too much noise," and the astonished basses did their best to come in softly.

That combination of gestures became a stimulus for "sing the next part softly." From then on, LaMarchina started "fading" the stimulus. "Fading" is lab jargon for replacing a big, obvious cue with a much smaller one, so as to elicit an action unobtrusively. LaMarchina used just the warning hand—not the whole crouch and pantomime—or just the crouch and a warning glance. We were conditioned and we responded correctly. Finally a mere flinch of the shoulder was enough to subdue volume in one part of the chorus, freeing both the conductor's hands to raise the volume in another section.

During the rehearsal the conductor also transferred the stimulus for "sing softly" by combining the stimuli we knew with other new gestures and then using only the new gestures. Soon he could draw on a wide variety of well-understood signals. Once he even transferred the stimuli for both softer and louder to his left elbow.

Well, I became a rehearsal buff. I have watched a lot of conductors running rehearsals with choruses, with orchestras, with opera singers, with all three at once. Good conductors are all master porpoise trainers, Skinnerian maestros as well as musical maestros. Every device I know for manipulating behavior has become a part of the conductor's repertoire.

Extinction, for example, is one way to get rid of behavior you don't want. It might be a natural mistake, something learned incorrectly, or deliberate misbehavior, such as a porpoise splashing you from head to toe on purpose.

There are lots of ways to extinguish behavior. Ignoring it is one. If the action has no consequences, good or bad, it may disappear. Thomas Schippers, a ferocious conductor, walks to the podium for a rehearsal with the New York Philharmonic, a ferocious orchestra. A cellist behind Schippers makes an incredibly human "Oh-oh" on his instrument, and in the tumult of tuning up a woodwind warbles "I wish I were in Dixie." Schippers ignores the horseplay and starts the work, and the cutting-up quickly stops.

Punishment or aversive control is another way to eliminate behavior. I sometimes slap the snout of a porpoise that is snapping at me. Conductors fine musicians, fire them, or throw things at them. Handel once tried to throw a misbehaving soprano out a second-story window. Humiliation in front of the rest of the orchestra is a common device of conductors.

A subtler way to eliminate behavior is to train an incompatible action, one that is impossible to perform while performing the other. In shows I ran in Hawaii, a large female bottlenosed porpoise named Wela took to harassing the girl who swam with little spinner porpoises in one part of the performance. We trained Wela to press a lever with her nose while the girl was swimming. The porpoise couldn't do that and simultaneously boost the swimmer into the air with her tail. The same technique worked at an opera rehearsal when our chorus and the orchestra suddenly fell out of alignment. The conductor instantly put his finger on the problem. The chorus inadvertently had learned one measure of music one beat short. This put us a fraction ahead of the orchestra and turned the subsequent music into chaos.

How to fix it? Re-training 60 people who had diligently learned the passage wrong would be next to impossible. "In your lyrics," said the conductor, "where it says 'the king's coming,' stress that 's.' King'sssss coming." We all dutifully sang "The king'sssss coming." It made a funny buzzing sound, but it slowed us down the necessary beat. We could not perform the new action and still rush through the measure too fast. The conductor had trained an incompatible behavior.

Another way of eliminating unwanted behavior is to bring it under stimulus control—to tie it to a cue—and then never give the cue. I used this method to prevent one of our more enterprising porpoises from coming out of the tank and skidding around on the cement training platform whenever she felt like it, a habit potentially hazardous to her. We trained her to do it for a reward, in response to a hand signal. She stopped skidding at inconvenient moments and, instead, waited patiently in the water where she belonged, for the hand signal that seldom came.

The comparable creatures in the orchestra are the musicians who play brass instruments—the horns, trumpets, and trombones; they love to play loudly. Left to their own devices, the brasses will cheerfully drown out the other instruments. Consequently, the conductor permits the horn players to go at full volume only when he has signaled them to do so, and this he rarely does. Richard Strauss, in a satiric list of rules for young conductors, said, "Never look encouragingly at the brass players." It is a joke among orchestras that all brass players are bad-tempered from having to hold in their breath so much.

The conductor has a vast range of positive and negative reinforcers with which to modify the orchestra's behavior, ranging from letting the musicians play without interruption to throwing the occasional temper tantrum. It does not really matter whether he touches his players in the pride, the pocketbook, or the heart (Bruno Walter sorrowfully said, "Gentlemen, what would Mozart say?"). What matters is his timing. A reinforcement must be contingent upon the behavior it is meant to modify, marking the action the instant it occurs.

The master conductor does not anticipate, rehash, or even discuss the orchestra's actions. He may use a little verbal prompting (Schippers, in time to the music: "Take-it-eas-y-take-it-eas-y;" Leinsdorf, rehearsing Mahler's Fifth: "More grim, more grim.") However, you will hear no pep talks before rehearsal, no post-mortems, no threats, no promises. The conductor never telegraphs his punches. He waits, like any good animal trainer, until a sin is committed and then he explodes. Michael Costa, with a display of anger, once sent a player home to change his muddy boots and then, when the musician returned, fined him for not being present. Costa dealt with the errors as they occurred.

Consistent, predictable praise leads to blasé, routine performance, just as too much punishment leads to sullen, mechanical performance. Both must be irregular and unpredictable, meted out sparingly with the apparent randomness that may seem unfair to players, but which keeps them motivated in the same way the occasional jackpot keeps people feeding quarters into slot machines.

Reinforcing his musicians one step at a time, the conductor shapes the orchestra toward that elusive perfect performance of his dreams just as foot by foot I shape a porpoise toward a 20-foot leap hardly imaginable from its first small bounce out of the water. The conductor never stops. With his orchestra he will take every opportunity to introduce new complications, more difficult music, higher criteria. The players may describe this tendency subjectively: "The bastard is never satisfied;" the audience poetically: "Our conductor is a genius, always striving for greater beauty;" the psychologists pragmatically: "Continual raising of criteria, while reinforcing behavior, increases the quality of performance."

Do they know what they're doing, these conductors? Of course. Talk to LaMarchina about shaping or to Leinsdorf about extinguishing and you get back an informal but accurate description of each process.

Anyone who must manage the behavior of others—school teacher, coach, horse trainer—incorporates reinforcement in his work. All but the very best of these make consistent training errors. They often fail to distinguish between what they do that is effective and what they do by habit that is ineffective or even detrimental. They must often spend time tomorrow repairing the mistraining of today.

The symphony conductor cannot *afford* to be ineffective. He is faced with a task of immense complexity and extreme time limitations. Sometimes rehearsal time barely exceeds performance time. Through experience and intuition a top-rank conductor must develop almost perfect Skinnerian techniques. Conducting is the most elaborate use of these techniques that I have seen in real life, and conductors use them because they work.

Music and reinforcement...

It's great, being a journalist, even a temporary one. On an east coast trip while working on this piece I got rehearsal privileges at the Metropolitan Opera; a backstage pass to New York Philharmonic rehearsals, with a chair in the wings so I could watch the conductor's face; and an interview with Leinsdorf (when I asked him about extinguishing unwanted behavior he cocked an eyebrow at me, considered the question, and then said feelingly, "Let me tell you about that bassoonist!")

After my own first choral experience I applied myself to learning to sing better. You cannot do anything about your basic instrument—your airspaces, vocal chords, and so on—but you can learn to use it more effectively. I took voice lessons. Did you know that many of us self-consciously close our throats when singing the words "I" or "me?" You can learn not to do that.

I became a regular in the Honolulu Symphony Chorus. After several tries I got into the opera chorus as well. The first opera I ever saw, I was in: a touring production of Boito's *Mefistofele*, with Norman Treigel. What an experience!

I did not apply myself to learning to sightread music, but across two seasons of choral work I learned anyway. It was an interesting experience in right-brain learning, unmediated by language. For example, *years* later, and quite by accident, I discovered that there are little commas in some choral scores, and that they mean "Breathe here." I then observed, singing with friends, that I always do take a breath when I go past one of those marks, even though I did not consciously know anything about them. So it was with the notes, and the rhythm, and the intervals, and probably a lot of other markings: once the music starts, my throat "knows" what to do. I went from hanging always on my neighbors' coattails to being one of those who come in first and drag the timid along with them. It was like waking up one morning and discovering I could speak Russian.

That "unconscious" learning is an important component of music and of dance. The behavior must be rapid and timely, and to do that you need to Not Think; stopping to think wrecks the timing. One can get to that level in two ways: by working out intellectually what needs to be done, and then practicing until the behavior is automatic; or by learning without cogitating, through the senses and muscles. Ultimately both paths are important, of course. Guess which is more fun.

Right-brain learning is, I think, what is going on during any shaping session with reinforcement, at least initially. The rules of effective shaping, therefore, are particularly useful in teaching and learning music and dance. One day I gave a talk on reinforcement to a parenting conference. Afterwards a woman came up to me and told me she was a piano teacher. She had read *Lads Before the Wind,* learned about behavior chains, and realized it applied to music. From then on, she taught all her students to memorize their pieces from the back end first, starting with the last page or section, then the next to last, and so on. Thus when the students sat down to play they started with the most-recently learned, least familiar section, and became more and more comfortable and confident as they progressed always towards better-learned passages, ending up with a sure thing they had learned long before.

"It put an end to recital nerves," the music teacher said, "not only for my students: for ME!"

Part Two

New York
1976-1981

A new city, a new job...with dolphins

After three years in the advertising business, I realized I could probably hold down a copywriting job somewhere other than Hawaii, for a lot more money. Why not New York? I had happy childhood memories of the city; from my standpoint it would be like going home. I began planning.

When both boys finished high school and were headed for college, I turned them over to their dad and took myself and my fifteen-year-old daughter Gale to Manhattan. A big garage sale and the *Psychology Today* check subsidized the move. People in Hawaii were horrified; "You can't take a young girl like that to New York!" I pointed out that quite a few people managed to raise daughters in New York without mishap and I probably could do so too.

Gale and I took to city living with joy. We found the perfect apartment. Gale got into a good school and went there every day on the subway. And I found a good steady job—not in the advertising world, as I'd expected, but once more in the world of dolphins.

Starting in the early 1970s the U.S. tuna fishing industry ran into tremendous problems with dolphins. American purse seiners based in San Diego had discovered a new way of catching tuna fish by surrounding dolphins in their huge purse seine nets. Tuna that swam with the dolphins were caught, and the dolphins were released. Unfortunately, initially at least, a lot of dolphins drowned in the nets before they could be let go.

A huge environmental outcry ensued. In Hawaii I had followed the controversy with some interest. The dolphins involved were not good old Flipper, the tough and self-reliant bottlenose, but flighty little spinners and spotted dolphins, the very species, I thought, most likely to panic in a net.

Sea Life Park was the only place in the world with any real experience of these animals. Our experience was not considered unusual, in Hawaii, but now that I lived in New York, I was an Expert! The day after I arrived in the city, the tuna industry called me. I met with their representatives and agreed to be their scientific advisor. I would give them half my time, in return for a monthly retainer. I would be on call when needed, and free to do whatever I liked the rest of the time.

Not everybody approved of this move. One distinguished environmentalist called me a "biostitute." But I thought it made sense to help the industry; they were the ones who were going to have to solve the problem.

There was a way to reduce dolphin mortality: good skippers could fish without entangling dolphins. Their skills, therefore, could be identified, and transferred. The larger problems were, in my opinion, behavioral. The problem existed because of the behavior of the tuna, the behavior of the dolphins, and the behavior of the nets. The solutions were complicated by the behavior of the five principal human groups involved: environmentalists, businessmen, government bureaucrats, scientists, and skippers. Some groups just wanted this complex systems problem to go away, and others tried to turn it into an simple adversarial issue that could be solved by yelling.

I was comfortable with all five groups. I began trying to bring them together. The "tuna-porpoise wars" would keep me peace-making and problem-solving—and more or less solvent—throughout the years that I lived in New York. Meanwhile, for both me and Gale, there were a lot of fine adventures and advantages ahead, in the big city.

Freelancing...

My father, the writer, Philip Wylie, made a major part of his living writing for magazines, and so did many of his friends. In his prime, the '30s and '40s, you could live for a year on the proceeds of a couple of magazine articles; now the money is in television, and a magazine article will barely cover a couple of month's rent. Still, extra money sometimes came in handy, and I wrote for several magazines while I lived in New York, including *New York* magazine, where this piece ran. An editor I had met at *Psychology Today* was now working for *New York*. I called him; he said "Bring me five ideas on the back of an envelope." I did; he bought three of them, and this was one.

This piece is about behavior: the behavior of wind. It is also about our cultural behavior-blindness; we look at objects very clearly (buildings, cars, humans) but we seldom look at what is going on, what is happening across time and space. In remote parts of Hawaii one often stumbles across the foundations of old Hawaiian homesites. These are invariably located in a sheltered spot, out of the wind but with a view. In New York, people were oblivious to the reality of the wind—not just architects and planners, who certainly should know better, but the rest of us, too. The corner just south of my apartment building often generated a whirlwind, right outside the bookstore, that could be seen a block away, spinning trash and papers up to the second or third story. I used to sit in my window and watch neighborhood residents walk right into what I called the Brentano Vortex, helplessly squinting their eyes against the dust, grabbing at their hats or flapping coats, year in, year out. No one seemed to notice that one could just as easily walk across the street, or closer to the building, and avoid this atmospheric mishap altogether. "Oh, what a windy day!" people gasped, coming into our building's lobby—but often it was only windy in that particular spot.

It is as if we are interested only in product. Process is something we avoid noticing or thinking about, something we regard as immutable and outside our attention. So it is with behavior; we explain it away, instead of paying attention to what is happening.

CHAPTER FIVE

The Wicked Winds of New York

By Karen Pryor[1]

You may think that the vicious gust of wind that just turned your umbrella inside out was an act of God. In fact, it may have been a by-product of some corporation's long-term capital investment program. You may think it is unavoidable that you live on a windy street, that you have to fight the door to get into your building, that you hesitate to go out on windy nights (of which there seem to be so many); but if you knew how to recognize a Venturi effect you might have chosen an apartment elsewhere.

Buildings — particularly densely packed, high-rise apartment buildings and the office towers that rise sheerly from a spacious plaza—have the power to alter the temperature, the rainfall, and the wind, sometimes dramatically. Macroclimatology is the science of general trends in the weather; the budding science of microclimatology explains how these trends get translated into the effect that hits you in the face when you walk out of your house.

In the dust dome

For example: New York, like all other cities, has what is known as high specific heat — asphalt, concrete, and stone in the city's

---

[1]Reprinted with permission from NEW YORK magazine, April 24, 1978.

pavement and buildings absorb and retain and only slowly return to the atmosphere the vast amounts of heat from the sun. New York retains far more heat than, say, Short Hills, where the ground is covered with grass and trees. (Plants give off water vapor, cooling themselves and the air around them.) New York also makes a lot of heat on its own: cars, factories, furnaces, lights, and human bodies all give off heat.

As a result, New York is an average of 5 degrees warmer than suburban and rural neighborhoods, though peak differences can be much greater. When, for instance, the mercury dips toward 10 above 0 in Connecticut, it may not even be freezing in New York. Last summer when it was 104 degrees at Lincoln Center, the temperature was 15 degrees lower in some country spots not an hour away. And temperatures vary within the city. On a hot summer day it is not only more pleasant in Central Park than on Seventh Avenue, it may be cooler too, because of the vegetation.

New York is also a "dust dome"—the city is dustier than the surrounding countryside. Dirt, pulverized pavement, and other particles which in the country would become part of the turf in the city turn into dust, drift through the streets, and rise in the warm air currents. This creates a dome of dust which reduces visibility and partially masks incoming solar radiation. For this reason, it may in fact be no warmer in Manhattan on a hot afternoon than on an unshaded lawn in Greenwich, though it almost always will be so by evening, when the lawn has cooled down and the city pavement is still giving back its accumulated heat.

New York's dust dome increases rainfall, since raindrops coalesce around solid airborne particles. Dusty city air hooks rain out of clouds that otherwise might have passed us by, especially during the afternoon rush hour in summer, when the clouds formed by the day's heat have had time to build up. The dust would engender more snow in winter—except that the warmth of the city often turns the snow into rain before it nears the ground.

The architecture of the city affects the wind too. Wind in the New York area averages more than nine miles an hour, which is relatively high; it usually comes in from the northwest from

November to April and from the southwest the rest of the year. The prevailing winds which pass unobstructed across the Hudson River create the gusts on Riverside Drive; these winds are so powerful that members of the co-op at No. 552 are exploring the possibility of cutting their electric bill by installing a wind-driven generator on the roof.

Hitting the heights

In most of the city, buildings—as well as trees and other obstructions — tend to slow the wind down; that's why wind velocities are usually higher above the ground than on it. But if a building is considerably higher than those around it, disagreeable and even dangerous wind effects can result. About a third of the wind will go over the top of the building or around the sides; as it rushes over the roof it can create a prodigious vacuum on the opposite side, sometimes strong enough to suck glass right out of the windows. The John Hancock Tower in Boston is perhaps the most famous and litigious case of a building afflicted with the problem of flying glass—many of its windows not pushed in by the wind but pulled out.

The rest of the wind, striking the face of the building, goes straight down, gathering speed as it travels, to spill out at ground level in gusts and eddies that may have three times the speed of the natural wind. The apartment building at 1065 Park Avenue creates so much wind straight down its facade that elderly people have to be helped through the wind barrier to the door.

Relative height, not absolute height, is what creates wind problems. Clusters of tall buildings in midtown or lower Manhattan may cause no problem at all, whereas a high building in a relatively lowrise neighborhood will make its presence felt. When wind strikes the face of a tall tower, it whizzes around the corners of the building as well as over the roof and down to the pavement. Both the speed and the direction of the wind on the street may be altered. Take a stroll on a warm day when the wind is blowing from the south onto the Beresford and other apartment buildings between Columbus Avenue and Central Park West on 81st Street. At first the wind is unobstructed because of the open space around the Museum of Natural History on the south and because of Central Park on the east. As you walk east from Columbus Avenue, the wind will blow strongly in your face, whereas when you arrive at about mid-block it will come from the south. When you get to the corner of Central Park West and 81st Street, there will be a virtual gale blowing at you from behind. There on a rainy day you may find discarded umbrellas, their ribs broken by the sudden change in wind direction.

Wind blowing around buildings can create eddies and vortices. Eddies are the irregular side effects of wind going around an obstacle, like water swirling around rocks. Winds blowing down Fifth Avenue sometimes make an eddy which knocks hats off and wipes the snow away from the front of 4 Washington Mews, while two houses farther on, the snow lies still and the air is quiet.

Vortices are miniature whirlwinds, common phenomena on Manhattan streets. A current of air suddenly becomes a spinning corkscrew, whirling papers into the air and dust into people's eyes. Times Square is one of the windiest spots in the city, not just because of the speed of the winds there but also because of the violence and capriciousness of its vortices, which can snatch packages from the arms of passersby and send trash flying to the rooftops.

The Monroe phenomenon

The Monroe phenomenon is engineers' slang for a wind effect common around the bases of some tall, sheer-walled buildings with plazas below them. The wind rushes down the face of the building, hits the sidewalk, and bounces up again. Any woman in a full skirt who walks into a Monroe effect finds her skirts blowing upward like Marilyn's in the poster from "The Seven Year Itch," hence the name. Lunchtime loungers in the Wall Street area and around the World Trade Center know which windy corners are likely to produce the Monroe phenomenon. Skirtlifting winds are also common around the Flatiron Building at 23rd Street, which gave rise to the old exclamation, "23 skiddoo!"

The Venturi effect

Another common reaction of winds to buildings is the Venturi effect, named for the eighteenth-century Italian physicist who demonstrated that the velocity of a given amount of fluid is inversely proportional to the diameter of the tube through which it passes. This means that wind (which behaves like a fluid) blowing against a building or through a wide space will suddenly and dramatically increase in speed if it is channeled through a smaller space. Architects often use the Venturi effect to cool houses by making a relatively small opening on the side facing the wind and a larger opening on the leeward side. The former admits the wind and increases its speed (and therefore its cooling effect), and the latter sucks it out again. The Venturi effect can have undesirable consequences, though. A breeze blowing down Central Park into the narrower canyon of Sixth Avenue can suddenly become transformed into a gale, and a relatively modest wind off the Hudson River, when compressed into the side streets west of the park, creates stiff, unexpected gusts.

Every narrow, straight street lined with buildings is capable of increasing the speed of the wind. Mike Fayne, assistant meteorologist in charge of the National Weather Service in Rockefeller Center, observes that sometimes when his weather gauges at La Guardia report moderate winds of 15 miles per hour or so, he can look out of his office window and see the lampposts quivering and pedestrians on 50th Street hunched over, battling winds of up to 30 miles per hour, in a Rockefeller Center Venturi effect.

Pedestrian passageways through buildings, such as the one through the Celanese Building on Sixth Avenue between 47th and 48th streets, or through miniature plazas or the arcades behind the McGraw-Hill and Exxon buildings, on Sixth Avenue between 48th and 50th streets, are subject to the Venturi effect as well. Occasionally, these spaces, intended for strolling and relaxing, achieve the environmental qualities of a wind tunnel. It's a designed-in flaw which one can see in newer buildings all over Manhattan: the stately outdoor spaces which people never seem to use for anything and where no plants grow. Yet the flaw is avoidable. The new Citicorp Center was designed so that there would be no passages or spaces where Venturi effects could develop.

Whistle down the wind

A variation of the Venturi effect—known as the chimney effect—can alter the "weather." Chimneys work because warm air rises, the shape of the chimney creates suction, and the air speeds up, whisking away the smoke. Chimney, or "stack" effects can cause serious problems. As warm air rises in a building, up the elevator shafts and stairwells, it creates a partial vacuum. Doors to the street can be sucked shut and virtually sealed by the low pressure in the building and the higher pressure outdoors. The taller the building, the worse the problem is likely to be. There have been days at the World Trade Center when two strong men were needed to open some street-level doors, and when a door, once open, let in such a ferocious blast of high-pressure air that closing the door again became almost impossible. (The inevitability of stack effects was foreseen during the design of the World Trade Center, and an elaborate air-lock system in the substreet levels prevents the problem from being as serious as it might be. It is often subverted, however, by employees who find it tiresome to go through several sets of pressure-equalizing doors.) Still, there are days when only the revolving doors on the street level, which are miniature air locks in themselves, are of practical use.

Chimney effects can also make noise. New York law requires elevator shafts to be vented at the top to allow smoke to exit in case of fire, The wind can create moans and wails in the elevator shafts as it blows across the ventilators—an effect analogous to blowing across the top of a Coke bottle. The Pan Am Building offers a superb example of howling elevators, which take some getting used to by people whose offices adjoin the shafts. Such winds also exacerbate the pressure differentials; the interior walls of the building creak nerve-wrackingly, and the elevator doors rattle. Shortly after the Pan Am Building was erected, all its elevator-door motors had to be strengthened so the doors would shut on windy days.

Noise canyons

First and second-floor apartments on a busy street are likely to be noisy, but surely it's quieter higher up? Not in a noise canyon. When buildings of equal height face one another across a street, they can create a noise canyon that can make street sounds as maddening on the tenth floor as on the second.

It's not steady traffic sounds that bother us; it's unusual sudden rises in sound levels—raucous laughter, accelerating trucks, screams, gunshots, things like that. Higher floors miss peak sounds, such as loud conversation, that may bother ground-floor tenants, but they gather peak sounds—trucks, sirens—from a much wider area. You can live on the thirtieth floor and find you can't think with the windows open, if the buildings across the way and along both sides of the block are as tall as yours.

One way to escape the noise-canyon effect is to live in a building that rises well above its neighbors. Then, of course, you will be exposed to an unimpeded flow of microwaves. But how much can you worry about at one time?

The climate of the city

Thus the city makes its own climate. The effects on day-to-day life are modest. We are all aware of the differences between city and country climates and know that we need umbrellas and air conditioners more than people outside the city do. But few of us—including architects—know how to recognize the avoidable man-made problems.

New York's tendency to alter the weather for the worse seems to be increasing. Until 1961 the zoning law encouraged setbacks on the upper stories of tall buildings, resulting in a wedding-cake shape that seldom produced weird winds. But current laws permit sheer towers, and they also allow extra height in return for plazas, which the wind effects of the building itself may render useless.

The architect Jaquelin Robertson, director of the Office of Midtown Planning and Development in the Lindsay administration, maintains that the three latest Rockefeller Center buildings—Celanese, McGraw-Hill, and Exxon—have changed the microclimate of Sixth Avenue. An engineer who works at Madison Avenue and 59th Street says that ever since the General Motors Building went up, it has been snowing sideways on his corner. Residents in the Columbus Circle area blame the Gulf &

Western Building for disagreeable winds in their neighborhood. Then there is the World Trade Center, with its hazardously windy plaza. The World Trade Center is being sued because of its alleged wind effect on 22 Cortlandt Street. And one cannot help wondering what will happen to the tranquillity of the Museum of Modern Art's sculpture garden if a planned new addition to the museum—a tall, sheer tower—goes up next to it.

Fortunately, it *is* possible to analyze in advance not just the effect of weather on a new building but also the effect of the building on the weather by testing models of the building in wind tunnels. Such an analysis was performed for the World Trade Center, with promising results. The hotel that was part of the test model has not yet been built, however. So until that gap in the skyline is plugged, the good news from the tests cannot be confirmed.

Not all weather is bad weather. Newly created breezes of moderate intensity can be advantageous if they come at the right time. The natural climatic cycle produces strong winter winds from the northwest and cool breezes from the south on hot summer afternoons. Why should buildings not be designed to protect us from the one and expose us to the other? Perhaps a more poignant message, though, comes out of the marriage between architecture and the weather. A whole decade of idealists in the 1960s packed their bags and tramped off to the woods—in order to "connect" themselves with the natural world. It is pleasantly reassuring—and slightly surprising—to find that however urban and overbuilt New York becomes, we are connected too.

How to be a New Yorker...

This piece was fun to write. Some of it came from my own experience and childhood knowledge of the city. Some came from friends. I asked everyone I ran into for wind stories; many of the specific items in this piece came from neighbors in my building and other parents at PTA meetings at Gale's school. The rest of it I dug up on the telephone, investigative-reporter style. I was astonished by how willing people were to talk to The Press, namely me. The architect of a very famous building freely told me the troubles they'd had with a "stack effect" that sucked all the elevator doors shut and made it impossible to get off the upper floors from time to time. I very kindly didn't print that, as I thought it would frighten the people in that building and do his reputation no good; but I was amazed that he told me, so guilelessly.

In the 1970's, *New York* magazine, not to be confused with the more literary *New Yorker*, was really very chic. I never met any chic people when I turned in my assignments, mind you, but the fact that I wrote for the magazine gave me a certain cachet. Some of my acquaintances (not writers, interestingly, but lawyers and architects) were jealous, and said so. This piece, as it happened, was the cover article. I made sure a copy of that issue went along with every book or article proposal I wrote from then on; it opened doors for me in editorial offices for *years*. It made me a New Yorker—one of "us"—and that was downright useful.

Zoos...

One day in New York I got a call from the Director of the National Zoo in Washington, D.C., Ted Reed. He had read *Lads Before the Wind*. He wanted to know if I would be interested in teaching a course for his keepers on dolphin-style training for zoo animals. I was very interested indeed.

I have always loved zoos. As Curator of Sea Life Park I had traded on my title to visit zoos and meet and chat with zoo directors and curators wherever I traveled. For years, therefore, I had been wondering why zoos didn't borrow dolphin training techniques. Oceanariums used the dolphin training methods to care for lots of wild creatures, such as seals and sea lions and birds. Why didn't zoo personnel do the same?

Furthermore I had always been intrigued by the problem of training trainers; and now I not only would have a new population of trainers but all kinds of new animals to play with. I worked out a financial arrangement with the zoo, and a schedule I could fit in around my commitments to the tuna industry and their many hearings and meetings. I had about two dozen keepers to start with, of which perhaps half got interested and stayed involved. For six months I spent a day every two weeks with these keepers and their animals at the National Zoological Park in Washington, D.C. The article that follows describes what happened.

Illustration by British artist Ronald Searle for "The Rhino Likes Violets."

Chapter Six

The Rhino Likes Violets

By Karen Pryor[1]

We sat on the ground just outside the rhinoceros enclosure. Mary, an adult rhino, put her very large head through the fence, resting it on the bottom railing so that her chin overhung my lap. Since I was sitting in a patch of violets, I picked some violet leaves and fed them into her huge jaws. She took them with apparent pleasure. She seemed, too, to enjoy having me stroke her mouth and face. The heavy skin that looked like armor plating felt like suede; it seemed to be very sensitive. Mary could not see which way to turn for more leaves, even if I held them up to her eyes, but if I touched her face with the greenery she oriented easily and folded in the leaves adroitly.

Mary's ears tilted calmly and pleasantly to keep track of the whereabouts of her baby and to follow the conversation between Melanie Bond, a keeper at the National Zoological Park in Washington, D.C., and me, a visiting consultant. We had just finished a training session with the great apes, part of an experimental program at the zoo, to see if modern, nonforce behavioral modification techniques could be of use in handling zoo animals. Now, while we took a break in the spring sunshine, Melanie was playing with Mary's baby. Using violets and petting

[1]Reprinted with permission from *Psychology Today,* April, 1981

as rewards, she had just taught the baby to pick up one of its front feet on command, as horses and elephants are trained to do. The baby was quite excited at discovering such an easy way to earn Melanie's attentions, and between bouts of foot raising it gamboled clumsily about, now and then bumping heftily into its mother.

The half-hour of play reinforced for me a concept I'd long been aware of. If you have something an animal wants, you can train virtually any animal. People often don't realize how easy it is to train even difficult, dangerous animals without knocking them around. I wouldn't have dreamed of going into the rhinoceros enclosure and trying to train either animal by force, like an old-fashioned circus trainer. But obviously one could shape rhino behavior with positive reinforcements: in this case, greens and, I think, attention and diversion.

Shaping behavior with positive reinforcement is a technique described in the laws of learning first defined by B. F. Skinner and generally called operant conditioning. In the last 20 years or so, the technique has revolutionized animal training. All dolphin shows are based entirely on positive reinforcement, not aversive control. Bird shows involving free-flying birds of many species have proliferated; birds, too, cannot be trained by force (they just panic) but will work hard and learn well for food rewards. In Hollywood, shaping with positive reinforcement is called "affection training," and it has produced results that in the past would have been considered impossible: the Hartford Insurance stag is one example.

I gained my background in the applied uses of operant conditioning as the head trainer and curator of Sea Life Park, an oceanarium in Hawaii, where we trained dozens of dolphins, small whales, birds, and other creatures for both public performances and research. Positive reinforcement, properly used, could produce spectacular shows. Sometimes, though, I was even more impressed with its practical value in the everyday maintenance of our animals. For example, some whales are too large to restrain by force, so when our whales needed veterinary attention, we trained them to present their tails and allow blood samples to be taken and shots to be administered, for a reward of food and petting. (The amount and kind of reward is not important; what is important is that the animal know exactly what it has to do to get the reward.) All of our animals were trained to move from tank to tank on command; they did not have to be chased or forced. Also we used training to relieve the boredom of dolphins that were being kept in solitude; for dolphins, boredom can literally be fatal.

I had then been asked to see if the same techniques could be applied to wild animals in a zoo; thus I found myself feeding violets to the rhino. Theodore Reed, director of the National Zoo, had read a book I'd written about my porpoise-training experiences and had decided that these techniques might be useful to his keepers. He mentioned specific behavioral problems to me: the polar bears that banged on their steel doors hour after hour; the giraffes that sometimes refused to go indoors before a cold snap and had to be chased about by 10 men with sticks in a slipping, kicking, cursing, and risky rodeo; the chimp that sat in a corner all day plucking the hair out of its arms from boredom.

Reed, a veterinarian, was also worried about boredom among the keepers. He prided himself, and justifiably, I was to discover, on a staff of intelligent, capable men and women who took serious interest in the animals they cared for. But a lot of the work of animal care is grueling drudgery: feeding and cleaning, cleaning and feeding. Reed thought that, for those who took to it, ongoing training interactions might add interest to the keepers' lives as well as the animals'.

I agreed to go to work for the zoo as a consultant, teaching a group of keepers as much as I could about training techniques. Twenty-five people came to the first class: young, old, male, female, black, white. I was intrigued not only by the variety of lively faces but also by the variety of animals they had to work with: birds, reptiles, apes, elephants, mammals I'd never even heard of, such as grisons and binturongs. I explained that it would not be my job to train animals nor to solve specific problems, necessarily, but to give the keepers methods by which they could do those things. I outlined a basic technique: you let the animal discover that every time you blow a whistle, it gets a piece of food. Then you let it discover that *it* can make you blow the whistle by, say, moving toward its den. Presto. You are training the animal to move into its den. Or *it* is training *you* to be reliable about whistle blowing and food giving, depending on the point of view.

Everyone had to pick an animal to practice on and a behavior to shape. I recommended choosing a lively, greedy animal. Melanie Bond, in the great ape house, had dandy subjects to start with—two juvenile orangutans. Keepers had been forbidden to play or interact with the apes, on the ground that it was dangerous, but now that rule would be relaxed so that Melanie could participate in the training class. Bela Demeter, in the reptile house, was dubious about training snakes or lizards, but I knew reptiles could be conditioned; the late reptile collector Grace Wylie had had a number of trained alligators years ago. Birds, reindeer, elephants—everyone picked good subjects. However, Art Cooper in the lion/tiger complex had fixed his heart on training his best tiger, Peela. [Actually Art and the other keepers called the tiger Ajax, but the Zoo insisted I use his official name in this article. KP]

"No, Art," the others protested. "That tiger never does anything! He just lies on the top of his hill all day. What are you going to reinforce?"

"Well, he's cool," Art explained. "He's saving his strength." Art intended to persuade this cool cat 1) to come down to the front of the exhibit, to the edge of the moat; 2) to get into the water in the moat; 3) to retrieve a floating beer keg that was sometimes put in the moat as a tiger toy (tigers like to swim, and like all other cats, they will play with moving objects); 4) to put the beer keg on the beach; and 5) to get back up on shore himself. A five-step behavior chain, and quite difficult even for a seasoned trainer, especially with a disinterested animal. I suggested doing something simpler, but Art's mind was made up.

Training is time-consuming, and some people found that they could not fit it into an already overcrowded day's work. Curators, too, sometimes objected to the keepers' frittering away valuable minutes on apparently trivial tasks. "I do not see the value," one curator huffed at me, "in training the panda to stand on its head to impress the other keepers." The value, of course, was in the process, not the product: the trainer was learning to train. What he or she chose as a practice behavior was irrelevant to me; I have found that first-time trainers make much better progress if they choose their own task rather than have one assigned to them, so I let them do what they like. But I could empathize with the practical zoo people who not only saw no point in the particular behavior (who needs a retrieving tiger, after all?) but felt that it interfered with the animals' "natural behavior" as well although, given the alien zoo environment, much of the behavior we see is not at all normal.

In a few weeks, some people had successes to demonstrate to the class. Melanie had trained Junior, one of the young orangutans, to clean up his cage and toss trash into her bucket in return, not for a food reward, but for the chance to blow on a whistle; Junior was fascinated by the whistle. Next to his cage there was a large female orangutan who seemed to me to be suffering from clinical depression. She sat slumped against the wall all day long, looking like an exhausted shopping-bag lady. Melanie, with food, taught her to play a simple Simon Says: I pat my head, you pat your head; I clap my hands, you clap your hands; I rub my stomach, you rub your stomach. To everyone's amusement, the orang discovered she could play this game with the public, especially with groups of schoolchildren. It was gratifying to see her, active and bright-eyed, clapping her hands, then rubbing her stomach, while a corridor full of hilarious children copied her.

Melanie also began playing the training game with melancholy Ham, the chimpanzee (our first U.S. chimp in outer space), now a grown male with formidable fangs. She paid him with food for various actions, and slowly, he began to participate. One morning, Melanie informed us, she was about to let Ham outdoors after having given him his breakfast. When he saw that she was going to open the outside door, he graciously rewarded her by handing her a piece of celery. He understood the game.

Grayson Harding, in the small mammals building, had trained a chinchilla to weigh itself by hopping in a basket which could then be put on a scale—a big improvement over chasing it all over the cage with a net to catch and weigh it. Bela, at the reptile house, had trained two thin green lizards about 18 inches long to take insects from the tip of a forceps. He then held the forceps higher, shaping an upward jump. By the time he showed the behavior to the class, the lizards ran to the cage door as soon as he opened it and then, eyes bulging and pink, toothy mouths agape, jumped two feet straight up to the forceps tip with a tiny ferocity that was funny to see. Bela really did have leaping lizards. He himself wasn't impressed, though I pointed out that this Olympic-effort, straight-up leap is the high point of all dolphin shows and is trained in exactly the same way.

Meanwhile, Art actually was making progress with Peela. Peela got into the spirit of things and came bounding down the hill when he caught sight of Art. He learned to get into the water and to get out. He played with the keg. Training sessions, however, took a long time, because Peela appeared to have trouble making up his mind. He could take 20 minutes to get into the water and 45 to get out again. It's a trait common to cats, as anyone knows who has ever opened a door to let an importunate house cat out and then had it stand in the doorway. Peela just did it on a bigger scale.

In the long run, Art did accomplish his behavior chain and, I am sure, acquired in the process training skills that can be applied henceforth to any animal in his care. By the end of the program, Melanie's work with the apes was generally recognized as valuable; Barbara Bingham had some partially trained reindeer and had discovered that currycombing was reinforcing to them. The giraffes now came indoors when the keepers rang an electric bell. A few keepers, a few animals had benefited. The program had been fun for the participants, but did it have any value for the whole zoo?

Six months later, I went back to see. In the elephant house, where training sessions had previously been brief, with fixed routines, and held before opening hours, training demonstrations were now being given daily for the public. In the great ape house, morose Ham now laughed, played games, and even let himself be tickled; gorillas opened doors and tidied cages on request; the zoo had sent Melanie to night school to learn American Sign Language; she was teaching Junior.

I found that keepers were being hired specifically for their training skills. A Hollywood-trained keeper had all the bears going indoors on command for a food reward; previously, it had sometimes been necessary to chase them in with fire hoses in order to clean the yards. A new seal and sea lion exhibit, Beaver Valley, which had been under construction during my time at the zoo, was being run by an experienced trainer. On the site where I had once stood and listened to a head curator worry about how they would ever catch an individual seal for medical care since the pool was so large, I was now able to look over the completed pool and its barking inhabitants and hear a curator tell me that every animal was being trained to come out of the water on command and that he considered training to be integral to the staff's daily work.

The polar bears had also come under the care of the Beaver Valley keepers. They had noticed, I was told, that one of the bears had a broken canine tooth. This called for veterinary attention, since a broken tooth can get infected. Customarily, the bear would have had to be "knocked down," or shot with a tranquilizer gun—and with a stiff dosage, too, since you certainly do not want a polar bear to wake up while you are examining its teeth. To spare the bear this risky and potentially even fatal procedure, keeper leader Kayce Cover and her staff trained the bear to stick its nose out through a slot in the door and allow its lip to be lifted. When the behavior was shaped, they called the vet, the trainer signaled the bear, the bear poked its nose out, and the vet inspected the tooth and pronounced it healed. No trouble at all. And they did it with raisins.

That, I thought, was exactly the use of training as a zoo-management tool that Dr. Reed had been hoping for. The incident had nothing to do with me or my class, directly. The keepers had learned their obviously excellent training skills from others. But their success depended on a favorable climate of opinion at the curatorial level, in which such keeper-animal interactions are not forbidden but permitted, perhaps encouraged, maybe even expected. There, I thought, our class may have broken the ice.

What about other zoos? At the New York Zoological Park—the Bronx Zoo—director William Conway and some of his curators have also been interested in operant conditioning as a zoo-management tool. They have installed some automated exhibits, such as a "honey tree" that makes bears stand to their full height and show off their long tongues to get the occasionally dispensed honey. They have also undertaken a pilot training program, hiring an experienced marine-mammal trainer, Jerry Winsett, to be trainer-at-large in the zoo for a year. Some of the behavior problems Jerry solved seemed routine to him, but they were serious to the keepers. For example, a certain gorilla took to sitting in his doorway, refusing to go in or out, when the keepers wanted to clean the cage. No amount of banana waving could coax him from that position, and with his huge strength he prevented the door from being closed. Jerry pointed out that banana waving is bribery; you are reinforcing behavior that hasn't occurred yet, and trainers know that doesn't really work. Jerry suggested ignoring the gorilla when he sat in the doorway and rewarding him when he went out by himself. Problem solved.

The Bronx Zoo has an exhibit of nocturnal creatures, "The World of Darkness," in which many small birds and mammals are displayed under a dim, or red, light going about their normal lives. It is difficult for the keepers to check on the health or even the viable presence of each specimen in the darkness. Jerry taught the keepers techniques for "shaping" animals to come to their hands. To coax a timid douroucouli (a nocturnal monkey) or galago (a tiny primate) to take food from your hand might take weeks of patience. To shape it to do so, however, by reinforcing every step closer to you with morsels of food, which at first are put in a dish or on a branch where the animal can reach them easily, is a matter of a few five-minute training sessions. Now almost every important specimen in that exhibit is shaped to take food from a keeper's hand every day, which not only allows the keepers to count and inspect the fragile creatures but also facilitates catching animals who must be doctored or moved.

The Brookfield Zoo near Chicago has experimented extensively with automated exhibits in which animals are conditioned to show natural behavior, such as hunting, and are reinforced by food from an automatic dispenser when the behavior is performed correctly. Moral and esthetic objections are often loudly voiced in the zoo community to this "mechanizing" of the animals, but surely it is kinder to keep them active than to let them doze their lives away in hopelessness and apathy. Properly designed, automated exhibits appear to be fun for the animals. Brookfield's cougar, which was conditioned to lie on a branch until an artificial marmot (a sort of ground squirrel) stuck its head out of a hole, and then to leap on the marmot before it disappeared again, would go on playing long after the food dispenser was empty.

Humanists often view operant conditioning, or any use of Skinnerian techniques, as inhuman, monstrous, Machiavellian. Yet with captive animals it is more often the failure to use the techniques that is inhumane. Positive reinforcement training constitutes an exchange of deeds for goods in which a pleasant communion arises, a salutary sort of equality between animal and trainer. One cannot work without the other, and both must do their part. That is reinforcing in itself, for both parties. I was just as pleased, just as reinforced, by Mary the rhino's taking violets from my hand as she was pleased to eat them. The baby rhino's learning to pick up its foot so quickly was reinforcing to Melanie. Operant conditioning in zoos is not only a benign addition to animal management practices, but rewards staff and animals alike. I am sure B. F. Skinner would not be surprised to hear that; he would just wonder why it took so long.

Animal minds...

I was glad when the zoo job was over. I thought the keepers I worked with were terrific. I think I helped them. But the bureaucracy of the zoo itself was a pain in the neck. Curators were suspicious and obstructive; gossip and paranoia were rampant. It was hard to get things done.

Nevertheless, that zoo has made progress, and reinforcement training is beginning to catch on in zoos all over the country. Marine mammal trainers have moved into the zoo world, or have spread their techniques from dolphin facilities within zoos. Elephants, particularly, are benefiting. In the '80s the public began protesting traditional methods of handling elephants by dominance, force, and restraint, with the elephant goad and leg chains. In many zoos elephants are now being handled by shaping and reinforcement, in a system known as "protected contact." The keepers can stay outside the bars and still get an elephant to do anything they want, from going through doors to offering a foot to be trimmed, using voice signals, a conditioned reinforcer, and food treats. The public likes it, the elephants like it, and it's a lot safer for the keepers.

I did meet some interesting animals at the zoo. You will hear more about Art's tiger in Chapter 22, and you'll meet an adorable hyena in Chapter 14. I thought the polar bears were interesting— very dangerous, but fun-loving and infinitely patient, as you might suppose of seal-stalkers. I had one fascinating training exchange with a young elephant; she was a practical joker, like some dolphins. I was quite taken with a wildebeest I spent an afternoon fiddling with; he was reinforceable, bold, intelligent, even sort of sinister, I thought, calculating how to outwit me as soon as he found out what I was good for—handfuls of clover pushed into his dusty pen. There's nothing like operant conditioning to give you a fast look inside an animal's mind, and the zoo was indeed full of new minds to explore.

Two false killer whales (Pseudorca crassidens) *jump simultaneously in opposite directions at Sea Life Park.*

The Clever Hans Conference...

New York is full of arcane amusements, and one of them is the New York Academy of Sciences, which puts on weekend conferences and evening lectures on various topics, often open to the general public. One night at a lecture I saw a notice of an upcoming conference on the "Clever Hans" phenomenon. Clever Hans was a German horse that apparently could do arithmetic. He could answer questions by pawing the ground the right number of times. Nobody, including his owner, knew how he did it. Learned professors came from all over, and many papers were written before the mystery was solved. Clever Hans was cued by minute physical signs his owner gave unconsciously when the horse got to the right number. It was not a hoax, exactly, because the owner was just as deceived as everyone else.

The "Clever Hans" conference at the New York Academy of Sciences would bring together all kinds of people interested in communication, especially deceptive communication. It would include some of the people experimenting with ape languages, some psychologists, and a magician.

I decided I had to be part of this conference, somehow. The dolphins had thrust me into the whole question of animals, language, and self-deception by researchers, and I had quite a bit to say on the subject. I called the Academy and offered to do anything — lick envelopes, if necessary. They brushed me off disparagingly and referred me to the conference organizer, a professor in the mid-West, Tom Scbcok.

I called Dr. Sebeok, expecting to be brushed off by him, too. "Karen Pryor! I've been looking for you everywhere!" he cried. It seems Dr. Sebeok had read "The Creative Porpoise," and wanted me at his conference just as badly as I wanted to be there. He asked me to give a paper. I thought up the title and gave it to him over the phone. The conference program was just going to press; he stopped it in time to put my title in. He also asked me to participate in a post-conference Working Group discussion, of just a dozen people or so.

In order to talk about *real* communication between people and dolphins, I had first to dispel a lot of popular myths. The paper began with that.

CHAPTER SEVEN

Why Porpoise Trainers Are Not Dolphin Lovers
Real and false communication in the operant setting

By Karen Pryor[1]

DOLPHIN LOVERS ABOUND. Everyone who has ever seen "Flipper" on television, visited an oceanarium, or read John Lilly's books thinks that dolphins are cute, playful, friendly, harmless, and affectionate to each other and to man, that they save drowning people, and that they are possessed of extraordinary intelligence and a rich communication system comparable perhaps to our own.

Porpoise trainers know otherwise (many prefer the word "porpoise" to "dolphin" because it differentiates the mammals from a pelagic fish, *Coryphaena hippurus*, which is also called "dolphin.") The novice trainer quickly learns that porpoises can be very aggressive. They are highly social animals, to which rank order is a matter of considerable importance. Aggressive interactions between porpoises, usually during dominance disputes, include striking, raking with the teeth, and ramming with the beak or rostrum, sometimes with serious consequences, such as broken ribs or vertebrae, or punctured lungs, in the

[1]Reprinted with permission from *Annals of the New York Academy of Sciences.* Volume 364. pages 137-143 (1981).

rammed animal. A dolphin that has become accustomed to humans shows no hesitance in challenging the human for dominance, by means of threat displays and blows; a person who is in the water with an aggressive porpoise is at a dangerous disadvantage. The sentimental view that these animals are harmless stems at least in part from the fact that they are usually in the water and we are usually on boats or dry land; they can't get at us.

Interaction with porpoises in a training situation, usually with the trainer at tank-side, also brings their vaunted intelligence under pragmatic scrutiny. A poll of experienced trainers reveals that some trainers, after working with many individual animals of several species for five years or more, were not willing to place porpoise intelligence levels above that of dogs; the majority of the respondents, however, agreed with the dictum that porpoise intelligence is "between the dog and the chimpanzee, and nearer to the chimpanzee" (by no means, however, does it appear to trainers to be equal to or superior to that of the great apes.)

A confounding effect of this question is that most of the porpoises kept in captivity are Atlantic bottlenosed porpoises, *Tursiops truncatus,* a coastal species which is highly adaptable, plastic in its behavior, and an opportunistic feeder, showing a marked tendency to play with and to manipulate objects, and some tolerance for solitude. Other genera of Delphinidae, such as pilot whales, belugas, and the small, pelagic, white-sided, spinner and spotter porpoises, exhibit quite different behavioral profiles. Spinner porpoises *(Stenella longirostris),* for example, show very little tendency to play and high avoidance of foreign objects. They have difficulty negotiating barriers or obstacles, seldom learn to tolerate (much less solicit) human touch, and become inappetant and in fact rapidly moribund if kept in isolation from species mates. It is perhaps unfortunate that the popular view of porpoises is based on the genus *Tursiops,* the bottlenose, which is in fact a rather anomalous member of the Delphinidae, behaviorally.

Nevertheless, whether the subject is an inactive pilot whale, a very active but timid spinner, or a bold, aggressive bottlenosed dolphin, the trainer can train it: not by loving it, or even liking it—

one may find oneself cordially despising a particular individual—but by operant conditioning (Defran and Pryor 1980).

People often ask a working trainer about "communication," John Lilly having established an apparently ineradicable mystique by holding that there is something unusual about dolphin communication (Lilly, 1961). The flippant answer is that anyone can communicate just fine with a whistle and a bucket of fish.

In fact what is "different" about porpoises, compared to other frequently trained animals, is the manner in which they are trained. Aversive methods are virtually unavailable. The porpoise trainer cannot use the choke chain, the spur, the elephant hook, the cattle prod, or even a fist, on an animal that can swim away if alarmed. As they cannot "get at" us, so we cannot "get at" them.

The laboratory psychologist's mind may at once turn to devising some arcane method of punishment. In fact, punishment is unnecessary. Other than the mild negative reinforcement of a brief interruption of the training session, (a "time-out") porpoise trainers achieve highly disciplined and complex responses entirely with positive reinforcement.

The proliferation of trained porpoise shows, as well as some rather limited use of trained porpoises as domestic animals working in the open sea, has paralleled in time the promulgation and increasing public awareness of the laws of operant conditioning described by B.F. Skinner and others. Unlike traditional animal trainers, porpoise trainers are not only at the mercy of these laws, they are aware of them, and use them consciously. The jargon of the porpoise trainer is the jargon of the laboratory: successive approximation, conditioned stimuli, variable schedules of reinforcement, and so on. Unlike the shaper working under laboratory conditions, however, the porpoise trainer, in addition to being largely limited to positive reinforcement, is interacting with the animal; he or she can see the animal, the animal can see him or her, and both can introduce changes in the training process, at will. It is a situation. both rigorous and admitting of spontaneity: a game.

The game has "rules" on both sides: "I will reinforce you only for jumps in which you do not touch the hoop as you pass through it;" "I have come to expect a fish for at least every three or four jumps, and will stop jumping if you let eight or ten responses go unrewarded." It is a game in which challenge is always present, as the trainer, mindful of the various techniques for maintaining response levels, raises criteria or introduces new criteria; but, at least in the hands of a skilled trainer, it is a game that the animal always, eventually, wins.

A dog or a horse learns responses because it must do so to avoid aversive stimuli; a pigeon in a Skinner box must work, because it is hungry; and when we train people, we generally use a mix of positive and negative, of praise and coercion, though sometimes covert. There is little coercion, however, in the porpoise-trainer interaction (even food deprivation is hazardous, and seldom used) and this has an effect upon both trainer and animal. The animal is, as it were, training the trainer to give fish, and thus is shaped towards finding new ways to elicit fish; it is shaped in fact towards innovative response. The trainer in turn may become a very skilled and imaginative user of Skinner's laws. Porpoise trainer shoptalk (as opposed, let us say, to racehorse trainer shoptalk) is generally concerned with ingenious shaping programs, or novel use of operant conditioning techniques and not with the personalities or achievement of individual animals. It is the fascination of the game that keeps porpoise trainers in their strenuous, low-paying jobs, year after year, and not the fascination of the animals themselves. Many trainers in fact come to prefer the more reliably conditionable pinnipeds, and some greatly enjoy working with birds, another group that cannot be trained aversively.

This is not to say that every porpoise trainer is a walking compendium of Skinnerian laws. The less educated trainer, or the self-taught trainer working in isolation, may be full of superstitious behaviors ("You have to wear white; dolphins like white") or may be unable to say how he is cueing his animals, and thus fall victim to Clever Hans phenomenon, maintaining, for example, that his animals respond telepathically. The animals of course quickly develop superstitious behavior too; for example, only responding to trainers in white clothes.

The nontrainer, interacting with dolphins, is also apt to misinterpret, especially in the matter of social signaling. He may, for example, interpret the gaped jaw, a threat display, as a "smile," or touches and jostling as affectionate play, when they are often dominance challenges. Dr. Lilly made much of anecdotes concerning a male porpoise making sexual advances to a human female, but male bottlenosed porpoises in captivity may exhibit sexual behavior towards almost anything; and it is a behavior which, after all, we do not find intelligent or endearing in male dogs (Lilly 1978).

The interactive, positive-reinforcement training setting is an excellent way to become acquainted with the nature and function of social signals in an unfamiliar species. You do not need months or years of observation to discover which gestures, postures, and acts are aggressive, which affiliative, and so on. For example, in spinner porpoises, an extremely loud echo-location click-train is a threat display. This may not be obvious the first time you swim with spinners; if it is immediately followed by a sharp blow of a dorsal fin to your upper arm, you will recognize it the second time you hear it, and prepare to take evasive action.

In the operant setting, most large mammals quickly direct their intraspecific social signals at the trainer. They are not begging; begging does not work; they are exhibiting frustration, making submissive or aggressive displays, and so on, both giving and garnering information. One of the commonest trainer-directed social signals is sudden eye contact, which can be described metaphorically as the "Am I on the right track?" eye contact. Verifying that the trainer is indeed watching, the animal then escalates the vigor or duration of the response, and thus earns reinforcement. This is not a behavior seen only in porpoises, although they make eye contact more often than many other mammals; I have experienced this specific social interchange of information in an operant conditioning setting with an elephant, a wolf, a hyena, several polar bears, and primates.

The wise trainer makes use of whatever social signaling he feels he can accurately interpret. The animal can make use of this communication link too. Porpoises, for example, probably do not care what we think of them, and, according to Gish, do not necessarily, in their own acoustic social signaling, increase volume to add emphasis; nevertheless porpoises can learn that human increased volume—yelling—means "I mean it!" and respond appropriately, not from fear or a desire to please, as a dog might, but from having gleaned the appropriate information in training interactions (Gish 1979).

The richness and detail of information available in the operant setting enables communication to occur on a level considerably exceeding that of the usual interactions between man and beast. The porpoise trainer, for example, can change his tankside location to indicate when he wants previously conditioned responses, and when the animal is at liberty to earn reinforcement through new responses. A porpoise can indicate through a series of totally wrong responses that the quality of the fish reward is not satisfactory; this device is not uncommon in research animals being fed from feeding machines, in which fish may dry out or spoil. The porpoise, through actions, and with eye contact, may deliberately test the trainer's criteria: take, for example, this episode (Pryor 1975):

> Two false killer whales *(Pseudorca crassidens)* have been trained to jump a hurdle simultaneously, in opposite directions. The behavior, used in daily public performances, has deteriorated, due to trainer carelessness. One whale now always jumps too late, spoiling the effect of the mid-air crossing of trajectories. A corrective training session was held, as follows:
>
> (1) Trainer presents cue (an underwater sound). Both animals approach hurdle. Animal A jumps from the left; the conditioned reinforcer (a whistle) is sounded, and the cue is turned off; animal B then jumps from the right. Animal A receives a handful of fish. Animal B returns to trainer but is not reinforced.
>
> (2) Trainer presents cue. Both animals approach the jump, jump simultaneously in opposite directions, hear the whistle, the cue is turned off, and both are rewarded with 2 pounds of fish, many small fish (>10) dumped directly into the animals' large mouths. These are very large animals, and that constitutes the usual reinforcement.
>
> (3) Trainer presents cue, and the first episode is repeated, with animal B jumping late, after the cue is off, getting no whistle, and no fish.

(4) Trainer presents cue and animal B does something quite unprecedented; it switches sides and jumps in synchrony with animal A, but from the left or same side, hearing the cue, and the whistle, but getting no fish.

(5) Trainer presents cue. Both animals jump, and from opposite directions, and animal B is just slightly late. Animal A receives 2 pounds. of fish, and animal B gets one little 2-ounce smelt. Animal B physically startles, and makes eye contact with the trainer.

(6) Trainer presents cue. Animal B increases swimming speed and makes a perfect jump, opposite to and in synchrony with animal A. Both animals are given 4-pound rewards. Both animals henceforth perform the response correctly, eight times a day.

Does this demonstrate these large delphinids' "intelligence?" Perhaps: One would not expect such methodical testing of the criteria by a spinner porpoise, which has a behavioral repertoire generally more limited and rigid than that of *Pseudorca*. However, the anecdote may demonstrate the kind of communication that can arise purely through operant conditioning and through using positive reinforcement flexibly. Nothing in the "rules" suggests that half a reinforcement should convey the information, "You're about half right." But whether or not that interpretation represents what truly happened, there was information in the unusually tiny reinforcement, information possibly accessible to an animal that had experienced the earning of many consistently larger reinforcements, information that the animal, to all pragmatic intents and purposes, recognized and made note of.

Gregory Bateson has stated that operant conditioning is a method of communicating with an alien species (Bateson, pers. comm.) Others have suggested that the various language acquisition experiments with apes are nothing more than glorified operant conditioning.

Whether what the apes do is related to language, as we use language, is beside the point to a porpoise trainer. Like the porpoises, the apes have experienced very elaborate operant conditioning programs, in a setting conducive to interchange of social signals and a setting which, while rigorous, is admitting of spontaneity on both sides. It is a training circumstance that is rather rare in the world at large. What seems evident, and is taken now almost for granted by many researchers, is that at least chimpanzees are capable of assimilating enormous numbers of signs—conditioned stimuli, if you will—and of attaching correct meanings to these signs. A signing chimp, or even an ape that merely recognizes some signs (such as some orangutans and gorillas now do at the National Zoo) is capable both of giving and receiving information that is far more subtle than that normally conveyed between a person and a pet animal or a caged specimen. Something is developed; it may or may not be language; it is certainly heightened communication.

Innovative responses, and increased communication, thus may be not so much an indication of unusual or near-human capabilities in a species, but rather an artifact of the effect of advanced techniques ("glorified," if you like) of operant conditioning in opening pathways for communication, including two-way and unpremeditated communication, between other species—perhaps many other species—and man.

References

Defran, R. H. and K. Pryor. 1980. The behavior and training of cetaceans in captivity. In *Cetacean Behavior,* L. Herman, Ed., Wiley-Interscience, New York, N.Y.

Gish, S. I., 1979. *Quantitative Analysis of two-way Acoustic Communication between Captive Atlantic Bottlenosed Dolphins (Tursiops truncatus Montagu).* Ph.D. dissertation. Univ. of California at Santa Cruz.

Lilly, J. 1961. *Man and Dolphin.* Doubleday and Co., New York, N.Y.

Lilly, J. 1978. *Communication Between Man and Dolphin.* Crown, New York, N.Y.

Pryor, K. 1975. *Lads Before the Wind.* Harper & Row, New York, N.Y. [Also 1987, Sunshine Books, North Bend WA].

The "Clever Hans" aftermath...

I was unaware that the Clever Hans conference had a hidden agenda. Some of the organizers were specifically interested in debunking the ape language experiments, and showing them to be misinterpretations. Since the experiments are for the most part valid, and the apes do indeed learn something about using words, the effort was not successful; meanwhile the conference was a fascinating experience and generated a lot of interesting controversy.

The conference attracted quite a lot of press, and my statements about the peccadilloes of dolphins made news. After the third or fourth reporter interviewed me I called a clipping service, and thus was able to paper my kitchen wall with headlines from around the country: "Dolphins can be dangerous, scientist says." "Don't fool with Flipper!" and so on. Professionally and economically I don't know that this brief exposure made any difference in my life, but I enjoyed it. I especially enjoyed a call from some reporter in Miami who was convinced dolphins are all sweet and docile, and had made arrangements to swim in the dolphin show tank at one of the Florida oceanariums so he could write a story proving me wrong. I don't know what kind of story he wrote, but he had the grace to call me back after his swim, a chastened soul; the dolphins of course had taken advantage of this neophyte and given him a terrible time.

After I'd given my talk there was a break, in which a short, thin man with the most remarkable, snapping black eyes came up to me and said the presentation was "brilliant," which of

117

course made me think he was brilliant. He was, it turned out, the sociologist Erving Goffman. In the Working Group after the conference, an all-day meeting around one big table, Goffman allied himself with me and we did battle with the "animals don't think, animals don't feel," crowd, arguing them to a standstill with such matters as how to embarrass a cat (laugh at it when it tries to jump to the mantelpiece and misses.) Goffman, though not a biologist, trusted my statements that animals reveal their emotions via behavior, probably because in a way that's what he studied in people; so we had fun keeping the discussions in the realm (in my opinion) of reality. Goffman died a year or two later. I'm sure I am not alone in wishing he were still around to discuss behavior with.

"Anything the animal is physically and mentally capable of doing...".

Marine mammal trainers like to brag about their shaping skills, saying "I can train any animal to do any thing that it is physically and mentally capable of doing." This is true, not because marine mammal trainers are better than other kinds of trainers, but because they understand how to break even very difficult behaviors into small enough steps so that the end goal can be shaped eventually, even if it requires a long series of reinforcements.

My father was an odd and delightful person. I love writing about him. Phil's learning to dance was a fine example of a long and difficult shaping task. Whether my father was indeed physically and mentally capable of the behavior of dancing seemed dubious, at first. It took a well-thought-out shaping program, and some powerful reinforcers, starting with the repair of wounded pride. Of course, like many skills, once acquired the behavior became self-reinforcing.

Magazine editor Carol Tavris had moved from *Psychology Today* to a magazine called *Prime Time*; she invited me to come in and talk about freelance assignments. They published this memoir.

Ricky and Phil Wylie in about 1948, at the peak of their dancing years.

Chapter Eight

Philip Wylie, Dancin' Man

By Karen Pryor[1]

Until the age of 43, Phil Wylie was a terrible dancer. He was not just your normal bad dancer, who rocks timidly from side to side in time to the music. He was a really rotten dancer, the sort that sweats, bumps into people, doesn't keep time, and steps on your feet. After dancing with Phil, you were relieved to be able to sit down.

Part of the problem was that although my father loved almost everything in the world that gladdens the senses—flowers and sunsets were invariably a big hit—he really did not love music. He owned a record player. There was a radio in the car. I do not recall that I ever saw him turn on either of them. He never discussed music and seldom recognized music he heard. He was not exactly tone-deaf; he could muster a strained tenor for "Happy Birthday," but I never heard him raise his voice in song in a general way, except satirically, as in a hymn of praise to a daughter who washed the dishes without being asked.

Another problem was the way he moved, either listlessly or frenetically, usually the latter. In his youth, he had prided himself on being an outdoorsman. He took long canoe trips in the Canadian woods, he swam vigorously, he learned fancy-diving;

---

[1]Reprinted from *Prime Time*, February, 1980.

that is, he could execute a number of aerial maneuvers off a diving board, with great intensity of purpose but not with grace. He was energetic rather than strong, and had none of the ease of movement of the natural athlete. He tackled physical tasks with a large and sometimes unsuitable expenditure of thought and willpower.

It made dancing with him an unusually disagreeable experience. He knew he didn't know what he was doing, yet also knew it was a thing everyone else seemed to do easily. Furthermore, standing up while others sat made him feel conspicuous, and he hated that. So he would shove his partner about the floor in a cross manner and at cross-purposes until she found some good reason to sit down.

One night in New York in 1945, he and my stepmother, Ricky, went to a dance given by friends at the St. Regis to welcome Ricky's sister home from the war. Ricky finally complained at the frequency with which Phil stepped on her toes, remarking, "You don't dance; you just wander around on the dance floor." Phil was furious.

He woke up the next morning with "I'll show her!" ringing in his mind, left their suite at the Westbury, and went to Arthur Murray's.

I don't know if you have ever been to one of these places. They are very good at teaching what used to be called ballroom dancing (to differentiate it from The Dance—ballet and so on). In mirror-lined rooms, attractive young instructors take their pupils, however juvenile or elderly or plump or incompetent, step by step through an absolutely foolproof system for learning to dance. Records, each one carefully selected for a strong and steady beat, and played on a turntable, provide the music. You have 20 minutes or so alone with an instructor in a private practice room, where no one else can watch you fumbling and tripping and forgetting steps, and then a few dances in the main room where other pupils are zipping about in the arms of their competent partners. It is good exercise and rather a lot of fun.

Dance "studios," as they are called, also have a nearly foolproof marketing system. Your first lesson, of course, is free. Then you are encouraged to sign up for a series of five or perhaps ten lessons.

Your charming teacher, male or female, whichever you aren't, is as thoroughly trained in selling as in dancing. If you want to go home and think it over, they'll call you up in a day or two, usually with an invitation to a party. Studios give frequent parties for their pupils, either on the premises or at hotels or nightclubs—a fine way for shy or lonely people to meet others and to have a respectable, yet merry, evening out.

If that doesn't tempt you, they have other bait—package deals and special George Washington's Birthday price reductions and so on. It is hard to avoid a course of lessons, once you get in there. And while the lessons are pretty pricey, they are private, and you do learn to dance.

Nevertheless, after having enjoyed his first free lesson, when Phil decided to sign up for a course, his instructor advised against it. "Mr. Wylie, perhaps you are one of those people who was not cut out to be a dancer; I really do not recommend that you take lessons." (Was she dreading the prospect that she might have to dance with him again?) Phil, of course, said that if something was capable of being learned, he could learn it.

"Mr. Wylie, you have absolutely no sense of rhythm. You cannot keep up a steady beat, and you cannot hear the rhythm in the music. It has been our experience that dancing is the one thing you cannot teach a person who has this particular limitation. It's like being color-blind. If you can't keep time naturally at least a little bit, we just can't teach you to dance."

Phil immediately bought 100 lessons. He took a full hour of instruction each day—two half-hour lessons back to back—six days a week. I don't know where he told Ricky he was going every day, but he fooled her. They were in New York for the winter, so he had plenty of time.

His teacher took the first ten lessons or so to teach him how to tap his foot in time to the music. For him to master learning to walk a straight line in time to the music required new miracles of coordination. He also needed lessons in stepping back and forth and sideways according to a pattern, a skill Phil was temperamentally unsuited for.

He was quickly able to assimilate the mechanics of leading a partner, and once he could forget about his feet and the beat, he found it easy to execute known maneuvers and to avoid dancing his partner into walls and furniture.

By about the 85th or 90th lesson, he progressed to the big room where other pupils and teachers were dancing, and where he zestfully took up the sport of monopolizing the dance floor without bumping into anybody.

After the 100th lesson, the teachers at the New York Arthur Murray Dance Studio had a cake and coffee celebration for him. He signed up for another 100 lessons and went home to invite Ricky to go out dancing for the evening.

She didn't want to go, of course, but he promised her he'd sit down the minute she asked, so they went to the Savoy Plaza, where they joined Phil's teacher. Then he got up and danced with Ricky.

Oh, boy. Have you ever experienced total surprise? Ricky Wylie has. Phil could dance. He could dance the fox-trot, both slow and fast. He could waltz a little. He could even do a creditable rumba. He was easy to follow. He led his partner with a little too much vigor, but with clear and consistent signals.

Ricky was a good dancer, whose stylish sense of fun made her a pleasure to watch. She loved to dance and had done a lot of it before she met Phil. But, O joy, O rapture unforeseen, unmitigated bliss, Phil now knew some steps she didn't know. So Ricky signed up for lessons too, and they began going to the studio together.

When I was 15 and went to live with Phil and Ricky, they were living in Miami. They'd switched their lessons from New York to Florida, and spent two afternoons a week dancing at the Murray studio on Biscayne Boulevard.

By that age I was a finished product of Miss Darling's Dancing School at the New Haven Lawn Club, where we wore white gloves to the Monday night classes. I could do the fox-trot, the waltz, the conga, the rumba, and the Mexican hat dance. Now, twice a week after school I started going to Arthur Murray's with the Wylies.

It was fun. The music, the wide, polished floors, the ballroom open to Miami's balmy afternoon air. At 15 I objected to dancing with strange men, especially those dances where you had to stay in bodily contact to accomplish the steps. Although I dreaded the tango practice, the teachers were pleasantly impersonal, and on the whole I enjoyed every minute.

By this time Phil and Ricky could do the fox-trot, the waltz, the rumba (in several variations, such as the merengue and the beguine), the tango, the Lindy (which I called jitterbugging, except it was very passé in my set—I knew no one my age who did that), the samba, and a number of specialty dances of the Rogers-Astaire type. Since the Murray teachers had, in fact, run out of things to teach the Wylies, they began sitting in on the teachers' training classes, which involved a lot more than dancing. Phil was especially interested in the wide range of methods for avoiding sweating, a real problem when you dance with strangers six or eight hours a day.

After the studios closed, the teachers liked to get together at night. To go dancing, of course. So the teachers, together with the Wylies and other select pupils, began making nightclub visits.

Though Cuba was still an okay place to be even in the fifties, there were a lot of Cubans in Miami, and so there were a lot of exciting Cuban bands to dance to. Sometimes I got to go along. It was my father himself who taught me to hear and understand the intricacies of Cuban rhythm. The basic meter was always 4/4, the rumba beat, but within the band one percussion instrument might be beating it thus—one, pause, two, three; then another one, two, three, pause; and with the bongos beating 5/4—five-four, interesting—you danced one-two-THREE-four-five within the space of four beats. Phil would snatch me out to the floor and dance the rumba, now following one beat, now another. I had to listen hard and switch to the new beat each time he did. It was difficult, and strenuous, but great fun, marred only by the expression on Phil's face—his eyes bulged, his forehead was corrugated, and his mouth was drawn down by the strain.

Arthur Murray himself, and his wife, Kathryn, came to Miami every winter to see how the studio was doing. By and by, it was with the Murrays that the Wylies went nightclubbing and dancing socko new Cuban dances far into the night. I was not included on these excursions, of course; they were adult parties. Once, dancing the Lindy with Kathryn Murray, to her astonishment and delight, Phil successfully accomplished one of those steps where the man whirls his partner around his head in the air.

After graduating from college, I returned to Miami and made arrangements for a large, traditional wedding. I walked down the church aisle on my father's arm. My husband-to-be was at the far end of the aisle, looking encouragingly at me. Everyone was staring. I was embarrassed in about 40 different ways at once; surely I'd feel better when I got to the end of this endless walk, and yet Phil kept holding me back. Finally we got to the altar and Phil relinquished me. Then the ceremony was over, and we plunged outside into the Miami sunlight.

A couple of days later I read in the *Miami Daily News* what Phil had been thinking about as we walked down the aisle: "I bought this girl thousands of dollars worth of dancing lessons and she can't even keep time to Lohengrin."

And by God he not only could now, but automatically did. Like a natural dancer.

Sidewalks and sentiment...

Part of the fun of living in New York, for me, was that all my parents had all lived in Manhattan at various times, and shared the same kind of city life I was enjoying now. I sometimes went to lunch at the Westbury Hotel, on 69th Street, where Phil and Ricky lived in the winters, just to relish the familiar setting; and I never walked past the Arthur Murray studios on Fifth Avenue without thinking fondly of the Wylies.

Phil Wylie had died some years before I left Hawaii. Ricky, who lived in Sarasota, Florida, died about a year after this piece was written. She did read it. She deplored my description of Phil's facial contortions while dancing, but didn't deny their accuracy.

Net work....

From the time I first heard about tuna boats encircling whole schools of spinners and spotters, I had a selfish thought: the huge enclosure of net would be a wonderful place, like a vast aquarium, to get a good look at pelagic dolphin schools.

However, in spite of all the time I put in for the tuna industry, testifying in Congress about dolphin behavior, talking to environmental groups, meeting with fishermen, I never expected to get a chance to see the fishing for myself. It took place thousands of miles from shore; there was no way to get there but on the tuna boats, and tuna boats were off-limits for women.

Then Ken Norris set up two trips on a government research vessel, the *David Starr Jordan*, accompanying a tuna fishing vessel. Women were (grudgingly) permitted on the government boat, so I got to go on the second trip, to see and in fact to dive in one set of a tuna boat's half-mile-long net around a school of spotted dolphins.

Coastal dolphins, such as the bottlenose, live in small groups and often traverse the same bays and coves year in, year out. They can be observed, even recognized as individuals, from shore, or from small boats. Pelagic dolphins, on the other hand, such as spinners and spotters, travel far and fast in the open sea. The observer is limited, by and large, to glimpses of dorsal fins as the school hurtles by.

Furthermore, spinners and spotters, the two species involved in the tuna-porpoise fishery, were reported to live in groups of hundreds or thousands, or sometimes tens of thousands. Were they just amorphous, anonymous gatherings, as one supposes schools of fish to be? It seemed unlikely. Spinners are rather democratic, but from what I knew of spotted dolphins in captivity, they are terrible snobs, and NEVER swim with some dolphin they don't know. Maybe these giant schools were like crowds in a football stadium: from the air it looks like a mass of anonymous people, but up close they are all divided into clusters of family groups, same-sex-same-age friends, courting couples, and so on.

When I finally got my day on a tuna boat, and went out into the net in a rubber raft and went underwater, the first thing I saw was a mother spotted dolphin calmly nursing her baby, right underneath me; and a look at the other dolphins all around us told me at once, yes, these spotters are in sub-groups, that is, they are all swimming with their particular friends. For that one glimpse I spent three weeks cooped up on the *Jordan* in bad weather with no company (since the other scientists were seasick) and continual hazing from the civil service crew, but it was worth it.

Then the tuna fishing industry, the environmental community, and the government got together and agreed on a joint project: a year of research aboard a fishing vessel refitted for scientific teams, and subsidized to carry out research as well as fishing: the Dedicated Vessel program. The National Marine Fisheries Service asked me if I would be one of the researchers, and study dolphin behavior in the nets. Their concern was that the dolphins might be dying of fright and shock, after they were released apparently unharmed. I was pretty sure the dolphins were not that frightened, but I jumped at the chance to see some more schools underwater.

I called Ingrid Kang, my replacement at Sea Life Park in Hawaii: would she come with me, if the Park gave her leave of absence? She would, and they did. There were some difficulties about our being women, but the captain's wife, Evelyn Silva, resolved them by going to sea with us, not to protect us, but to protect the crew! The first mate and navigator moved into crew quarters and chivalrously gave us their cabin for the voyage. In June of 1979 we sailed out of San Diego on the *Queen Mary*, with four other scientists and a crew of nineteen fishermen, mostly Portuguese-American, for a month in the eastern tropical Pacific, 1500 miles from land.

Did we have to witness a lot of suffering dolphins? Not at all. Though we encircled thousands of dolphins, in seventeen sets of the net, the crew were highly skilled, the dolphins appeared to be experienced, and there were only two mortalities. Often, in the net, the dolphins were simply resting or going about their business. When the time came for release from the net, they all went to the release point and waited quietly, like cattle at a gate. They knew what to do.

Was it dangerous for us? Yes, especially on rough days. Getting on and off the fishing boat was always a bumpy experience. Also there were sharks, both inside and outside the net, though we seldom saw them. We divided the duties: Ingrid worried about sharks. I worried about broken bones and drowning. The captain worried about everything.

Was it fun? You bet. I hope some day to write about the human side of that trip; meanwhile, here is the science.

Karen Pryor and Ingrid Kang on the bridge of the tuna purse seiner Queen Mary, *1500 miles from land in the Eastern tropical Pacific, with speedboats keeping pace off the bow.*

CHAPTER NINE

Social Structure in Spotted Dolphins (*Stenella attenuata*) in the Tuna Purse Seine Fishery in the Eastern Tropical Pacific.

by Karen Pryor and Ingrid Kang Shallenberger[1,2]

Introduction

Along the west coast of South America, reaching north from the Galapagos and 1,500 miles out toward Tahiti, lies a million-square-mile area of ocean known as the eastern tropical Pacific, or ETP. A peculiarity of the ETP is that while in this region the

[1]Reprinted with permission from *Dolphin Societies: Discoveries and Puzzles*, K. Pryor and K.S. Norris, Eds., University of California Press, 1991.

[2]This study was undertaken as a portion of the 1979 Dedicated Vessel Program, under the joint direction of the Marine Mammal Commission, the National Marine Fisheries Service, and the U.S. Tuna Foundation. The research was supported by National Marine Fisheries Service Contract No. 01-78-027-1043.

We would like to thank William Perrin and Warren Stuntz, of the Southwest Fisheries Center, Ethyl Tobach, American Museum of Natural History, and Rosamund Gianutsios, Adelphi University, for assistance in designing the data acquisition system and the initial analysis and interpretation of the data (SFC Admin. Rept. LJ-80-11C). We are very grateful for the kindness, cooperation, and support of Captain and Mrs. Ralph Silva, Jr., and the crew of the *Queen Mary*, without which this work would have been impossible. Our special thanks to Philippe Vergne, Living Marine Resources, who managed our small boat and swam as shark guard. This chapter was reviewed, and greatly improved thereby, by Kenneth Norris, William Perrin, Kevin Lohman, and Erich Klinghammer.

sea floor is thousands of meters below, the warm, productive surface water is shallow, sometimes only 10 m deep. This surface layer, in which temperatures are typically greater than 24.5°C, is cut off from the water beneath by a thermocline, a "floor" or discontinuity, below which the water is not only colder but higher in salinity and unusually low in oxygen. Therefore, the sea life that in other tropical oceans is often spread through a much deeper water column, is here concentrated in the shallow surface layer (Au et al. 1979). Vertical discontinuities and confluences of water bodies along and within this surface layer attract enormous concentrations of prey and predator, most conspicuously, dolphins, tuna, and tuna fishing vessels.

Schools of dolphins in the ETP, principally of the genus *Stenella,* are often accompanied by schools of yellowfin *(Thunnus albicares)* and skip-jack tuna *(Katsuwonus pelamis).* The association, which appears to be involuntary on the part of the dolphins, is probably due to the behavior of the tuna, which tend to join up with dolphin schools in the daylight hours. Presumably, this increases their foraging efficiency; while dolphins do not eat everything tuna eat (e.g., pelagic portunid crabs), tuna eat dolphin prey (Perrin et al. 1973). The association may also include several species of seabirds, sharks, and other fast-swimming predators such as marlin. Such mixed-species foraging groups are a phenomenon related to areas of rich but patchy resources (McArthur and Pianka 1966).

Tuna fishermen, using hooks and poles, had long known that the "porpoise," as they call all species of small cetaceans, could be an indicator of the presence of tuna. After World War II, the American tuna fleet, based in San Diego, developed techniques for using large purse seine nets to surround tuna and dolphins both, gathering in the tuna and releasing the dolphins. Initially, dolphin mortality was extremely high: pelagic animals are not behaviorally adapted to avoiding or surmounting obstacles, and the nets were fatal to hundreds of thousands (Pryor and Norris 1978).

Although the ETP dolphin populations were postulated to consist of many millions, they could not sustain this kind of loss for long (Perrin et al. 1982). Techniques were developed and adopted by the industry for safe release of encircled dolphins; the federal government established detailed regulations governing the fishing procedure; and by 1982, mortality caused by the U.S. fleet dropped to biologically acceptable levels (unfortunately, annual mortality caused by domestic and foreign fleets had climbed again to an estimated 120,000 by 1986). Meanwhile, the National Marine Fisheries Service undertook extensive research into the biology of the dolphins. In 1978, a consortium was formed between the U.S. tuna industry, the National Marine Fisheries Service, and other interested groups to use a tuna purse-seining vessel exclusively for scientific research on the tuna-porpoise problem. The *Elizabeth C.J.*, a large seiner, was chartered experimentally. Then a middle-sized seiner, the *Queen Mary,* (150 ft., 500-ton capacity) was refitted to accommodate up to six scientists for a full year of research during 1979, the "Year of the Dedicated Vessel." Six research voyages of four to six weeks each were accomplished in the eastern tropical Pacific. During these voyages, the vessel located and encircled schools of tuna and dolphins, in the usual manner called fishing "on porpoise," but scientific tasks and requirements took precedence over fishing success.

In January 1979, the authors contracted with the Southwest Fisheries Center to join one voyage of the Dedicated Vessel to study the behavior of encircled dolphins by making underwater observations within the net. The principal species of dolphins involved in the tuna fishery are the Pacific spotted dolphin (*Stenella attenuata*) and the spinner dolphin (*Stenella longirostris,* so-called for its behavior of leaping into the air and spinning on its long axis). Spotted and spinner dolphins have been maintained successfully in captivity only at Sea Life Park in Hawaii. Karen Pryor was head trainer and curator at this oceanarium from before its opening, in 1963, until 1971. Ingrid Kang Shallenberger was second-in-command from 1965 until 1971 and was head trainer and curator from 1971 until 1990. Both authors were also trained as ethologists, Shallenberger at the University of Stockholm and the University of Washington, Pryor at Cornell, New York University, and Rutgers University.

Between 1963 and 1979, the authors personally adapted to captivity, maintained, and trained many individuals of several pelagic species of cetaceans, including over forty spinner and spotted dolphins (Pryor 1973, 1975). Spinner and spotted dolphins were maintained as performing and research animals, in groups of two to eight individuals, throughout this period.

Training as a tool for the ethologist

George Schaller has been widely quoted as saying that to describe the behavior of any species of animals in the field, one needs "5,000-hour eyeballs," meaning that it takes considerable looking before one can understand or indeed even notice the crucial but often small events that constitute social communication. If this is true of terrestrial animals, whose signals—a growl, a threatening posture—are often at least partly familiar to us, it is much truer of the cetaceans. For example, the lay literature abounds with egregious accounts of dolphins "laughing," "smiling," and "acting playful," when what the author witnessed were the gaped jaw and head movements that in dolphins signify aggressive intent (Nollman 1987).

We had, individually, considerably more than Schaller's requisite 5,000 hours of looking at the behavior of spinner and spotted dolphins as well as several other species (Pryor 1973, 1975; Defran and Pryor 1980). Furthermore, we had looked at these animals from the special viewpoint of the trainer.[3] Training animals in a group, as we did with spinner and spotted dolphins, provides excellent opportunities for learning about social relationships and the nature of social signaling (Lorenz 1975; Pryor 1981, 1987). For example, we dolphin trainers have a straightforward technique for identifying an animal's place in the dominance hierarchy: if a fish falls between two dolphins, who gets it? The dominant animal (barring the rare gesture: a dominant male spotted dolphin at Sea Life Park, named Hoku, sometimes deliberately gave a fish to his female con-specific, Kiko; see Pryor 1975).

---

[3]For detailed discussions of dolphin training methods, see Karen Pryor's *Lads Before the Wind* (Harper & Row, 1975; Sunshine Books, 1987) and *Don't Shoot the Dog.* (Bantam Books, 1985).

Knowledge of the dominance hierarchy is of practical importance to the trainer.[4] It also opens a window to the ethologist. Knowing which animal in a pair or group is dominant, one can then learn to identify aggressive and submissive displays and other indications of relationships, often in rather fine detail. As an example, a common threat gesture in spotted dolphins (not seen in bottlenose dolphins) is a rapid nodding of the head, sometimes with jaws open, and sometimes accompanied by burst-pulse sounds (dubbed "snitting" by Sea Life Park trainers). The male spotted dolphin mentioned above, Hoku, routinely used this threat to force an adult female false killer whale *(Pseudorca crassidens)* ten times his weight to give him some of her fish. When we looked at wild spotted dolphins underwater, at sea, and saw groups of males "snitting" at each other, we knew this to be an exchange of threats, not, say, affiliative greetings, however much it might have looked like "nodding and smiling."

Social organization in captivity

Studying our captive animals, we learned to identify many individual behavioral events, from postures and gestures to stylized bubble releases, and to recognize their significance at least in part (Defran and Pryor 1980, Pryor and Kang 1980). Of major importance in our captive school was the dominance hierarchy, to which the animals devoted much time. Behavioral indications of this hierarchy are many: we have observed that the dominant animal often swims slightly in advance of the others, or above them; subordinate animals in a group tend to swim closer to equals and a bit farther away (wider interanimal distance) from animals dominant to them; subordinate animals move aside from dominant animals and can be displaced from feeding or work stations. Gregory Bateson found that our *Stenella* group sometimes rested in "rank order," with the superior animals cruising at the surface and the most subordinate at the bottom of the school (Bateson 1974). He also observed that changes in the hierarchy (introduc-

---

[4]All too often, novice trainers dismiss a nonperforming animal as "untrainable" when it is merely at the bottom of the hierarchy, being prevented from earning reinforcement by more dominant animals. These animals may actually go hungry if not given special attention.

tion of new animals) or transgressions by subordinates (stealing fish, for example) sometimes produced open conflict, blows, and ramming attacks that could be quite severe.

In any established group of captive dolphins, a network of affiliative connections is, as it were, thrown across the dominance hierarchy. Affiliative relationships can be expressed by unison swimming and respiration; by close interanimal distances; by frequency and duration of swimming together; and most conspicuously, by contact, especially by animals petting, touching, or rubbing each other with fins, flukes, rostrum, or body (Defran and Pryor 1980, Norris et al., 1985). We observed repeatedly that in the Sea Life Park *Stenella* group, individuals newly introduced into the school were not included in affiliative exchanges. In fact, a stranger, unless highly dominant, was likely to be shunned and avoided for days or even weeks before becoming part of the affiliative network (Defran and Pryor 1980; Pryor 1973, 1975).

Research goals

Of primary interest to the National Marine Fisheries Service in our research at sea were evidences of stress that might or might not be evinced by encircled animals. Their hypothesis was that animals encircled by tuna nets might be undergoing hazardous levels of stress, perhaps leading to mortalities additional to those observed during the fishing process.

Of primary interest to us, however, was the question of social organization. At sea, these species can be found in aggregations of hundreds or even thousands of animals. It seemed likely that some sort of finer-grained social organization continues to be maintained in these large schools. Subgroups of two to perhaps six or eight animals or so could sometimes be seen even in aerial photographs of these aggregations. But what might the nature of those subgroups be? And how might they relate to each other? The brief confinement of whole schools of these ever-traveling pelagic animals in a purse seine was an unprecedented opportunity for behavioral observation. We hoped our familiarity with the interactions between individual captive animals would help us investigate the next step up the ladder of social behavior:

the nature of the subgroups and the interactions and relationships between them.

METHODS

The fishing method

A tuna purse seiner cruises until a school of dolphins is sighted (some larger vessels carry helicopters to spot schools). Several speedboats are then lowered overboard which chase, turn, and herd the dolphins, like cattle, back toward the ship. Tuna accompanying the school usually remain with it during this process. The captain directs the herding by radio from the top of the mast.

The seine net, which is 200 m deep and sometimes nearly a mile long, is stacked on the back deck of the ship, fan-folded so that it will run into the water smoothly. The location of winches and other gear requires the net to be set on the left or port side of the vessel. When the dolphins reach the port side of the ship, a heavy open boat, the net skiff, is dropped off the stern of the vessel, pulling one end of the seine net after it. The fishing vessel then travels in a circle until the net is paid out, or set, around the animals.

Once the circle of net is complete, a cable running through steel rings around the bottom of the net is drawn tight, thus pursing or closing the net underwater. The top of the net, or cork line, is kept open in a circle, by the way in which the net is set relative to the wind and current and if necessary, by speedboats pulling the cork line outward; this allows the dolphins room to swim and breathe. The vessel is now temporarily immobilized by the inertia of the net in the water.

The dolphins usually cluster at or near the water surface and as far from the vessel as possible. The tuna, meanwhile, move constantly about in the net throughout the time the net is in the water. Unlike the object-shy dolphins, if the tuna find a hole in the net, they will rapidly escape.

The net is then "rolled," or pulled back aboard the vessel, through a power winch at the top of the boom. Crew members

Fig. 1. Taken from the mast of the fishing vessel, this photograph shows the completion of the backdown procedure. The vessel has pulled the net until the cork lines at the far end sank, passing under the dolphins. White splashes in the distance are made by the released dolphins. A school of tuna "boil" inside the cork line, which is now at the surface again. The speedboat driver is examining the area to make sure all dolphins have been released. (Photo courtesy of the United States Tuna Foundation.)

restack the net below the winch on the deck. When approximately three-quarters of the net is back aboard, the vessel starts its engines and begins backing up, hauling the remaining bowl-shaped net through the water. The net elongates, and in due course, the cork line in the portion of the net farthest from the boat is pulled underwater. This area of the net is lined with special fine-meshed net, the "Medina panel," which prevents accidental entanglement of dolphin fins or beaks. When the cork line sinks, the backward movement of the vessel slips the net out from under the dolphins, releasing them unharmed. (Figure 1.) Many dolphins appear to have learned to expect this procedure, called "backing down;" they wait quietly in the backdown area and swim out or allow themselves to be sluiced out.

When all the dolphins have been released, the remainder of the net is rolled aboard. The tuna are "sacked up" in the last of the net and scooped aboard the vessel to be frozen in tanks of brine in the hold. Sharks and other unwanted animals in the catch are disposed of overboard. Cleaning and other processing of the fish is done later by canneries onshore. A single set of the net may take two or more hours to complete, requires a crew of about twenty, and may catch no tuna, a few fish, or 30 tons or more (Orbach 1977).

Investigators' procedures during a set

The fishing procedure allowed a period of one to two hours, during pursing and rolling of the net, when the seiner was stationary and underwater observations were possible. Once the seiner had halted and the two ends of the net had been drawn together, we lowered an inflatable, outboard-powered rubber raft over the side, climbed into it, and crossed the cork line into the net. It was usually possible to approach the school very closely by moving slowly and by flanking the school rather than heading right at it. A third member of the scientific party, Phillippe Vergne, launched and handled the raft for us and dove with us as shark guard. First mate Ralph Silva, Jr., also dove with us when duties permitted, and other members of the scientific party sometimes assisted us from the surface. (Fig. 2.)

We then entered the water using snorkeling gear and collected data and photographs and made observations until backdown was about to begin. The clarity of the water and the approachability of the dolphins made SCUBA gear unnecessary. The water temperature, approximately 80°F, was not a limitation on observation time. (Fig. 3.)

Fig. 2. Investigators make observations in a school of spotted dolphins, near the corkline. One shark guard swims behind them while another watches from the surface.

Fig.3. Ingrid Kang Shallenberger taking data underwater, using a plastic slate and ordinary lead pencils. The pair of spotted dolphins directly behind her are "columning," or diving vertically after surfacing to breathe. Bubbles, at left, were released by a whistling animal.

During backdown, as the dolphins were released from the net, we tied the raft to the cork line in the backdown area, next to the release point. We continued observations underwater until ordered into the raft (to avoid being sluiced out into open sea; Pryor did get backed out of the net once). We then returned to the vessel, transferred and recorded our data and observations, and prepared for the next set.[5]

Species, age, and sex recognition

Spotted and spinner dolphins in the ETP are easily separated by coloration, spotters having a dark cape and in adult animals, light and dark speckles or spots, while spinners are unspotted and either all gray or gray with white bellies. Also, spotted dolphins have falcate or sickle-shaped dorsal fins, and spinner dolphins have triangular fins, making them easily separable even in silhouette or at a distance.

Conveniently for the investigator, spotted dolphins change their color pattern as they age. William Perrin, studying specimens taken during tuna fishing, divided spotted dolphins into five maturation stages, based on size and on the degree of spotting: neonatal (gray with ivory belly), two-toned (dark gray above, light gray below), speckled (with a few dark ventral spots), mottled (spotted all over, with spots overlapping below), and fused (heavily spotted, with a black mask, and spots below fused and faded; Perrin 1969). We divided the spotted dolphins in the nets, by size, into five age groups—neonate, calf, juvenile, young adult, and large or fused-pattern adult—that corresponded to the differences in coloration as defined by Perrin (Table 1). While transitional animals undoubtedly existed, in practice, we found we could readily assign animals to their age groups based on Perrin's five color pattern groups and on size relative to nearby animals.

---

[5]Care must be taken if the tuna come into the backdown area while the dolphins are being released. Speedboat drivers are assigned to signal if the tuna head toward the opening, whereupon the vessel halts temporarily and the cork lines pop to the surface until the tuna swim away. Crew members also assist any dolphins that may be in difficulties and inspect the net underwater for stragglers.

Table 1. *Color Pattern Changes with Age in Pacific Spotted Dolphins* *

Age group	Size	Coloration	Pattern type
Neonate 1–2 weeks	80–110 cm	gray and ivory	neonatal
Calf 2 weeks–1 year or 3/4 adult	100–160 cm	dark gray above, light gray below	"two-tone"
Juvenile 1–3 years	150–180 cm	dark above, light below with a few ventral spots	"speckled"
Young adult 3–6 years	160–190 cm	spotted all over	"mottled"
Large adult 6 or 7+ years	170–200 cm	black mask, heavily spotted, spots fused and faded below	"fused"

*Age estimates are based on sizes and color patterns of captive spotted dolphins of known ages. Size estimates are adapted from Perrin *et al.*, 1976, based on measurements of animals killed during fishing. Pattern type is derived from Perrin, 1969.

Sex identification was usually possible in large adult spotted dolphins. In fused-pattern adults, the sexes are dimorphic: the most conspicuous difference is that males have a postanal bulge, or keel, and a thickened caudal peduncle (Perrin 1975). Since this keel is more pronounced in ETP spotted dolphins than in Hawaiian spotted dolphins, the keel on large male dolphins in the nets seemed quite conspicuous to our eyes; it is not, however, as conspicuous as the keel in large male ETP spinners, which is almost grotesque. Nevertheless, to verify that the individuals we identified as males were indeed males, we tested our assumptions on a group of fused-pattern animals that was resting at the surface (rafting) by verbally agreeing on the presumed sex of an animal and then taking turns visually checking its genital area. Those with postanal keels were indeed males, and those without were females. In addition, adult animals closely associated with a calf were usually assumed to be female, based on behavior.

Solitary animals and younger animals could not be sexed unless circumstances provided a close look at the genital area (males have two visible swellings, at the anus and penis, while females have a single genital slit, flanked, in adults, by two small mammary slits). We never succeeded in sexing a calf or a juvenile.

Recording data

We recorded data underwater on lightly sanded plastic slates made of 3/16-inch Lucite, cut into 9-inch-by-12-inch sheets and painted white on the reverse side to improve legibility (the white surface was then painted over again with black to reduce visibility to sharks). The writing tools were ordinary No. 2 soft lead pencils. Each slate was drilled with two 1/4-inch holes, one for a string to tether the slate to the investigator, and one to tether the pencil to the slate. About twenty extra pencils and slates were carried in the raft for each dive.

We used Focal Animal Sampling as one data collection method (Altmann 1974). Based on our experience with captive animals,

Fig. 4. a. Surfacing to breathe, two fused-pattern Pacific spotted dolphins exhibit the postanal keels of mature males. The third animal accompanying them is an adult female. Rafting animals are visible in the background.

Fig. 4. b. In a group of spinner dolphins of mixed ages and sexes, the nearest animal shows the "backward" dorsal fin and exaggerated postanal keel of mature male spinners in the eastern tropical Pacific.

we selected five minutes as a representative sample of an animal's activity when viewed underwater. Insofar as possible, we spread our focal animal selection over both sexes, all age groups, and over active, inactive, solitary, and grouped animals. To record focal animal samples without taking our eyes off the animals, we listed events vertically, moving the hand down the edge of the slate after each entry. If two animals were interacting or swimming in unison, we could sometimes watch two focal animals at a time.

Each set also provided a wealth of observational data other than the behavior of focal animals. We tape recorded our other observations and discussion immediately on returning to the ship after each set. Written field notes and taped observations were also made whenever possible during the chase and the early part of the set, from shipboard on sets in which we did not dive, and during and after backdown. Weather, location, time at start of chase, and shipboard school size estimates were taken from the ship's log.

Recognition and labeling of behavior

Before going to sea, we constructed a "dictionary" of all the behavioral events known by us to occur in spotted dolphins in captivity and the social or communicative significance of these events when known (based on a previous survey of senior trainers: Defran and Pryor 1980). We used standard terms where they existed and coined terms if they did not, especially for behavior specific to these species, such as certain leaps and aggressive displays. Each behavior was assigned a two-letter, mnemonic code (BR for "breathe," DV for "dive," TS for "tailslap," etc.) to facilitate data taking underwater and subsequent computer analysis of focal animal samples. We augmented the dictionary and codes in the field as needed (Pryor and Kang 1980.)

Sets made

Between July 23 and August 13, 1978, the M.V. *Queen Mary* made seventeen sets of the net in the eastern tropical Pacific. (Fig. 5.) The investigators dove in the net on fourteen sets (omitting two night sets and one set in which sharks were visible

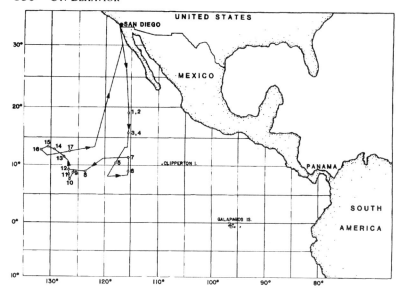

FIGURE 1: CRUISE TRACK AND SET LOCATIONS

Fig. 5. Cruise track and set locations.

in the net). In two more sets, data could not be collected under water because of rough seas, though the attempt was made. Details of each set are given in Table 2.

A total of over 4,000 dolphins were encircled and released during the voyage; three mortalities occurred. Spotted dolphins were present in all seventeen sets; spinner dolphins were present only in nine sets. A total of 119 focal animal samples were completed (table 3).

Table 2. Set-by-Set Overview

Set	Spinners present	School size	Time (at chase start)	Agitation levels[a]	Social activity[b]
1		23	12:36 P.M.	1,1,2	III
2		60	3:30 P.M.	2,2,4	II
3		60+	9:45 A.M.	1,1,1	III
4		45	1:00 P.M.	1,1,1	II
5	✓	180	7:12 A.M.	1,1,3	III
6		300+	4:58 P.M.	4,4,4–5	II
7	✓	300–500	2:21 P.M.	2,3,3	—
8	✓	—	11:19 A.M.	2,1,3	—
9	✓	300+	11:22 AM.	1,1,2–3	III
10	✓	500+	11:18 A.M.	1,1,2	IV
11	✓	100	6:23 P.M.	2,1,2	—
12	✓	220	7:59 A.M.	2,1,2	IV
13		120	12:51 P.M.	1,1,2	—
14	✓	350	9:15 A.M.	1,1,2	III
15		50–100	12:37 P.M.	2,3,3	—
16	✓	1000	4:40 P.M.	3,3,3	—
17		450+	7:45 A.M.	3,3,2	III

[a]Types of surface activity during pursuing, rolling, and backdown. See text for details.
[b]Degree of social interaction underwater. See text.

Table 3. Focal Animal Samples

	Spotted Dolphins	Spinner Dolphins
Adult male	26	13
Adult female	16	2
Adult, sex unknown	5	1
Juvenile	23	—
Calf	5	—
Females and calves in pairs	22	6

FINDINGS AND DISCUSSION

Dolphin aggregations underwater

Excellent visibility prevailed on most dives during our cruise (30-75 m, gauged by the distance at which the net walls and floor were visible). We could often view the aggregation of animals as a whole, at least until the crowded conditions before backdown.

We follow Norris in defining a school as any aggregation of animals that swim together as a unit, separated from other aggregations (Norris and Dohl 1980). If spotted and spinner schools were both present, they occupied the same general area in the net but did not mingle; no social interactions were observed between species. The aggregations of each species in the net might be further divided into several separate groups containing from 20+ to 100+ individuals. For example, Set 3 initially contained three groups of spotted dolphins that stayed separate for half an hour. Set 9 contained two separate groups of spotted dolphins, a cluster of about 30 mostly stationary animals and another of about 60 actively swimming animals, as well as three separate groups of spinners. In these multiple-school sets, the groups kept to themselves as neatly as if they were contained in invisible plastic bags, what Norris aptly calls "the school envelope" (Norris et al. 1985).

Once within the net, spinners have been reported to group themselves in a circle, with animals in the middle engaged in "rafting" (floating in a somewhat vertical posture near or at the surface) and more active animals moving protectively in a "ring of aggression" around the central group—what one might call the musk-ox model. But spotted dolphins did not, in our underwater observations, appear to arrange themselves in this manner. In nine of the eleven sets in which we could see the whole school, spotted dolphins were arranged in a truncated cone (likened by Norris to an upside down tea cup). The top of the cone, the smallest portion, was the area at the surface, where rafting animals, if present, were indeed gathered; rafting animals might be of any age, including large adult males, except neonates. Here, also, other animals in the school surfaced to breathe.

Meanwhile, most of the rest of the group, including large and small adults and juveniles, circled and cruised below this apex, in a pyramidal mass that might extend 20 or more m downward and widen to 30 m or more at the base. In the center of this mass, a column of animals were moving upward and downward vertically, rising to breathe and diving again in a column, and then joining the animals cruising horizontally at various depths.[6]

Rather than staying in the middle of the school , a la musk-ox, females with calves under one-year size tended to remain, during rolling and pursing of the net, at the outside perimeter of the bottom of the mass of animals. Female-calf pairs on which focal animal samples were taken in this location surfaced to breathe, of course, but then returned to the bottom rim of the school, staying, as it were, out of the crowds.

Fear and stress

While social organization and the role of males in spotted dolphin schools is our principal topic, it seems appropriate to discuss, first, the question of fear and stress in the nets, so as to respond to the not uncommon supposition that one could observe little or no normal social behavior in such frightening circumstances.

When each dolphin school was finally driven into the net by the pursuing speedboats, the animals were certainly agitated and, if the chase had been a long one, probably severely fatigued. All schools, when set on, took up a similar position in the net, described as a "node" of minimum fear, as far from the ship as possible without coming into actual contact with the net (Norris et al. 1978). Whether aggregation in the net consisted of a single group or of two or more separate groups, all the animals

---

[6]The picture was very different in spinners (present in 9 of 17 sets), which seldom rafted and which surfaced to breathe in long, horizontal arcs rather than vertical columns. Spinners also moved faster and over a wider area throughout the sets (Pryor and Kang 1980).

We saw only two neonates, identifiable by visible fetal folds, on this cruise; in both cases, the mother and neonate, viewed repeatedly by both observers during the set, were moving rapidly, continuously and well beyond the perimeter of the school.

responded to any alarming stimulus, such as a speedboat motor, by moving away.

At the beginning of some sets (9 out of 17), we saw signs of agitation at the surface, such as headslaps, tailslaps, thrashing, and "bunching" (animals traveling rapidly, grouped tightly together, and breathing in sharp puffs). In captive *Stenella* spp., these are all signs of fear, stress, excitement, or frustration (Pryor 1973, 1975; Norris and Dohl 1980). In most sets, these agonistic displays diminished partially or entirely during pursing and rolling but sometimes increased again just prior to backdown (Table 2).

Presence or absence of behavioral events can be used as an index of the state of an organism, as is done in many physiological assessment scales (King-Thomas and Hacker 1987). Norris and his associates observed that some types of surface behavior in spinner dolphins increased in frequency prior to the school's traveling from a rest area to offshore feeding sites. Ranking of these behaviors enabled them to predict when the departure was imminent (Norris et al. 1985).

Similarly, we created an agitation scale, using surface-visible behavior related to fear and stress in *Stenella* in captivity, to rank the evidences of stress in the schools (Table 4). We rated each school on the Agitation Scale three times, at the beginning, middle, and end of the set (Pryor and Kang 1980). Schools varied from being highly agitated throughout (Set 6) to being very calm, with no surface displays even at backdown (Sets 3 and 4; see Table 2).

Table 4. Agitation Levels

Level 1: No aerial behavior, Animals moving quietly.

Level 2: Rapid swimming; rolling or leaping across surface ("porpoising"); loud exhalations ("chuffing").

Level 3: Level 2 plus some headlaps, tailslaps, rostrums in air.

Level 4: Level 2 and 3 activity plus fluking, tailwaves, sideswipes, charging; whistling audible in air.

Level 5: Level 2, 3, and 4 activity plus panicky dashing about, charging the net, struggling.

Except for the animals in Set 6, we saw no panicky dashing about or blundering into the nets, scenes that had been described by many observers in previous years. We also saw no "sleepers," animals lying on the bottom of the backdown channel (Norris et al. 1978), though we were able to scan the backdown area through face masks in most sets. It is our surmise that this difference was a result of experience on the part of the animals we happened to observe. There seems to be no doubt that some dolphins in the ETP have learned what to expect when set on and can develop accommodating behavior (Stuntz and Perrin 1979). We think it probable that those schools showing the most agitation were those with the least experience; highly agitated schools also showed the most incompetence at backdown, going out of the net sideways, swimming back into the net, and so on, whereas calmer schools sometimes left the net very efficiently, some individuals even slithering over the cork lines before they sank.

As the intensity of fear and agitation varied from school to school, so did evidences of fear and stress in individuals. Some cruised slowly as captive animals do when resting or engaged in social activity; others showed signs of stress, such as sinking briefly or whistling repeatedly. One individual, a large adult male, caught our eye by lashing out in all directions for about 10 seconds. The other animals gave him a wide berth (this was the only event of its kind that we observed in 11 underwater sets).

Rafting

The behavior of rafting, or hanging at the surface with just the blowhole exposed, was recorded in animals of both sexes and in all age groups except neonates and small calves (which, according to Sea Life Park staff, never lie still at the surface in captivity, either). Percentage of animals rafting varied from none to over half the animals in a given set; there was no correlation between agitation levels and the percentage of animals rafting.

It is our guess that rafting may combine elements of both fear and adaptation in individually varying amounts. Nearby rafting animals appeared alert and could be seen inspecting us and our equipment attentively; yet in several sets, we swam among rafting animals, touched them, and even moved them about. At Sea Life Park, newly captured *Stenella* specimens are often extremely passive, allowing themselves to be caught, force-fed, and even inoculated without resistance, until they learn to feed, whereupon they become hard to catch again. Some rafting animals may be exhibiting this "learned helplessness." However, in captivity, spotted dolphins that are not otherwise occupied sometimes loaf or rest in the rafting position. It is possible that some animals were doing so by choice. And some animals may have been rafting simply in mimicry of others. One focal animal case describes a juvenile repeatedly nudging its rafting mother (a play invitation). When the female gaped (a threat display), the calf finally gave up and rafted beside her.

Social activity levels

The *Stenella* school at Sea Life Park tended to engage in abundant social interaction in intermittent bouts, alternating with rest periods (in spinners, aerial displays often occurred at night and were reported by night watchmen). Bouts of leaping and social interaction in the dusky dolphin *(Lagenorhynchus obscurus)* commonly occur following feeding episodes (Würsig and Würsig 1981). The social activity observed by us in spotted dolphins in the net also appeared to be occurring in bouts. Either a lot was going on or very little. Whatever the state of socializing in a particular set happened to be, that level of activity remained constant throughout the set until just before backdown.

While actions of individual animals—leaps, tailslaps, and so on—can be seen from the surface, one needs to be under water to see and record the small but significant interactions between two or more animals, such as a pectoral pat or a gape and the reaction to it. Therefore, we can report on spotted dolphin social activity only in the eleven sets we observed underwater. We created a scale for assessment of the intensity of social activity, similar to our scale for agitation levels, as shown in table 5.

In three sets, social activity was at a minimum. In six sets, social activity was commonplace. The remaining two sets were very high in social activity. The social activity level for each set seen underwater is given in Table 2.

Table 5. Social Activity Levels

Level I:	No apparent social activity; animals *not* in visible subgroups.
Level II:	Animals in subgroups, rafting, columning, and/or cruising. Social interactions not conspicuous.
Level III:	Level II activity plus social interaction between individuals, such as affiliative exchanges, aggressive display, and adult-calf play.
Level IV:	Level II and III activity, plus extensive social interactions of long duration or involving several animals.

Social activity levels, agitation levels, and time of day

If spotted dolphins feed at dawn and dusk, and if social activity normally follows feeding as in the dusky dolphin, we might expect time of day to affect social activity levels. All sets observed underwater before 1:00 P.M. were ranked for social activity at Levels III or IV; the two sets observed after 1:00 P.M. were low (Level II) in social activity. Given our limited data, there is nevertheless a significant visible trend toward social activity in the morning. (Fig. 6a.) We also compared agitation levels for all seventeen sets to time of day and to size of school and found a random scatter and no correlation. (Fig. 6b.)

It has been suggested that some of what we considered to be normal social activity, particularly male-male aggression, was a by-product of fear and stress. We compared social activity levels to agitation levels for the eleven sets observed underwater. We found a highly significant inverse correlation of social activity to agitation levels: sets with higher levels of agitation showed less incidence and less variety of social activity; sets with high levels of social interaction (including male-male conflict) were, conversely, low in surface signs of agitation (Spearman rank correlation = 0.84; n =11; 0.002 < P < 0005; Zar 1984).

Spotted dolphin subgroups: general observations

We define subgroups as a relatively small (<20) group of animals oriented and traveling in the same direction, maintaining close interanimal distances (usually <2 m), and, typically, separated from their neighbors by a wider gap (>3 m). Subgroups usually surfaced to breathe all together. Some subgroups moved in physical contact and in complete unison, tailbeat matching

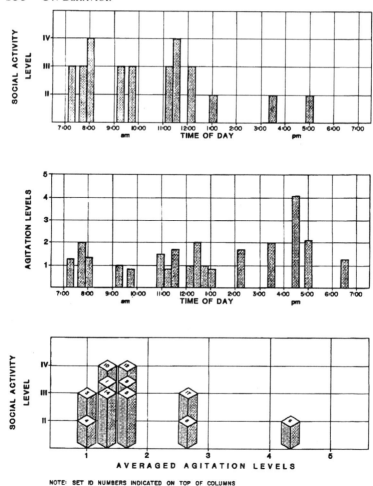

Fig. 6 a. Social activity levels compared to time of day.
Fig. 6 b. Agitation levels compared to time of day.
Fig. 6 c. Social activity levels compared to agitation levels.

tailbeat. In the schools we observed, subgroups constituted about half the animals; most of the remaining half moved in a single loose congregation.[7]

_____

[7]A few animals moved about individually but rarely for long: of 14 focal animals selected for being solitary, only 4 failed to join another animal or group even in the brief five minutes of case study.

Female-calf pairs

Focal animal sampling was the technique that helped us tease apart the subgroup structure. We began by taking five-minute study cases on the most obvious and identifiable animals, the female-calf pairs that stayed in one location on the perimeter of the school. These pairs were easily recognizable not only by their size difference but also by behavior; rather than cruising or resting side by side as adult pairs might, they often oriented toward each other, rubbing heads or fins or bodies, even when cruising or surfacing to breathe. Studies of the reproductive tract indicate that female spotted dolphins do not normally have a new calf every year but may keep a single calf with them for two, three, or even four years. Therefore, we could expect that some females would be accompanied by quite large young, even juveniles in the speckled state (Kasuya et al. 1974; Hohn et al. 1985). In fact, we did occasionally see the somewhat irregular swimming pattern and the frequency and types of contact that characterized females and calves in pairs consisting of a mottled or fused-pattern adult and a speckled juvenile. Based on these behavioral patterns, we considered these to be mother-young pairs, even though the size difference might no longer be appreciable. It is possible, however, that such pairs may also be siblings (Perrin pers. comm.)

Female-young subgroups

Female-calf pairs did not always remain alone; sometimes they joined other animals or were joined by them. We noted the animals female-calf pairs associated with and thus identified another type of subgroup—female-young. These groups, when inspected animal by animal, consisted of adult females in the mottled or fused pattern, each accompanied by a calf or two-tone or speckled juvenile. Sometimes female-young groups did include a single, large, fused-pattern female without a youngster. Spotted dolphin schools sometimes contain a few (> 1%) truly postreproductive females (Myrick et al. 1986). It seems at least possible that, as in many terrestrial animals, older females that are neither pregnant nor lactating may remain in social association with their daughters and their offspring.

Female-young groups were by no means static organizations: the numbers in such groups changed constantly as animals joined and

Fig. 7. A female-young subgroup. The calf in the center is traveling from the adult female at left to the two female-calf pairs at right. The net floor is visible below these animals as they in turn pass below the investigator floating at the surface.

left. However, the separation of the group from other nearby animals and the composition of the group remained constant. Female-young groups never seemed to contain any other classes of animals, such as independent juveniles, young adults, or large adult males, and the presence of even one calf seemed diagnostic. Whenever we inspected all the animals in a group with a calf in it, all appeared to be adult females with associated young[8] (Fig. 7).

Juvenile subgroups

Juvenile subgroups, which were not seen in every set, consisted of three to six two-tone individuals, smaller than adult size and quite without spots, characterized by minimum interanimal distances and near-perfect synchrony of breathing and swimming. In fact, the behavior of these juvenile subgroups was strikingly similar to that of adult male subgroups: both swam shoulder to shoulder in precise formation, both moved through the schools at a constant speed and on their own course, and both appeared to remain intact throughout sets, neither gaining

---

[8]In examining photographs of schools in the nets, Norris et al. (1978) found that any group with a calf in it had smaller interanimal distances, overall, than groups without calves.

Fig. 8. A juvenile subgroup "rafting head-down" near the bottom of the net. These five juveniles persisted in this behavior, exhept when surfacing to breathe, throughout the set until backdown. Two adult male subgroups were seen rafting head-down in other sets.

nor losing individuals. Also, a peculiar behavior we called rafting head-down was seen only in juvenile and adult male subgroups (Pryor and Kang 1980) (Fig. 8).

Juvenile subgroups were never seen to join other subgroups, although once a juvenile subgroup was joined by an adult female that exchanged body rubs and pectoral pats with one of the juveniles. Juvenile subgroups did not appear to gain or lose animals; focal animals in a juvenile sub-group studied in Set 10 were seen repeatedly, their behavior and numbers unchanged,

Fig. 9. *An adult male subgroup crusing through the school. An individual in another male subgroup rising from below gapes his jaws in a threat gesture at the group passing over him.*

until backdown. We had no explanation for why some juveniles formed these closely associated subgroups, while others, as large or larger, were still paired with adult females.

Adult male subgroups

The most conspicuous subgroups, seen in every school, were made up of adult males. These were groups of three to eight large, fused-pattern males, all with heavy keels, dark coloration, black facial masks, and white rostrum tips, the fully developed mature pattern of the largest animals in Perrin's scale (Table 5.1; Perrin 1969). These animals characteristically moved in unison, often shoulder to shoulder with pectoral fins overlapping and no individual in advance of another. They cruised slowly through the school without swerving or altering speed, while a path opened up before them; even rafting animals bestirred themselves to move aside when these dominant animals passed through (Fig. 9).[9]

---

[9]We identified similar subgroups of large, heavily keeled males in some (not all) spinner schools; they did not exhibit the tight unison of spotted male groups but swam in loose clusters and echelons, as has been reported for Hawaiian spinners (K. Norris pers. comm.)

Every school observed contained at least one adult male subgroup. If the aggregation in the net was divided into separate schools, each such school contained one or more of these conspicuous groups. In Set 12, among 200+ spotted dolphins, we counted eight adult male subgroups.

These subgroups did not seem to fluctuate in numbers as, for example, female-young subgroups did. We sometimes recorded a fused-pattern female (slender and keelless) joining an adult male subgroup to exchange affiliative gestures (patting, body rubbing) with one (or in one case, two) of the males, but the visit was always brief; conversely, an individual male might leave its subgroup, perhaps to interact with another individual or to investigate one of us, but in all recorded observations these individuals returned to the subgroup they came from, usually in less than one minute. In three sets, we noted an adult male subgroup containing a marked or scarred individual that could be positively identified throughout the set; in each case, the numbers of males in that subgroup remained the same.

Young adults

The rest of the school, the amorphous mass of animals that were not in clear-cut subgroups, proved to consist of speckled juveniles and mottled-pattern young adults. We never saw fused-pattern animals or calves in these larger aggregations. Young adult gatherings differed from the smaller subgroups in size, up to fifty or more individuals, but they were similar to the smaller groups in that interanimal distances were small (about 1 body width), and exchanges of affiliative displays were abundant.[10]

Other associations

In addition to the subgroup types recognized above, we observed many kinds of transient associations between two or more animals that we did not consider as subgroups, such as male-female pairs, animals engaged in aggressive interchanges, and triads, two adults with a young calf sandwiched tightly between them.

---

[10]Again, the picture was very different in spinners. In some spinner schools we saw large, heavily keeled males, females, half-grown animals, and calves jumbled together in a big mass of animals throughout the set.

Fig. 10. An adult male subgroup positions itself between the main part of the school and the investigators. Another adult male subgroup of four animals cruises behind these three. Two of the first group cock their heads stiffly to study us with both eyes; these pelagic dolphins do not have the head-neck mobility of coastal bottlenose dolphins. Note the conspicuous white rostrum tips of the mature males, also visible on a large, fused-pattern female in a female-calf subgroup, lower right.

The behavior of adult male subgroups

The behavior of adult male subgroups differed from the behavior of all other animals in the school, perhaps most conspicuously in the way they carried out so much of their activity in synchrony. Synchronized behavior is a particular skill of dolphins, and episodes of unison breathing, leaping, and so on, are not uncommon. Usually, however, this unison behavior is a transient event. These adult male subgroups took it to extremes. In unison, they rose to breathe, and dived again. Together, they investigated us; an adult male subgroup was often our first sight, positioned between us and the school, when we entered the water. (Fig. 10.)

If one adult male subgroup met another, they made threat displays in unison.[11] Often, we could identify adult male

---

[11]Senior male subgroups even scouted out the unknown together. In Set 13, just before backdown, we observed a group of four make a simultaneous high-speed excursion 200 m back toward the ship to investigate some research gear being hauled up from the net floor; together, they circled the gear tightly, twice, before returning to the school.

subgroups, even at considerable distance underwater, by the stereotyped precision of their swimming formation. This "military" unanimity, which has been remarked on by other observers, seems to us to be peculiar to this species (James Coe pers. comm. Brower and Curtsinger 1981).

Social aggression

We feel that it is important to differentiate between noninteractive agonistic behavior (such as headslaps and breaching), which is often fear or stress related, and agonistic behavior directed at another specific individual animal (such as a threat display or actual blow), which constitutes social aggression.

Social aggression in captive animals is usually related to dominance disputes. As such, we consider it normal social behavior. We were not surprised, therefore, to see episodes of social aggression occurring, along with many other sorts of social behavior, in schools engaged in social activity. The principal aggressive behavior we recorded in focal animal sampling was gaping. Females sometimes gaped at calves. Solitary animals, whether adults or juveniles, sometimes gaped at other animals investigating or approaching them. Animals in young adult subgroups occasionally gaped at newcomers (but in reviewing data from all sets, young adults were about three times more likely to greet animals joining them with a pectoral pat). We recorded only one instance of threat between males in an adult male subgroup; two males in a subgroup of five exchanged two rounds of gapes and head noddings. Even including this modest exchange of threats, in data compiled from all sets, aggressive signaling was recorded less often within adult male subgroups than in female-young and young adult subgroups.

Outside of focal animal sampling, however, we collected numerous observations of more extensive episodes of social aggression, almost entirely between adult males. There were three exceptions: once a female reprimanded a lively calf in the backdown area by knocking it into the air with her head three times before it settled at her side; in Set 10, a female drove another female out of an adult male subgroup with gapes; and in Set 12, three pairs of young adults engaged in noisy and bubbly bouts of toothraking, which may or may not have been aggressive behavior.

We saw three interchanges between spotted dolphins which we would describe as fights, each time between a fused-pattern male and a younger individual (a juvenile in the speckled phase in Set 1 and mottled-phase young adults in Sets 3 and 8). The animals exchanged threat signals and burst-pulse sounds and whirled around each other head to tail, until the younger animal swam away (with the older male, in one case, in aggressive pursuit). These episodes took place in clear water and about 4 to 5 m from the observer, so the color pattern differences were distinct, but the sex of the younger animal could not be identified positively.

In Set 12, Pryor recorded a confrontation between two adult male sub-groups. An adult male subgroup of four animals and another of three met face to face, came to a halt, and exchanged open-jawed burst-pulse threat displays for about 10 seconds before the smaller subgroup ducked under and both continued on their previous courses. In Set 14, two fused-pattern males, with a fused-pattern female between them, fenced with open jaws across her bows as they cruised; the clash of teeth was audible.

Little aggression was manifested toward divers. On seven occasions, a male spinner or spotted dolphin directed a loud click train and sharp eye contact at an investigator, a signal pairing that in captivity is sometimes followed by a feint or a blow. Once, in Set 17, the nearest animal in a subgroup of four adult males threatened an observer with jaw shaking and burst-pulse sounds but deflected his course when threatened back.

Affiliative behavior in spotted dolphin schools

Much of the typical behavior of individuals within subgroups, such as unison breathing, unison swimming, close interanimal distances, and body contact, could be characterized as affiliative. Therefore, the very existence of subgroups might be considered to be affiliative behavior. In captive spotted dolphins, such affiliative activities are engaged in largely or exclusively by individuals that recognize each other and have established relationships. One may deduce that the animals seen in spotted dolphin subgroups in the nets are well acquainted with each other.

In addition, we observed many occurrences of affiliative behavior between animals that were not in the same subgroups. The most frequently recorded events might be termed greeting behavior and consisted of an individual briefly joining another individual or group and exchanging body rubs or pectoral pats. Specific instances were recorded between calves and other calves, between calves and more than one adult female, between adult males on meeting (in Set 4, two large adult males exchanged pectoral pats), between solitary juveniles encountering each other (rostrum touches, Set 4), between young adults, between large adult males briefly joining females in female-young groups, and between females and individual males in adult male subgroups. In summary, we saw greeting and affiliative behavior between every category of sex and age in the school except adult males and young adults and adult males and calves.

One unusual example of affiliative behavior occurred in Set 17, shortly before backdown. Both investigators were recording animals in adult male subgroups when a speedboat engine started up suddenly nearby, alarming the animals (the boat was attempting to drive animals away from a pocket in the net). Each group of males bunched together and speeded up, and each was simultaneously joined by females, calves, and young adults, crowded above, below, and beside the males. One group thus increased briefly from three males to ten individuals and the other, from eight males to seventeen individuals.

Conclusions

The sample size of this study is small—seventeen sets, of which only eleven were studied underwater. Nevertheless, we feel that subgroup identification was reliable, thanks to the focal animal sampling approach. The wealth of observational material allows some hypotheses on spotted dolphin organization.

Each autonomous aggregation of spotted dolphins in a set contained female-calf pairs, female-young subgroups, young adult subgroups, and adult male subgroups; some also contained juvenile subgroups. Because of the frequency and widespread nature of affiliative exchanges, we suspect that the spotted dolphin groups that we saw, or at least most of the animals in those groups, knew each other and had been in association for prolonged periods.

The adult male subgroups, in particular, exhibited unusually uniform behavior and constancy. In captivity, we have seen spotted dolphins (but not spinners) form fixed, long-term associations that excluded other individuals (Pryor 1975). We suspect that adult male subgroups will eventually prove to be neither temporary nor opportunistic but long-term associations of particular individuals.

What could be the function of such an alliance? Perhaps it facilitates breeding. In spotted dolphins, anatomical studies have demonstrated that fused-pattern males are the breeding animals (Hohn et al. 1985). About 50 percent of the females are reproductively mature in the mottled stage (and 4 percent in the speckled stage), but the testes size and function in many hundreds of samples show that mottled-pattern males are reproductively immature (Perrin et al. 1976; Perrin and Reilly 1984; Hohn et al. 1985). Therefore, what we identify as adult male subgroups are likely to be the principal reproductive males in their schools.

In examining specimens collected from four different schools, Perrin found several variations of color pattern between schools. For example, in one school, the darkish band from jaw to flipper, seen in all age groups, was narrow and simple, and in another, it was wide and complex; in one school, the adults had white rostrum tips, and in another, they did not (Perrin 1969). Behavioral evidence suggests to us that spotted dolphin schools could be stable enough to provide an environment favoring the perpetuation of genetic relatedness. Males within such a school might not need to compete with each other physically for dominance or access to mates. And, indeed, the amount of status conflict within adult male subgroups seemed to us to be very low. One can speculate, however, that defense of the group against other adult male sub-groups, or maturing, younger males, would confer reproductive advantage. Again, our glimpses of social aggression by fused-pattern males and adult male subgroups are consonant with this premise.

There are many successful species of pelagic cetaceans. Spinners and spotted dolphins are among the most numerous. Their behavioral ecology is probably similar in some respects and different in others. For example, in the ETP in a year, spinners may travel no more than 300 miles, while spotted dolphins may move 1,000 miles or more, traveling 30 to 50 miles a day (Perrin et al. 1979). Possibly, a more rigid school structure is beneficial to the more nomadic spotted dolphins.

Several studies in progress at the Southwest Fisheries Center suggest that there are two kinds of spotted dolphin schools in the ETP. Some schools are breeding schools, generally numbering under 300 animals (Barlow and Hohn 1984, Myrick et al. 1986). These schools (which are the kind we saw in our research) are characterized by the presence of fewer males and more females and young than would be expected by chance and by a partly *missing* age class consisting of prepubescent animals (Hohn and Scott 1983). These juveniles are sometimes completely absent from the records of a given school, although young adults, the next age group, are present in expected proportions (Perrin and Myrick 1980).

The missing age class apparently forms the bulk of the second sort of spotted school: these are small groups, mostly male and mostly juvenile, which are often found in association with very large schools of spinners (Barlow and Hohn 1984, Hohn and Scott 1983). Since very large groups of spinners rarely carry tuna, they are seldom set on by tuna vessels; thus, fewer records exist of these animals that seem to have left the parental association. How and when (and if) these juvenile schools rejoin the breeding groups is at present only a matter for speculation.

References

Altmann, Jeanne. 1974. Observational study of behavior: Sampling methods. *Behaviour* 49: 3.

Armitage, Kenneth B. 1987. Social dynamics of mammals: Reproductive success, kinship and individual fitness. *Trends in Ecology and Evolution* 2: 9.

Au, David W. K., Wayne L. Perryman, and William F. Perrin. 1979. Dolphin distribution and the relationship to environmental features in the eastern tropical Pacific. *Southwest Fisheries Center Administrative Report* No. LJ-79-43.

Barlow, J., and A. A. Hohn. 1984. Interpreting spotted dolphin age distributions. *U.S. Department of Commerce NOAA Technical Memo* NOAA-NMFS-SWFC-48.

Bateson, Gregory. 1974. Observations of a cetacean community. In: *Mind in the Waters,* Joan MacIntyre, Ed. New York: Scribner's.

Bertram, B.C. R. 1976. Kin selection in lions and in evolution. In: *Growing Points in Ethology,* P. P. G. Bateson and R. A. Hinde, Ed. Cambridge: Cambridge University Press.

Brower, Kenneth, and William Curtsinger. 1981. *Wake of the Whale.* New York: E. P. Dutton.

Defran, R. H., and Karen Pryor. 1980. The behavior and training of cetaceans in captivity. In: *Cetacean Behavior: Mechanisms and Functions,* Louis Herman. Ed. New York: John Wiley- Interscience.

Douglas-Hamilton, Ian, and Oria Douglas-Hamilton. 1975. *Among the Elephants.* New York: Viking Press.

Hohn, A. A., J. Barlow, and S. J. Chivers. 1985. Reproductive maturity and seasonality in male spotted dolphins in the eastern tropical Pacific. *Marine Mammal Science* 1(4):273-293.

Hohn, A. A., and Michael D. Scott. 1983. Segregation by age in schools of spotted dolphin in the eastern tropical Pacific. In: *Abstracts:* Fifth Biennial Conference on the Biology of Marine Mammals. Marine Mammal Society.

Kasuya, T., N. Muazaki, and W. H. Dawbin. 1974. Growth and reproduction of *Stenella attenuata* in the Pacific coast of Japan. *Sci. Rept. Whales Research Institute* 26: 157.

King-Thomas, Linda, and Bonnie Hacker (Eds.). 1987. *A Therapist's Guide to Pediatric Assessment.* Boston: Little, Brown & Co.

Lorenz, Konrad. 1975. Foreword. In: *Lads Before the Wind,* Karen Pryor. New York: Harper & Row.

McArthur, R. H., and E. R. Pianka. 1966. On optimal use of a patchy environment. *American Naturalist* 100(916):603.

Myrick, A. C. Jr., A. A. Hohn, J. Barlow, and P. A. Sloan. 1986. Reproductive biology of female spotted dolphins, *Stenella attenuata,* from the eastern tropical Pacific. *Fishery Bulletin* 84: 2.

Nollman, James. 1987. *Animal Dreaming*. New York: Bantam Books.

Norris, Kenneth S., and T. P. Dohl. 1980. The structure and function of cetacean schools. In: *Cetacean Behavior: Mechanisms and Functions*, ed. L. M. Herman. New York: John Wiley and Sons.

Norris, Kenneth S., Warren E. Stuntz, and William Rogers. 1978. The behavior of porpoises and tuna in the eastern tropical Pacific yellowfin tuna fishery: Preliminary studies. *National Technical Information Service* PB-283 970.

Norris, Kenneth S., Bernd Würsig, Randall S. Wells, Melany Würsig, Shannon M. Brownlee, Christine Johnson, and Judy Solow. 1985. The behavior of the Hawaiian spinner dolphin, *Stenella longirostris*. *Southwest Fisheries Center Administrative Bulletin* LJ-85-06C.

Orbach, Michael K. 1977. *Hunters, Seamen, and Entrepreneurs: The Tuna Seinermen of San Diego*. Berkeley and Los Angeles: University of California Press.

Perrin, William F. 1969. Color pattern of the eastern Pacific spotted porpoise, *Stenella graffmani* Lonnberg. *Zoologica* 54: 12.

—1975. Variation of spotted and spinner porpoise (Genus *Stenella*) in the eastern tropical Pacific and Hawaii. *Bulletin of the Scripps Institution of Oceanography*, vol. 21.

—1984. Patterns of geographical variation in small cetaceans. *Acta Zoologica Fennica* 172: 137.

Perrin, William F., James M. Coe, and James R. Zweifel. 1976. Growth and reproduction of the spotted porpoise, *Stenella attenuata*, in the offshore eastern tropical Pacific. *Fishery Bulletin* 74: 2.

Perrin, William F., W. E. Evans, and D. B. Holt. 1979. Movements of pelagic dolphins *(Stenella* spp.) in the eastern tropical Pacific as indicated by results of tagging, with summary of tagging operations, 1969-1976. *NOAA Technical Report* NMFS SSRF-737.

Perrin, William F., R. B. Miller, and P. A. Sloan. 1977. Reproductive parameters of the offshore spotted dolphin, a geographical form of *Stenella attenuata*, in the eastern tropical Pacific, 1973-1975. *Fishery Bulletin* 75: 629.

Perrin, William F., and A. C. Myrick (eds.). 1980. Age determination of toothed whales and sirenians. Rept. Int. Whal. Comm. Special Issue 3.

Perrin, William F., and S. B. Reilly. 1984. Reproductive parameters of dolphins and small whales of the family Delphinidae. In: *Reproduction in Whales, Dolphins, and Porpoises*, W.F. Perrin, R.L. Brownell, Jr., and D. P. DeMaster, Ed. *Rept. Int. Whal. Comm.* Special Issue 6.

Perrin, William F., Michael D. Scott, G. Jay Waler, and Virginia L. Cass.1985. Review of geographical stocks of tropical dolphins *(Stenella* spp. and *Delphinus delphis)* in the eastern Pacific. *NOAA Technical Report* NMFS 28.

Perrin, William F., T. D. Smith, and G. T. Sakagawa. 1982. Status of populations of spotted dolphin *(Stenella attenuata),* and spinner dolphin *(S. longirostris),* in the eastern tropical Pacific. In: *Mammals in the Seas,* FAO Fisheries Series No. 5, Vol. IV.

Perrin, William F., R. R. Warner, C. H. Fiscus, and D. B. Holts. 1973. Stomach contents of porpoise, *Stenella* spp., and yellowfin tuna, *Thunnus albicares,* in mixed-species aggregations. *Fishery Bulletin* 71:4.

Pryor, Karen. 1973. Behavior and learning in porpoises and whales. *Naturwissenschaften* 60: 412.

—1975. *Lads Before the Wind.* New York: Harper & Row.

—1981. Why porpoise trainers are not dolphin lovers: Real and false communication in the operant setting. *Annals of the New York Academy of Sciences* 364: 137.

—1987. Reinforcement training as interspecies communication. In: *Dolphin Cognition and Behavior: A Comparative Approach,* R. J. Schusterman, J. Thomas, and F. G. Wood, Eds, Lawrence Erlbaum Associates, Hillsdale, NJ.

Pryor, Karen, and Ingrid Kang. 1980. Social behavior and school structure in pelagic porpoises *(Stenella attenuata* and *S. longirostris)* during purse seining for tuna. *Southwest Fisheries Center Administrative Report* LJ-80-11C.

Pryor, Karen, and K. S. Norris. 1978. The tuna/porpoise problem: behavioral aspects. *Oceanus* 21: 2.

Stuntz, Warren E., and William F. Perrin. 1979. Learned evasive behavior by dolphins involved in the eastern tropical Pacific tuna purse seine fishery. *Abstract,* 3rd Biennial Conference of the Biology of Marine Mammals. Seattle, Wash.

Tayler, C. K., and G. S. Saayman. 1972. The social organization and behavior of dolphins *(Tursiops aduncus)* and baboons *(Papio ursinus):* Some comparisons and assessments. *Annals of the Cape Provincial Museums* 9: 12.

Würsig, Bernd, and Melany Würsig. 1979. Day and night of the dolphin. *Natural History* 88: 3.

Zar, J. H. 1984. *Biostatistical Analysis,* 2d ed. 718 pp. Englewood Cliffs, N.J.: Prentice-Hall.

Dolphin-safe tuna? Maybe...

This research was well received, at least in New York. The biologist Donald Griffin, whom I'd gotten to know because of his daring book on animal awareness, invited me to give a presentation at Rockefeller University, to a large and formidable audience that included the ethologist Peter Marler and Roger and Katie Payne; and I must have showed my slides to every biology graduate department in the New York area, at one time or another. Getting the research published was another story, however. In my spare time I was a graduate student in the zoology department at Rutgers University. I intended to use this open ocean research as my Ph.D. thesis, publishing it as a dissertation. Before I got that far, however, my life once again turned in a new direction. Ten years would pass before this paper finally got published, in a book you will read about in Chapter 16.

Meanwhile the tuna-porpoise controversy continued. While American ships became more skillful at reducing dolphin mortality, inexperienced foreign boats were entering the fishery. Eventually most of the American purse-seining fleet scattered, sold out, or turned to other methods of fishing. The public distress erupted again in the early '90s, this time directed at Central and South American fishing fleets. Most tuna sold in the U.S. is now labeled as "dolphin-safe," and has presumably been caught by methods other than "fishing on porpoise."

Part Three

North Bend, Washington

Riverbend
1981-1985

Leaving the city...

I used to joke that there was neither the man nor the job that could take me away from New York. I had in fact turned down several pretty good out-of-town jobs, including the directorship of the new National Aquarium then being built in Baltimore. (Brr! Can you imagine running a huge staff and a complicated physical plant full of fragile animals, while also working for the government? No thanks!)

Now, however, changes were happening. I was busy writing up my research and going to graduate school, but the tuna industry problems seemed to be abating, and I knew that sooner or later my consulting job with them would be coming to an end. Furthermore, much as I loved the city, I missed country life too. I envied people I saw in magazines who had dogs and fireplaces and woods to walk in. I wanted a garden. Houseplants didn't satisfy that urge, and besides, the cats ate them.

Now, also, I was without family responsibilities for first time in many years. In the autumn following my voyage on the tuna-fishing boat, Gale went off to Cornell. From then on she was in Ithaca most of the year, and in Hawaii during the summers; the cats and I all missed her merry company. Michael had come and lived with me or nearby in New York for a couple of years while going to art school; but now he was back in Hawaii. Ted was in Europe, working for a bank. In spite of friends, work, and the city's many amusements, I was lonesome. And I was dating a man who did not live in New York.

A pioneer in aquaculture, and particularly in salmon farming, Jon Lindbergh advised clients all over the world. We had met in the Sea Life Park days, when Jon worked for an underwater salvage company. We had in fact at one time submitted a joint proposal to the Navy to use dolphins to locate lost airplanes underwater (the Navy said no). Now Jon's family, like mine, was grown, and he spent much of his time in South America, occasionally passing through New York. It was fun being in the city with Jon. His quiet demeanor did not deceive New Yorkers; headwaiters always showed us to great tables, and muggers wisely gave us a wide berth. But Jon was uncomfortable in the city.

In 1980 I rented a house in Vermont for a summer of writing. Jon visited. He showed me a mother and baby porcupine. He knew where the deer were and what they were doing, even when they were out of sight in the underbrush. He was as much at home in the woods as I was on East Tenth Street.

Jon would never live in a big city by choice. As a writer, however, I could easily live in the country. All I needed was a quiet room, an electrical outlet, a nearby post office...and the right companion.

Jon's consulting business was equally portable. So when the decision was made to be together, we realized we could live anywhere we wanted, as long as it was a country setting: but where? We settled it in a morning. No foreign countries; Jon's business entailed all the foreign travel one could want. No tropics; we wanted the four seasons we both grew up with. No inland states; we wanted an ocean somewhere nearby. Jon also wanted a location accessible to wilderness so he could hunt and fish. There was one more requirement: we both needed to be no more than forty-five minutes from a major international airport.

Which coast to live on? Jon's six children and my three were grown and scattered from Paris to Hawaii. No matter where we lived, we would be near to some and far from others. For climate and wilderness access, Vermont was nice, but travel was difficult in winter. The alternative was the Pacific Northwest. Jon had lived in the Seattle area for many years, and some of his children were still in the area. We settled on his terrain in the little mountain town of North Bend.

This piece was written later, for a collection of essays by nature-writers; it began, however, during the transition between New York and a new life.

Jon and our border terrier puppy.

Lago Llanquihue, in Southern Chile, with Volcan Osorno in the background and clumps of kila grass in the foreground.

CHAPTER TEN

A Gathering of Birds

by Karen Pryor[1]

I have been studying animals and their behavior all my life. I spent my childhood summers catching butterflies and hunting minnows in Connecticut. I have since then floated over coral reefs to see what the fish are doing. I have dived amongst wild dolphins and watched mothers nursing calves and rival males fighting. I have seen flamingos feeding in freezing salt lakes in the high Andes. I have exchanged remarks with a signing chimpanzee. I have gone to school and published papers and even books about behavior.

While the behavior I watch might be interesting, even thrilling, it has seldom been inexplicable; courting, fighting, feeding, tending babies, communicating; these are activities common to many sorts of living things.

The first truly baffling piece of animal behavior I ever saw occurred in the yard of a house I rented one summer in Vermont. I had been living in New York for some years, earning a living as a writer and occasional scientific consultant. One spring day I took a walk, noticed a buttercup blooming in a vacant lot, and felt my eyes fill with tears. I thought about that, and decided I

---

[1]Reprinted with permission from *The Nature of Nature,* William H. Shore, editor, for Share our Strength Hunger-Relief Programs; Harcourt Brace NY 1994.

was homesick for the New England countryside of my childhood. I wanted fields, brooks, woods, ponds, dappled sunlight on dirt roads; cicadas buzzing; Queen Anne's Lace.

I was working on a book on learning and behavior which was giving me unexpected difficulties. New and quiet surroundings might help. So I made a foray to Vermont and rented the house of a schoolteacher who planned to be away for the summer. The house stood on a dirt road, surrounded by lawn, then hayfields and woods. There was a brook across the road. Buttercups in the grass. Cicadas and Queen Anne's Lace would surely come in August. Perfect.

I packed up the cat and my typewriter, drove north, and moved into my new territory just as the birds were moving into theirs. While I wrote, they sang.

When I'd finished my work each day, I wandered around in the fields and woods looking for wildlife. I saw a mother and baby porcupine. I saw a businesslike red fox that trotted off to work across the top of the hill in the afternoon. I saw a pine marten, a rare and thrilling sight to me, trying and failing to raid the nest of a pair of kestrels in the top of a huge maple behind the barn (the clamor of the parents drew my binoculars to the event, and successfully drove the marten off, too.)

I located, I thought, all the nesting birds on the premises: a pair of flickers in the old butternut tree in the pasture; the redwinged blackbird with his three wives down the road in a patch of cattails; the catbird, robin, and warbler families in the underbrush; and several other species.

There were bluebirds raising a family in a nest box put out for them by the schoolteacher, and they showed me something I'd never heard of or read about, though no doubt it is old news to ornithologists: bluebirds can catch grasshoppers in their wings. Here's the technique: spotting a grasshopper in the lawn, the bluebird spreads its wings and stalls out, as it were, fluttering vertically down onto the grass like a falling leaf. The grasshopper doesn't read this as an attack, at first. When it does jump, it's a moment too late. The grasshopper thumps into the inside of a spread wing, from whence the bluebird, by ducking its head, neatly snaps it up. I watched the bluebirds doing this from the kitchen window, and so did the cat, making "k-k-k-k-" hunting sounds and lashing her tail.

The Vermont sojourn was good for my country nostalgia and good for my work too; after a couple of weeks of false starts I found the tone I wanted and began making real progress on the book. But being alone in the country was not really good for me. I became profoundly, ferociously lonely: lonely, it seemed to me, not for any one person, but for my own familiar cluster of humanity, my neighborhood.

My fourth-floor corner apartment in Manhattan overlooked two small but busy streets in Greenwich Village. From my window I could see what kind of sandwich Reuben was making in his delicatessen, and for whom. If my upstairs neighbor, the wine critic, came out of the butcher's with a large package, I knew he was giving a dinner party. I saw the cops whooping their patrol car sirens at their girlfriends. I saw old ladies walk their dogs, and often I knew the name of both the walker and the dog.

All these people knew me, too. We were not social friends, but we recognized each other—we were all part of the neighborhood. If some event of interest occurred, we all took part in it. For example, there was the day Duke caught the mugger. Duke was an elderly harlequin Great Dane belonging to the antique shop in my block. Like a lot of big dogs, he had hip trouble, and rarely moved more than he had to; mostly he lay in the shop doorway. He was always polite to customers. He never needed a leash.

One day I heard screams, real screams, coming from the street. I rushed to the window in time to see a smallish person in white running down the sidewalk, carrying a big black purse. The screamer was a woman at the far end of the block, presumably the owner of the purse. The thief, hotly pursued by a plump bearded gentleman who was losing ground, reached the street corner just as gimpy old Duke, walking beside his owner, reached the corner from the other side of the building. Surprised to see someone running, Duke gamboled forward in play (it was probably the first time in years he had run even a step, himself).

The mugger, terrified, attempted to change direction in mid air and fell to the sidewalk, kicking. Duke, now looking confused and a little worried, put his big mouth carefully over one of those kicking legs, whereupon the mugger became still as a statue, enabling the bearded gentleman to catch up. He very sensibly sat down on the mugger.

A small crowd gathered, a crowd in which I could see several familiar people. Duke sat by his owner. Reuben came out of the deli and gave Duke a pound or so of pastrami, which he ate. Bob the butcher came out of his shop and gave the dog a steak, and he ate that, too. The cops drove up and took the mugger away, and the crowd dispersed. Later, someone in my building who'd been in the crowd told me one thing I'd missed from the window: the mugger was a woman.

In our city neighborhood, this was an entertaining rather than an alarming event. Petty crimes exist, and our neighborhood put a complete stop to this one, in an interesting and satisfactory way. Just so, some country event such as the butchering of a hog mightbe traumatic to an urban person while being mildly interesting and even ultimately beneficial (the mugger was caught) to locals.

Now, in the country silence, I missed not only the eventful life of the city, I missed having those many familiar people all around me. The quiet countryside seemed dangerous, without my neighbors. The result was acute insomnia. I couldn't get to sleep, I couldn't stay asleep, I couldn't even nap without startling awake at every sound. Alcohol made it worse, exercise made no difference, and I knew better than to try pills.

One morning I woke up about 4 A.M., too late to go back to sleep, too early to start writing. In a mood of irritable despair I made a cup of tea and took it outdoors. I sat down on the lawn on the east side of my rented house, the side facing the road, to watch the sky. It was part of the yard I ordinarily avoided, since sitting there might entail talking to the occasional stranger passing by on that narrow dirt road, and I felt unwilling to do that. But dawn was just breaking and passersby seemed unlikely at dawn.

At the edge of the lawn about twenty feet from me was a little dead tree, hardly bigger than a sapling, the only leafless tree in the yard. By and by I noticed that there was a bird in the tree: a veery. I often saw two veeries feeding along the road. As I watched, a catbird flew in from the thickets where I knew it had its nest. With it came two of its fledglings. Then a redwinged blackbird landed in the upper branches, presumably the male from the patch of cattails down the road. I was surprised; he seldom strayed this far from his own premises. Next, into the little tree's bare branches came a male Canadian warbler, with his tidy necklace of black spots on yellow vest showing up in the increasing daylight: perhaps the very one who was nesting in the bushes down by the brook.

Then I saw the male flicker sail in from the butternut tree in the pasture. The flicker landed on the trunk of the sapling, hanging on vertically as woodpeckers do, right next to the warbler. They weren't six inches apart. A flicker is quite a big bird, almost pigeon-sized, and I myself would be a bit nervous that close to its wicked woodpecking bill; but the warbler, not much bigger than a golfball, didn't move. This was getting incredible; why were these diverse species gathering in one tree? Why were they being so sociable? They were not feeding, they were making no sounds, they were just gathering.

For that matter, what birds, nesting on this old farm, were *not* in this one little tree? Robins, I thought, and sure enough, here came both the male and the female robin, with their disheveled, noisy fledglings. And then a bluebird. What *was* going on here?

Then from the sky, fluttering onto the lawn at the foot of the little dead tree, came a scrap of black and white and shocking pink—a rose-breasted grosbeak, a bird I had not seen since childhood and did not know was nesting on the place. (I later realized why I'd overlooked him; I was locating nests by the birds' songs, and the grosbeak's song was so similar to the robin's that I never trained my binoculars on him, assuming I already knew who he was.)

The whole thing, this little tree at daybreak, cluttered at final count with one or more each of eight species of birds, was incomprehensible; and the grosbeak somehow was the last straw. I got up and took my teacup indoors, shutting this bizarre sight out of my mind for the time being.

That fall, however, when I got back to New York, I went out to the zoology department at Rutgers University in Newark where I knew some topnotch young naturalists, nowadays called behavioral ecologists. I described this gathering of birds to them and asked them what was going on.

They accepted that I had seen what I said I saw—and I was glad, because some professors would not have—but they had no idea what the birds were doing. One mentioned something about migration. The others simply shrugged. It would be four years before I found out for myself what was happening—and the solution would come 6000 miles away.

The following summer, I married an old friend, Jon Lindbergh; the decisions and changes involved in this step may have contributed to that Vermont insomnia, I now suspect. Jon's business as an aquaculture consultant took him to southern Chile several times a year; on some trips, I went along.

We spent a lot of our time in Chile in remote rural areas, usually as guests of the owner or manager of a fish farm belonging to one of Jon's clients. Jon worked all day, and I often had a lot of time on my hands. Luckily for me Ken Norris, a dolphin researcher and old friend who had spent a lot of time in Chile himself, had lent me his rare copies of Johnson and Goodall's "Birds of Chile." A.W. Johnson was an English mining engineer who spent much of his adult life as a businessman in Santiago, Chile. His real life work, however, was birding, and he accomplished many years of field work. With his friend, J.B. Goodall, an amateur painter, he created and published two volumes covering every species of bird in that Andes-isolated land: volumes distinguished by Goodall's delightful naive watercolors and Johnson's even more delightful (and very sophisticated) behavioral observations.

I had never before seen any of the species of birds in Chile except English sparrows and some migratory shorebirds. So Johnson and Goodall became my constant companions. When I was tired of reading novels or practicing my ersatz Spanish I went out into the woods and fields and looked for birds.

In the south, along the chilly, lonely shores of Seno Ultima Esperanza (Last Hope Cove), I saw Chilean flamingos, and flightless "steamer" ducks, so-called because they flee by running across the water, beating with both wings like a paddle-wheeled steamer; several spectacular species of Andean sheldgeese; and blacknecked swans with their babies riding on their backs. In the vast and unpeopled national park, Torres del Paine, we saw condors, Darwin's rheas, the huge magellanic woodpecker, and wild parrots. In tumultuous Andean rivers we saw torrent ducks, calmly bathing themselves in the seething rapids. In the villages and towns of the coastal islands I learned the names of the common songbirds in people's gardens—gardens very like those of home, with roses and cabbages and apple trees—but with other birds standing in for New England's robins and blackbirds.

On our fifth or sixth trip we spent part of the Christmas holidays in the Lake District of Chile, staying at the lakeside vacation house of one of Jon's fish farming clients. The client's family had preserved a nice patch of native forest behind their house, in what was otherwise largely farmland; this made for splendid birding. I saw the big, wine-colored native pigeon there for the first time. I spent numerous hours in the woods, crouching near a stream trying to spot the chucao, a sort of waterbird. The chucao has a magnificently loud gobbling song which, alas, it can throw like a ventriloquist, making it impossible to find out where the bird actually is, though one is being deafened by his racket.

One morning I got tired of this fruitless hunt and instead went out across the lawn to the rail fence along the bluff, to look for ducks on the lake below. The acres-wide mowed lawn was not usually a good place for birds, except for the omnipresent queltehue, a big ploverlike bird that likes open fields, lives in pairs, and rises with a flash of white-banded wings and a loud clamor when disturbed. (The queltehue is such a noisy alarmist that Chilean farmers have been known to pinion them and keep them in the farmyard as watchbirds.)

I stopped by the fence next to a six-foot clump of kila grass, a bamboo-like native shrub, left by some gardener's whim to stick up from the well-mowed verge of the bluff on the other side of the fence. I looked out over the beautiful lake, Lago Llanquihue, with its highly ornamental snow-covered volcano, Osorno, on the far shore. It is a famous view; our host's house and every other summer villa on the lake is oriented to take in the sight of the lake and Osorno's snowy cone.

Great scenery. No ducks. Gradually, however, I became aware that there were some little birds very close to me in the kila grass; three or four jilgueros, little yellow sparrow-like birds. Then here came a diuca, the gray singing finch that in Chilean gardens takes the slot filled in North America by the song sparrow.

Then a couple of zorzals, the Austral version of our robin, flew into the kila clump, followed by a handsome little red and black cometocino. All of them sat in the kila thicket, saying nothing, doing nothing, and amazingly close together. I looked over my shoulder to see that even the suspicious queltehues had tiptoed within ten yards of me, although when I looked back they hurried away, pretending they weren't involved.

As a finale, a little fire-crowned hummingbird landed in the topmost twig of the kila grass and glared about with the typical hostile stare of male hummingbirds, raising his spiky crest so that he looked like a furious version of the bird in "Peanuts." With the vast blue lake and the snowcapped cone of Osorno for a background, the clump of kila grass, crammed with a dozen species of birds, looked like a bad museum display: "Songbirds of Chile."

I realized I was looking at just what I had seen in Vermont: a gathering of birds. Christmas is summertime, below the equator; and, just as in Vermont, this gathering consisted of the males, and sometimes the females and young as well, of small territorial birds all nesting on our host's property. This time, however, the birds were only two yards away, the sun was shining, I had my wits about me, and it was obvious what the birds were doing. They were looking at me.

I was a novelty. Men pushing lawnmowers, they knew about. The property owners, coming and going in cars, no doubt with children and dogs, they knew about. But presumably nobody ever strayed down to the lawn's edge for no reason. That was new. And while I of course cannot pinpoint exactly what was especially novel about me to the birds, they appeared to be looking most particularly at the object hanging from my neck—my binoculars. I had drawn a crowd. It was just like the day on Tenth Street when Duke caught the mugger and neighbors gathered to see the interesting sight; only this was a neighborhood of birds.

That is also, of course, what the birds in Vermont had been doing: gawking. Their neighborhood Person was in the wrong place, at the wrong time of day, with the wrong object— a teacup—in hand (the Vermont birds presumably *expected* my binoculars.) So they came to see what was going on. Here I had been feeling so isolated and alone, and I was a well-observed member of a neighborhood after all; I just hadn't known it!

The phenomenon called mobbing, in which various species of small birds join forces to attack a predator such as a hawk or owl, is well known; but then aggression is gaudy and obvious behavior, and has been a focus of much behavioral research. The phenomenon of neighborliness, however, has I think been rather overlooked. In both Vermont and Chile I am sure it was not just *any* small birds that came to gawk at my odd doings; it was those specific birds in that specific neighborhood. Being territorial defenders, each one would have driven off any member of its own species that tried to set up housekeeping nearby; but they didn't mind other species. Just so, Reuben the delicatessen owner on Tenth Street probably felt no animosity toward the Bob the butcher or Sam the dry cleaner but might have been distinctly upset if another delicatessen had opened on his block.

I was witness to the fact that these birds shared neighborhood duties and events easily with each other. I judged, from the relaxed behavior and physical closeness of the birds, that they knew each other by sight, maybe even as individuals; in my experience, even in captivity small songbirds usually avoid sitting with birds they don't know. Maybe they drew comfort from each other's familiarity: oh, that's just "our" flicker, "our" catbird, "our" redwinged blackbird, "our" diuca; I know him. Would a strange bird, from another farm or field, have caused consternation? Maybe so.

The day after I saw the gathering of Chilean birds, I went out with a camera at the same hour, hoping to photograph my audience. The birds were having none of it; they'd already checked me out and lost interest. Not a single bird showed up. But I was elated, anyway, to have solved my mystery.

The bird gathering fixed itself in my mind as an example of a strong evolutionary phenomenon across many species that I think is almost completely overlooked, at present, by science — by physical ecologists, by ethologists or behavioral biologists, and by all brands of psychology. We don't even have a technical term for the phenomenon, so I can give it only anthropomorphic human names: Neighborliness. Friendship. A good area for serious investigation: the seeds of social peace might be in it.

Scientific nomenclature of species mentioned in "A Gathering of Birds"

North American mammals
pine marten *Martes americana*
porcupine *Erethizon dorsatum*
red fox *Vulpes vulpes*

North American birds
Redwinged blackbird *Aglaius phoeniceus*
Eastern bluebird *Sialia sialis*
Catbird *Dumatella carolinensis*
Flicker *Colaptes auratus*
Rosebreasted grosbeak *Pheucticus ludovicianus*
Kestrel *Falco sparvarius*
Robin *Turdus migratorius*
Veery *Hylocichla minima*
Canada warbler *Wilsonia canadensis*

South American birds
Andean sheldgeese *Chloephaga spp.*
Black-necked swan *Cygnus melanocoryphus*
Chilean flamingo *Phoenicopterus ruber chilensis*
Chilean pigeon *Columba araucana*
Chucao *Scelorchilus rubecula*
Cometocino *Lessonia rufa*
Condor *Vulture gryphus*
Darwin's rhea *Pterocnemia pennata*
Diuca *Diuca diuca chilensis*
English sparrow *Passer domesticus*
Fire-crowned hummingbird *Sephaniodes sephaniodes*
Jilguero *Spinus barbatus*
Magellanic woodpecker *Campephilus magellanicus*
Parrot *Microsittace ferruginea*
Queltehue *Belanopterus chilensis*
Steamer duck *Tachyeres pteneres*
Torrent duck *Merganetta armata*
Zorzal *Turdus falklandii magellanicus*

A new life...

The Zoology Department at Rutgers imposed one final condition on my earning a doctorate: a full year in residence on campus. This was now impossible. Jon and I certainly weren't going to spend a year in Newark so I could complete a degree which I had until now gotten along nicely without. I bowed out of the graduate program.

Jon rented a house in North Bend, Washington, a little logging town in a bowl of snow-covered mountains in the Cascades, about an hour from Seattle (and forty-five minutes from Seattle's major international airport.) In March Ted Pryor, who was putting himself through Columbia Business School, moved into my now vacated apartment in New York. The cats went to live with Gale, who had graduated from college and was working for a publishing house, and I packed up the books and some furniture and moved to North Bend.

We started a garden. We bought a terrier puppy. We got considerable amusement from the aerial battles of hummingbirds around the feeder we hung on the porch. Our children came to see us, and we went to see them.

And I finished another book.

Don't shoot the dog! The editor, maybe...

Shortly after moving to New York I acquired a new literary agent, Julian Bach. I talked to Julian about the training book I still had in mind, and I produced several proposals which Julian shopped around without success.

The version that worked actually began at a dinner party. I was sitting next to my hostess's tennis pro. He said, "I hear you're a dolphin trainer. Do you know about Skinner and all that?" I said yes.

"Well," he went on, "Where can I get a book about Skinner that will help me be a better tennis coach?" Good question! There wasn't one.

I told Julian Bach about this conversation. He leapt from his chair like a startled gazelle and said "Go home and write a letter to that tennis coach. Tell him what he needs to know. That will not be the book but it will get you started."

What a good idea! When I'd written that letter, I saw how to organize the book and what should be in it. Julian sold the book to an editor at Simon & Schuster on the basis of a chapter and an outline. I wrote some of the book in Vermont, and the rest of it during the first two years in North Bend.

When I turned in the manuscript, I got a surprise. The editor who had bought it was horrified. "What's all this stuff about training? I thought this was supposed to be a joke book. This isn't funny at all!"

Oh-oh. I had given him, as my initial sample, a chapter called "Eight Methods for Getting Rid of Behavior you Don't Want."

The first method was called "Shoot the animal." (This definitely puts an end to the behavior problem; you will never have to deal with that behavior from that individual again. Firing a lazy employee, or putting a thief in jail, are examples of Method One solutions; the subject learns nothing, but you are rid of the behavior.) The editor had thought that chapter was funny. That's was the only reason he bought the book! Help! What to do now?

Fortunately Fate intervened. Two weeks later, that editor retired. My orphan book was handed over to another editor, Don Hutter, who understood what it was about, who liked it, and who let it be published.

I had called my opus "The Training Book." The Sales Department rejected that title on the grounds that it would make people think of potty-training. I thought up about seventy five more titles. Hutter finally settled on "Positive Reinforcement." Under that title the galleys went to Dick Snyder, the head of Simon & Schuster.

"What is this, this will never sell!" he is reported to have yelled.

When Jon and I were next in New York on business, my new editor took me to the Algonquin lobby, bought me a drink, and told me the publisher had decided to call the book "Don't Shoot the Dog!"

What! My nice book about positive reinforcement with a hostile, negative title— Don't? Shoot? Dog? Exclamation Point? Aaaargh! I fumed all the way west on the plane. I kept Jon up all night, fuming some more. I wrote a seventy-five dollar telegram. No use. The book had gone to press. Some people thought the new title was catchy. I guess it is. Certainly Simon & Schuster had given me every chance to come up with something both positive and catchy, and I hadn't. The book came out and the *Readers Digest* published this excerpt.

DON'T SHOOT THE DOG!

THE NEW ART OF TEACHING AND TRAINING

KAREN PRYOR

AUTHOR OF NURSING YOUR BABY

25388-3 ★ IN U.S. $5.59 (IN CANADA $6.99) ★ A BANTAM BOOK

CHAPTER ELEVEN

The Power of Praise

by *Karen Pryor*[1]

Tired of nagging at your spouse, your kids, your dog? Try "positive reinforcement," says this expert on behavioral science, and watch them jump.Condensed from "Don't Shoot The Dog!"

- A teacher habitually harangued a painting class over failure to complete homework. Tired of being scolded, one student gently suggested that the teacher praise those who *did* assignments instead of heckling those who didn't. The teacher tried it. In three weeks, he not only doubled the number of homeworkers but also had a far happier class.
- A young woman married a very bossy and demanding man. His father, who lived with them, was equally given to ordering her about. She established a practice of reacting minimally to their commands and harsh remarks, while responding with approval and affection to any pleasant or thoughtful action—such as helping carry in the groceries—by either man. Within a year she had turned them both into decent human beings.
- A girl liked to take her dog for walks, but often the dog ran off and refused to come when called. Then the girl started making

[2]Reprinted with permission from *The Readers Digest.* © 1984 *The Reader's Digest Association, Inc.* Pleasantville, N.Y.

a huge fuss over the dog—praise, baby talk, hugs—whenever it came to her unbidden. Now the dog comes gladly the instant it's called.

These are all examples of training with "positive reinforcement." I first learned about it at Hawaii's Sea Life Park oceanarium, where I signed on as head dolphin trainer in 1963. Positive reinforcement—primarily via buckets of fish—was our only tool.

The techniques we used, variously known as reinforcement, operant conditioning or behavior modification, are largely credited to Harvard psychologist B.F. Skinner. A reinforcement, in Skinner's experiments, is anything which, occurring in conjunction with an act, tends to increase the probability that the act will happen again. But it's not mere reward or punishment. These usually come *after* an act is completed. Reinforcement occurs *during* or immediately upon the conclusion of the behavior the trainer wants to affect. Correctly timed, it changes the behavior.

But we had a problem getting reinforcement to our dolphins the instant they did what we wanted. If I was training a dolphin to jump, I couldn't get a fish to it in midair, so how would it know which jump I liked? For this we used a "conditioned reinforcement," some originally meaningless signal—a sound, a light—that had been deliberately associated with a primary reinforcement such as fish. Dolphin trainers often blow a whistle at feeding time, until the sound becomes a reinforcement by itself. I have seen animals work for an hour or more to hear a whistle—with little or no *primary* reinforcement.

I found myself fascinated with how much could be communicated between the dolphins and me by this kind of training. And I began to apply what I learned in my daily life. For example, I stopped yelling at my kids, because it didn't work. Instead, I watched for behavior I liked—such as help with the dishes—and then reinforced it with a hug or a word of praise. It worked a lot better and kept the peace, too.

There are two categories of reinforcement: positive and negative. A positive reinforcement is something the subject wants, such as food, petting or praise. A negative reinforcement is something he wants to avoid—a spank, a frown, an unpleasant sound (like the warning buzzer in cars if you don't fasten your seat belt).

Behavior can always be intensified with positive reinforcement, provided that it is already occurring. Suppose you want someone to telephone you. If he doesn't call, there isn't much you can do. You can't reinforce behavior that is not already occurring! But if, when your friend *does* call, you act delighted, chances are he will call more often. If, instead, you scold him, you are applying the negative reinforcement of punishment—training him not to call at all.

Several years ago at the Bronx Zoo in New York City, keepers couldn't get a particular gorilla out of an indoor cage when it needed cleaning. The gorilla just sat in the doorway; when keepers waved bananas enticingly, the ape ignored them or snatched the food and ran back inside. A staff trainer pointed out that banana waving was an attempt to reinforce behavior that hadn't occurred yet. (The name for this is bribery!) The solution was to ignore the gorilla when it sat in the doorway, but reinforce it with food whenever it *did* happen to go out by itself. Problem solved!

Reinforcements are relative, not absolute. A reinforcement must be something the subject wants. Rain is a positive reinforcement to ducks, negative to cats. Food is not a reinforcement if you're full. Thus, it's useful to have a variety of reinforcements for any training situation.

At Sea World, killer whales are reinforced in many ways—with fish, with stroking and scratching, with social attention, with toys. Whole shows are run in which the animals never know what behavior will be reinforced next with what. The "surprises" are what challenge the performers. A reinforcement is information: it communicates. It tells the subject exactly what it is you like. In coaching athletes or training dancers, the instructor calls out, "Yes!" or "Good !" to mark a movement *as it occurs*. That truly gives the needed information—not the debriefing later in the dressing room.

Watching football and baseball, I'm often struck by the beautifully timed reinforcements the players receive. When a touchdown or a run is scored, there's a frenzy of mutual reinforcement among the players—plus the roar of the crowd.

It's quite different for on-stage actors, with the applause coming long after many dramatic scenes.

Reinforcing too late is a real problem. "Gee, honey, you looked great last night." ("What's the matter, don't I look great *now?*") But so is reinforcing too early. We do this often with children, under the misimpression that we are encouraging them. ("Atta girl, you almost got it right.") What we may be doing here is reinforcing *unsuccessful* behavior, and that can be confusing. Wails of "I can't" may be symptoms of being reinforced too often for unsuccessful tries.

Timing is also important with negative reinforcement, such as when parents or teachers nag a child. If the nagging doesn't cease the instant that desired results are achieved, it is not reinforcement and it is not information. In communication theory, it is "noise."

Constant reinforcement is needed only in the learning stages. Teaching a kid to ride a bicycle may require a stream of "That's right, steady now!" But your child would think you were crazy if you went on praising him once he had really learned to ride. To maintain an already learned behavior, use reinforcement only occasionally.

This is what psychologists call a variable schedule. Random, unpredictable reinforcement is far more effective than a constant, predictable schedule. If every time a dolphin jumps I give it a fish, very quickly the jump becomes as perfunctory as the animal can get away with. If I then stop giving fish, the dolphin quickly stops jumping. But if I reinforce jumps at random, the behavior is much more strongly maintained. This in turn allows me to reinforce the more vigorous jumps selectively, thus shaping improved performance.

Reinforcements occur all the time in real life, often by coincidence. Find a five-dollar bill in a trash basket, and I defy you to walk past that basket the next day without looking it over closely. If, while taking an exam, you happen to be chewing a pencil when you get a right answer, this will reinforce pencil chewing. Many behavior rituals arise from such accidental reinforcements. I've seen a baseball pitcher who goes through a nine-step chain of behavior every time he gets set to throw the ball. He's been conditioned to believe he's a better pitcher with his sequential delivery.

You can deliberately use positive reinforcement on yourself. I once met a Wall Street lawyer who is an avid squash player and shouts to himself "Way to go, Pete, atta boy !" for every good shot. He says it has improved his game tremendously since the days when he cursed himself for his errors all the time.

But reinforcing ourselves is something we often neglect. Either it doesn't occur to us, or we demand too much of ourselves. As a result, we often go for days without letup, moving from task to task, unthanked by ourselves! Deprivation of reinforcement is one factor, I think, in anxiety and depression.

You can and should reinforce yourself in healthful ways—with an hour off, a walk, a talk with friends, some self-approval. I like performer Ruth Gordon's suggestion: "An actor has to have compliments. If I go long enough without getting a compliment, I compliment myself, and that's just as good, because at least then I know it's sincere."

Keeping a book alive...

Don't Shoot the Dog! had an endorsement from B.F. Skinner on the cover. Simon & Schuster gave me a grueling book tour, made sure the book was available everywhere, and sent it out for review. Ted, Gale, and Jon's daughter Kristina organized a wonderful book party in a blizzard in a medieval meeting hall at the Cathedral of St. John the Divine, where Jon and I had been married.

But keeping a book alive takes hard work and luck, too, especially if, like *Don't Shoot the Dog!*, it is on a new topic and not like any other book. Hardbound sales were going slowly.

While I was writing the book a writer friend, Diana Korte, who had just published a book with Bantam, called me from Denver to insist I go introduce myself to her Bantam editor. Taking my courage in both hands, I did so, and Toni Burbank and I had an interesting visit, followed up by a phone call from me when I'd thought of an answer to how to get her four-year-old to dress himself faster in the mornings.

When *Don't Shoot the Dog!* was published, Simon & Schuster put it out for bid to the paperback companies. Toni Burbank made an offer. So, thank heavens, the book went it into paperback. Like *Nursing Your Baby,* this book, I felt, could only really do its job in paperback where people could afford it, and more than that, afford to buy two copies and press one on a friend.

I wrote new jacket copy for the paperback, something publishers are often very happy to have authors do. I made another book tour. I gave talks and did radio shows from home.

I did everything I could think of to get the book to the ultimate markets I knew it had — parents, pet owners, businesses, and maybe psychology classrooms.

La Leche League, the nursing mothers' organization that had sold jillions of copies of *Nursing Your Baby*, liked this book too, and put it on their parenting list in spite of the title (one psychologist friend told me that she loved the book but she just couldn't tell parents to read a book about child raising called "Don't Shoot the Dog!" I didn't really blame her!)

The paperback began to move, by word of mouth. Starting in the year it came out, 1985, it sold 800 to 1000 copies a month. Who was buying it? How did they hear about it? I didn't know, then. But Bantam was happy, and kept the book in print.

Positive reinforcement....

One reason people like *Don't Shoot the Dog!* is that it offers a realistic alternative to punishment. This is not an obvious aspect of Skinner's discoveries, and in fact many behavioral psychologists don't place much value on positive reinforcement as opposed to other ways of influencing behavior ("I never saw anything wrong with a little electric shock," one experimental psychologist said to me.) We dolphin trainers, however, are very much aware that you don't need to frighten or hurt or even impress an animal to get great results, and highly reliable results, *if* you know what to do with the tools of reinforcement. This article, in *Mothering* magazine, was also based on *Don't Shoot the Dog!* but aimed very specifically at parents.

"Naughty Kitty." *The angry child with raised hand, the dead bird, the unrepentant cat...a perfect example of why punishment doesn't work. I inherited this picture from Ricky Wylie; it was painted by her great-aunt sometime before 1900.*

CHAPTER TWELVE

Why Punishment Doesn't Work

by *Karen Pryor*[1]

The kids are fighting, or making too much noise in the car; your toddler deliberately runs out into the street; your teenager flouts the household rules. And you have to put a stop to it. Whether the problem is dirty words, dirty clothes, or dirty tricks—in every household there are some behaviors that just cannot be tolerated. What do we do when these behaviors arise? We punish. We threaten, we coerce, we scold, we deprive. We may even strike out. When pushed hard enough, nearly every parent on the planet has felt the urge to slap and yell; and most of us have done it at least once.

Did you ever notice that it does not really work? Behavior that is punished may stop for an instant, but it will not necessarily stop forever. Nevertheless, punishment is humanity's favorite method of stopping behavior. We scold the child, beat the dog, dock the paycheck, fine the company, torture the dissident, invade the country. Yet, the child goes on whining, the dog still chases cars, the employee is tardy, the company is dishonest, the dissidents still protest, and things are not serene in Afghanistan.

---

[1]Reprinted with permission from *Mothering* magazine, Summer, 1986.

And what happens when we punish someone and then they go out and do the same thing again? Do we say, "Hmm, punishment isn't working. Let's try something else?" No. We punish harder. If a little scolding or penalty does not have an effect, why not try a bigger one. If whipping doesn't convert the heretic, try thumbscrews, or the rack. The worst thing about the escalation of punishment is that there is absolutely no end to it. The search for a punishment so intense that "maybe *this* one will work" has preoccupied humans since history began, and probably before.

Why Punishment Doesn't Work

One of the rules that psychologists have discovered about behavior is that whatever you do to change behavior must occur *during* the behavior, and not afterward. For example, a positive reinforcement, or pleasant consequence of an act, must be timed right in order to produce learning. Suppose you are in a hotel room and trying to turn on an unfamiliar TV. You touch all the likely-looking buttons and knobs until one of them produces a click and a picture, or at least a hum. From then on, this is the one that you will probably use. But what if each button took 15 seconds to work? You would have a difficult time figuring out which one produced the picture, and might have to continue trying them all every time you wanted to catch the news.

We can also change behavior with undesirable events, or negative reinforcement. Here too, the event must coincide with the behavior in order to produce learning. Suppose you are cooking in someone else's kitchen. The negative reinforcement of pain from the heat will quickly teach you which pan handles require a pot holder. From this experience you will develop learned behavior to protect yourself from the handles that get hot. If you could not feel the heat at the moment of contact, you would not know that you had been badly burned until later, when the blisters develop. So, without the immediate sensation of pain, you would have a hard time learning which objects on the stove are safe to touch and which ones are not.

Punishment is an unpleasant consequence of a behavior. But, like a burn that is not noticed until it blisters, it often does not coincide with the behavior closely enough to produce learning. Spanking a roaming toddler after he returns to the sidewalk may intimidate or frighten him, but he will be more likely to connect the spanking with the sidewalk than with the traffic. Even if the child understands the verbal message explaining why he or she is being punished, the desired improvement may not take place. For example, a child who is punished for a bad report card cannot mitigate the punishment in the present. This is because people cannot change their actions of the past; one cannot do anything about a bad report card that one has already received. Furthermore, punishment teaches the child nothing about how to achieve better report cards.

The most any punisher can hope for is that the child's motivation will change, and that the child will try to alter future behavior in order to avoid punishment. That is a lot to ask, even of intelligent adults. We know that society's punishments and threats do not prevent adult misbehavior. Moreover, if a child's behavior is strongly motivated—snitching food when hungry, being part of the gang in adolescence—what the child does learn is to try to not get caught. Evasiveness increases rapidly under a punishment regime—a sad situation in a family setting, and not so great in society either.

How The Punisher Gets Reinforced

One reason why we keep thinking that punishment works is because sometimes the punished behavior stops, at least temporarily. *Punishment has the best chance of halting behavior if the subject understands which action is being punished, if the behavior is not well-established, and if the person can control the behavior in the first place.* (For example, punishment does not cure bedwetting.) The punishment is also more likely to be effective if it is a novel experience for the subject, a shock to which the person has not become hardened. A child who is scolded sharply the first time he or she crayons on the walls may stop defacing the house. A citizen who gets caught and fined for cheating on his income tax may not cheat again.

My parents punished me exactly twice throughout my upbringing. They scolded me once at age six for pilfering and once at age fifteen for skipping school, which caused everyone to fear I'd been abducted. The extreme rarity of the punishment experience contributed vastly to the effect. Both behaviors stopped instantly.

When a punishment effectively halts a behavior, the sequence of events can be quite reinforcing for the punisher. The punisher may tend to sally forth confidently to punish again. I have seen punishment exhibited and defended by disciplinarian school teachers, bullying athletic coaches, domineering bosses, and well-intentioned parents. Often they reenact old harsh methods despite meager successes and many disappointments. And often they tend to neither notice nor accept the good results of others around them who are not using punishment at all. The repeated use of punishment by such practitioners can produce nasty side effects in the punished ones: fear, anger, resentment, resistance, and even hate—mental states definitely *not* conducive to learning improved behavior!

Alternatives That Work

One promising way to change behavior without punishment is to reinforce behavior that you *do* like. Sometimes this requires a lot of self-discipline. It is easy to call out "I told you not to slam the door!" every time the children come home with a bang; but it is another matter entirely to alert yourself to notice and say "thank you" when they come in quietly. Sometimes the behavior that needs reinforcing can be subtle and easily misunderstood. For example, a teen-ager who is testing the limits of family rules may really be trying to participate in family life in newly adult ways. Youngsters in this transition stage need to be responded to for making conversation, for being helpful, for the good things that they do.

All too often, parents assume that because doing chores pleasantly is expected of their children, the behavior deserves no comment or attention. Eventually the behavior may dwindle. After all, the child reasons, if I love my parents and want them to notice me, and if the only comment or attention I get is for being horrible, then this is the way I will be.

Three negative ways to change behavior, besides punishment, may occasionally be appropriate. The first, the "Shoot the

Animal" method, is to get rid of the doer, temporarily or permanently. Send the child to his room if he is disrupting company; tie up the dog so that it cannot chase cars. This method stops the undesirable behavior, but it does not teach desirable alternatives. Negative reinforcement can also provide a solution. With a load of cranky, tired, noisy kids in the car, I have been known to pull off the road and park on the shoulder until everyone is quiet enough to permit me to drive safely again. Simply ignoring the misbehavior until it goes away by itself is often the easiest way to cope. Parents sometimes tend to correct every annoying little thing that their young children do, without realizing that some behavior is self-limiting and will disappear on its own.

Of more value are the ways in which you can use positive reinforcement to get rid of behaviors that you do not want. For example, you can *substitute and reinforce permissible behaviors to take their place.* One mother told me that her 18-month-old son developed the habit of splatting his hands in his food on the high chair tray when he'd finished a meal, thus sending food all over the kitchen. Naturally, this brought his mother on the run—but always too late to prevent the mess. So, she watched him carefully and soon arrived at an incompatible behavior. She taught him to throw his arms in the air and cheer when he was finished eating. This brought Mama on the run too, but with laughs and hugs instead of a cross face and a washcloth. The substitute behavior turned out to be easier on the baby, the mother, and the kitchen.

You can also *reinforce the absence of the undesirable behavior.* When I have to spend time with children who have developed bad (parent-trained) habits such as whining or teasing, I pay a lot of attention to the times when they are quiet or pleasant. This way, they tend to be quiet and pleasant more and more often.

Finally, the most fundamental method of changing behavior without punishment is to *eliminate whatever is causing the behavior in the first place.* Take, for example, the familiar disaster of the toddler having a tantrum in the supermarket. Frequently, the underlying cause of the tantrum is hunger. The child may be specifically yelling for the brightly displayed candy, but what he or she needs is food—and the sight and smell of all these edibles, now that the toddler is old enough to recognize them, is more than he or she can handle. Solution: Feed the children before you market.

The laws of how reinforcement changes behavior were worked out in psychology labs by research scientists. Applying these laws in real life, however, is a task for creative and imaginative teachers and parents. It requires imagination, thoughtfulness, self-discipline, and attention to your children. Good parenting always did, but reinforcement theory adds a few new tools to the problem-solving kit. Using reinforcement is fun, too. And, properly used, reinforcement always works; you need never revert to punishment in the hope that maybe just this once it will not backfire. Perhaps this generation of parents will really work out ways of using reinforcement to supersede the old and regrettable traditions of force and punishment— once and for all.

The behavioral viewpoint...

I wrote this about ten years ago. If I were writing it now, I wouldn't change anything, but I might add another definition of punishment. My definition of punishment, in *Don't Shoot the Dog!,* was something unpleasant that happens too late to do anything to change it. That is not the official behaviorist definition of punishment, which is something that *stops* behavior, rather than generating alternative behavior. In my opinion, that's part of it too, if not all of it; and the fact that punishment (sometimes) stops behavior in its tracks can make it highly reinforcing for the behavior of the one doing the punishing.

Just kidding....

Two of my children were still living in New York. Ted had graduated from Columbia Business School and had a job with the Bank of America. Gale was an editorial assistant at William Morrow, a publishing house. They both called me in North Bend, often just to pass on the latest jokes—hence this piece, which was published in *The Sun*, a fearless counterculture magazine.

CHAPTER THIRTEEN

My Favorite Joke

by Karen Pryor[1]

"What's yellow and dangerous?"
"A two thousand pound canary."

"What's yellow and dangerous?"
"A canary with a machine gun."

My favorite jokes are two-liners. I guess technically they are riddles, except you're not really supposed to guess the answer; you're just supposed to wait for it. And the answer is usually both silly and macabre.

Interest in this kind of joke tends to peak around the fifth grade. As my children passed through this age period, I relished the two-liner jokes they brought home. Elephant jokes. Lightbulb jokes. Dead baby jokes. Helen Keller jokes ("What did Helen Keller do when she fell down the well? She screamed her hands off.")

In 1976 I moved to Manhattan and found that New Yorkers too specialize in two-liners, usually topical, often in refreshingly bad taste. Whatever was on the front page of the newspaper, that's what people were telling jokes about. A cardinal from Warsaw was elevated to the papacy; by the next day I'd heard

[1]Reprinted with permission from *The Sun*, Chapel Hill, NC, Summer, 1984,

four Polish Pope jokes. Grace Kelly died? Grace Kelly jokes. A horrible new disease appeared? So did the jokes. "What do you call a person with herpes and AIDS?" "An incurable romantic." Now are you sorry you asked?

It was not until my oldest son, now grown, became a New York banker that I found out where these jokes come from, and why they seem to be all over Manhattan within hours of the precipitating event. They come from the financial district: from the brokers, the foreign exchange desks, the arbitrageurs, the merger and takeover teams — a population of highly intelligent people working at top speed under great pressure, with the possibility of disaster, either personal or corporate, always at hand. Jokes, especially gruesome jokes, are natural in such circumstances; surgeons make similar jokes in the operating room. And the financial district provides the other necessity, an incessantly active and widespread communications system which spreads the jokes around.

Once again my kids amuse me by passing on the latest jokes, this time from their office telephones. A man the press called the Subway Vigilante shot four muggers who were threatening him with sharp tools; here's one my son picked up from Goldman Sachs, the brokerage, the next morning.: "How do you make a vigilante cocktail? A screwdriver and four shots." And then, after a Union Carbide chemical plant exploded in India, with many fatalities, there's the Union Carbide theme song: "One little, two little, three little Indians..."

Gregory Bateson said that we are never so serious as when we are joking. I think about that sometimes. Perhaps the reason I cherish this gallows humor is that my life has always involved a lot of risk-taking. And what does it tell us about life in the fifth grade? Never mind. Of all the two-liners I've ever heard, here is my very favorite, one of the fifth-grader contributions:

"What's yellow and dangerous?"

"Shark-infested custard."

Over to you...

Are you wondering what this has to do with "behavior?"
What's your favorite joke?

Thinking about animals thinking...

Even though I had said good-bye to the tuna industry and its problems, moved to the mountains, and began looking at terrestrial creatures entirely— hummingbirds, Stellars' jays, chipmunks — the dolphins didn't leave me alone. The Office of Naval Research sponsored a "multi-disciplinary" conference in San Diego to discuss the question of dolphin cognition, or, Do Dolphins Think. Sigh. The wrong question, as usual. Of course they think, now and then—like us. The important thing to look at is thinking in all animals. Elephants. Wildebeest. Mice.

The reason dolphins get singled out as special, I have always thought, is two-fold: a) people (the Navy, for instance) don't know enough about other animals, and b) since dolphins get trained with shaping and reinforcement, instead of correction and punishment, they show us their real natures, and give us their very best; so they look unusually "smart." If you train other animals by these methods, they become "smart," too.

I had little hope of converting anyone, but it seemed to be my duty to try, so I reluctantly left Jon in North Bend and went to the conference in San Diego. Participants included Ken Norris, John Lilly, Don Griffin, and another two dozen folks. We each gave a paper. Then we sat around a big table and argued for a couple of days. Then the organizers turned the whole thing into a book, of which this was one chapter.

Since this meeting consisted largely of biologists, who would not be familiar with work I had published in psychology (such as the "Clever Hans" paper, Chapter Seven) I began with a little review.

CHAPTER FOURTEEN

Reinforcement Training as Interspecies Communication

Karen Pryor[1]

Dolphin domestication

Most of the large mammals that are trained to perform useful work for man, whether horse or dog, camel or yak, were brought into captivity and successfully domesticated by the dawn of recorded history. The dolphin, therefore, is a very recent addition to the roster of man's animal partners. We may think of dolphins primarily as performers, like circus animals. However, beginning in the early 1960s, dolphins have also become established as at least semi-domesticated animals, capable of performing useful tasks in their natural environment, the ocean. For example, at the United States Naval Ocean Systems Centers in San Diego and in Hawaii, dolphins have been trained to carry burdens and (as have sea lions) to seek, locate, and aid in the recovery of underwater objects.

Dolphins differ, however, from horses, dogs, and most other domestic animals, not only in being aquatic but in the methods by which they are trained. The training of behavior in terrestrial

[1]Reprinted with permission from *Dolphin Cognition and Behavior: A Comparative Approach.* Edited by Ronald J. Schusterman, Jeanette A. Thomas, and Forrest G. Wood. Erlbaum Associates, Hillsdale, N.J. 1986.

domestic animals is almost always accomplished by means of negative reinforcement, coercion, and restraint; and it is enforced with punishment. The ox moves forward to avoid the goad, and thus pulls the wagon. The dog must obey the leash, the horse the bridle. The sheep which will not move with the other sheep will be barked at or even bitten by the dog, and the dog which does not chase sheep when told to will be beaten by the shepherd. The dolphin, however, is not easily trained by these negative methods. The dolphin thus has become one of the few large mammals with which we have had extensive experience in the shaping of behavior primarily, and indeed in most cases almost exclusively, by the use of positive reinforcement.

Although a few dolphins were kept as aquarium specimens as early as the 1860s, routine maintenance of dolphins in captivity first occurred just before World War II (for a history of dolphins in captivity, see Defran & Pryor, 1980.) Thus techniques for the maintenance and training of dolphins were being developed during roughly the same decades in which experimental psychologists were reaching an understanding of the laws of operant conditioning, and the ways in which behavior could be modified by using positive reinforcement—the area of research associated most prominently with B. F. Skinner.

Several behavioral psychologists, students or colleagues of Skinner, were closely involved with the development of dolphin training techniques in the early decades of dolphin use and research. Keller Breland, under the auspices of a visionary Naval research director, William B. McLean, was instrumental in the development of the Navy's dolphin research programs and in the uses of operant techniques for both basic and applied research with dolphins by Navy scientists. R. N. Turner, working with Kenneth Norris at Marineland of the Pacific, developed reinforcement training techniques for some of the first dolphin sonar research, and was the original source of operant conditioning techniques for innovative work at Sea Life Park and the Oceanic Institute in the 1960s. Kent Burgess provided a sound scientific grounding for the training program at Sea World during its early years. Many contributions to methodology have since been made by trainers at these and other organizations (Schusterman, 1980; Turner, 1964).

Positive reinforcement training and cognition

In traditional force-training of domestic animals, the subject typically is not given choices (other than the implied choice, "Obey, or else!") For example if one asks a horse pulling a wagon to turn left, one wants only that behavior, and no other: not a right turn or an increase in speed, and certainly not some self-initiated behavior such as standing on the hind legs or jumping in the air. However the training of dolphins by positive reinforcement techniques often gives the animal freedom to demonstrate whatever capabilities it may have. During the training process the animal is at liberty to initiate its own behavior, as well as interactions with the trainer, in a way that is almost impossible in the restrictive circumstances of traditional training of domestic animals (or, for that matter, in the "whip-and-chair" aversive training traditionally used with circus animals.) To a certain extent it is this circumstance, rather than some intrinsic characteristic of the dolphin, which has given the public and scientists alike such respect for the animal's cognitive abilities: We get more chances to observe cognitive processes in these animals than in most others.

Reinforcement training is interactive: What the trainer does depends on what the animal does. The trainer can, and often does, develop behavior without making any attempt to prompt or cue the animal, but instead by watching, reacting, and reinforcing behavior that does occur. Thus the animal discovers that various actions of its own may result in reinforcement. One might say that as the trainer is developing behavior, the animal in effect is training the trainer to give fish.

Opportunity is thus provided for an animal to utilize cognitive skills. A well-known example is the much-anthologized "creative porpoise" experiment at Sea Life Park in which a rough-toothed dolphin *(Steno bredanensis)* was taught to respond to the criterion "Only behavior which has not previously been rewarded will now be reinforced." In each training session a behavior was selected for reinforcement which had not previously been a conditioned behavior. Within a few such sessions, the normal behavioral repertoire was exhausted. After a period of confusion, the animal began offering novel behaviors such as aerial flips, spitting, and swimming in corkscrew patterns, thus fulfilling the criterion—and demonstrating a capacity not only for complex learning but also for a certain amount of creativity (Pryor, Haag, & O'Reilly, 1969).

Another example of insightful behavior is the ability of some experienced animals to "check out" training criteria by running through a series of variations on a learned behavior. A false killer whale *(Pseudorca crassidens)* at Sea Life Park did this when trainers attempted to correct an error in a routine in the performance. Two whales had been trained to jump over a hurdle simultaneously in opposite directions; however one whale had taken to jumping late. When the trainers held a practice session and did not reinforce the late jumper, it "tested the premise" by a series of five jumps: (l) it made a perfect jump and was reinforced; (2) it made a late jump and was not reinforced; (3) it made a perfectly timed jump, but from the wrong side, traveling parallel to the other whale rather than in the opposite direction, an unprecedented event for which it had never been reinforced; (4) it made a correct jump that was just a little bit late, and received a very small reinforcement; and, finally, (5) it made a correct jump that was also perfectly timed, received a large number of fish, and performed correctly from then on (Pryor, 1981b).

Another not uncommon example of cognitive activity in trained dolphins is the deliberate wrong response. Ronald Schusterman has described an experiment in which a bottlenose dolphin *(Tursiops truncatus)* was being asked to make a series of choices, and after many correct responses, one day made a long series of completely wrong responses. The animal was being reinforced by fish dispensed from a feeding machine; examination revealed that the fish in the machine had dried out and become unpalatable. When the fish were replaced, the dolphin resumed making correct responses (Schusterman, personal communication).

Within the context of a positive reinforcement training session it is not just dolphins that can use the rules of the game to "train the trainer." During a project at the National Zoological Park in which I taught reinforcement training to a group of keepers (Pryor, 1981a), primate caretaker Melanie Bond was using food reinforcement to shape behavior in a chimpanzee. When the session was over, she moved to open the door and let the chimpanzee into its outside run, whereupon the animal reinforced this desirable behavior by handing her a piece of celery. During the same project, I was training a juvenile elephant to retrieve objects tossed into its pen. In the first session, the elephant quickly trained me to give it only the preferred reinforcement, sweet potatoes, from an assortment of food. When that was successful, it used the same methods—eye glances and trunk movements, primarily—to try to get me to unlock the cage door. I have seen similar grasping of both concept and opportunity in a wolf (Pryor, 1984). It is perhaps worth noting that this kind of event occurs frequently only in the training of those species which are commonly thought to be the most "intelligent," such as apes, dolphins, elephants, and some parrots.

Because these kinds of events take place within a training situation, they are often amenable to replication (the "creative porpoise" experiment described above was a replication of a serendipitous event that occurred during public performances.) Thus reinforcement training constitutes an excellent tool for the investigation of animal cognition.

Reinforcement training and intraspecific signals

Another consequence of reinforcement training is that the animal may—in fact almost invariably does—direct its own intraspecific social signals at the trainer. Reinforcement training thus becomes a marvelous tool for the ethologist. Suppose one is looking at a tankful of dolphins, and a single animal leaps into the air and comes down sideways, a behavior known as breaching. In a tank of captive dolphins, one might be able to speculate about why the animal breached, based on past observations and the concurrent behavior of the other dolphins; but a great many observations might be needed to speculate correctly. Also, since breaching in dolphins appears to have several functions, from removal of remoras to driving of prey to various kinds of social signals, it might also take long observation to be able to state with some confidence what the function of a particular breach might be in a particular circumstance. Suppose, however, that I am engaged in a training session with a dolphin, shaping some particular behavior, and, either accidentally or deliberately, I fail to reinforce some action which previously has invariably resulted in the arrival of a fish. If the dolphin then leaps up in the air and comes down sidewise in such a way that it soaks me from head to toes—then I can say, from just that one experience, that at least in certain circumstances a breach is an aggressive or agonistic display, and a pretty good one, too.[2]

It is not just with dolphins that reinforcement training is a useful tool to the student of animal communication. While working at the National Zoo I saw several magnificent examples of animals directing intraspecific social displays to their keepers/trainers. Hyenas, for instance, are quite transformed by the throes of a greeting display: The tail goes in circles, the dorsal hair stands on end, the ears come up, the mouth opens with the tongue hanging out, and the animal makes an incredible variety of sounds, giving the effect (to portray the behavior with an anthropomorphic metaphor) of a person exclaiming, "My dear, where have you *been*, I haven't seen you in ages, you look *wonderful*, well don't just stand there come *in*, tell me what's happening!" I have seen a polar bear respond to a reinforcement during a training session by bouncing down on its elbows and offering its trainer, on the other side of the bars, a clear-cut play invitation: a piece of communication which one might not

---

[2]In this circumstance, familiar to most dolphin trainers, the training context not only illuminates the nature of the social signal, but also allows the signal to function as communication. For example, if the breaching animal is young or inexperienced, and especially if my failure to reinforce (thus putting the animal on an extinction schedule) was inadvertent, I would at once modify my own behavior and reinforce more liberally, in order to reduce the animal's distress lest it interfere with the progress of training.

expect to see in an adult of that species in a lifetime of watching. It is the context provided by the training situation that allows one to interpret behavior with considerable accuracy. As ethologist Konrad Lorenz has put it, one can use "the subtlety of conditioning not only as an end in itself... but as a tool to gain knowledge about the animal as a whole." (Lorenz, 1975.)

Reinforcement training and human-animal communication

In this rich setting of mutual interaction and the mutual exchange of reinforcement (the animal's successful responses are the trainer's reinforcement) we can communicate a remarkably various and detailed set of information to the dolphin, as demonstrated by the performance of many research, display, and working animals all around the world. However the training context also gives the dolphins a fine opportunity to communicate with us, and thus to allow us fleeting but real glimpses of both the animal's state of affect and of cognitive processes in action. At Sea Life Park in Hawaii in about 1965 I was working with a newly captured rough-toothed dolphin, an unusual oceanic species about which little was then known. I was beginning to initiate this individual into the rules of the training game by teaching it a few ways to earn a rein-forcement. The first step, teaching the animal to associate the sound of a whistle (a conditioned reinforcer) with the arrival of a fish (a primary reinforcer) had been accomplished. Now, as I watched at tankside, the animal happened to leap from the water. I blew the whistle, and tossed the animal a fish. Within a few minutes the animal was leaping repeatedly, earning one fish after another.

Then the animal happened to make a noise, a little squeak. Unlike many other species of dolphins, rough-toothed dolphins rarely make audible sounds, and I had never heard this individual make a noise before; curious to hear more, I reinforced the emission of the sound. The animal made the sound several times and I reinforced the noise-making several times. I was surprised and pleased that a newly captured animal with so little training experience could learn to repeat a new behavior so readily.[3] Then the animal leaped again, and I made a training mistake. I was more interested in the unusual noise-making, now, than in leaping, which I felt sure I would have other opportunities to reinforce, as the animal did it often. So I did not respond to the leaping.

The animal became visibly upset. A very "green" animal, it had had no previous experience of failure to earn reinforcement in a training situation, and it rushed around the tank breaching and then went over to the far side of the tank and turned its back on me. "I don't want to play this game any more."

The next day the animal was swimming around the tank, and again it offered the leaping. Now a clarification of the rules was needed, a signal that would define when leaping would be reinforced. I raised my hand, to act as a cue, and reinforced leaping when my hand was up, but not when it was down, several times. In a few minutes the animal was exhibiting the correct behavior in the presence of the newly established cue (again, in my opinion, a rather impressive rate of learning in a novice subject).

Then the animal happened to make the noise again. I reinforced the noise, and immediately also lifted my hand so it would have the opportunity to get reinforced for leaping too, which it did. The animal then initiated and carried out the sequence of "noise, conditioned reinforcer, signal for leap, leap, and primary reinforcer" several times. It then swam to the other side of the tank, but without apparent agitation, so I took advantage of the pause in the proceedings to put my arms in the water and rinse the fish juice off my hands.

As I was doing this, the dolphin came over, and with one flipper stroked my arm up and down, very vigorously, an

---

[3]Usually, in reinforcing spontaneously occurring behavior in an inexperienced dolphin, one expects to have to reinforce the behavior several to many times, perhaps over a period of days, before the animal "realizes" what action is being reinforced, and offers the behavior repeatedly. Often one must condition two or three kinds of responses before the individual generalizes, i.e. becomes capable of immediately repeating any new response as soon as it is reinforced more than once. This animal had learned to offer not just one but two new behaviors, with high frequency, in its first real training session. At Sea Life Park we were to find that rough-toothed dolphins seem to be unusually good at acquiring and exhibiting such rule-governed behavior.

affiliative signal frequently seen between dolphins but never, in my experience, from dolphin to person. In this context it might be loosely interpreted as "Okay, stupid, I understand what you mean now, and you're forgiven" (Pryor, 1974).

This kind of event, a real communication, can be an emotional experience for man and beast alike. When this individual, Malia, later to become a rather well-known research and performance animal, rubbed my arm, I was touched, and dumped all the rest of the fish into the tank. However, this and all similar anecdotes are not so much an indication of some quasi-human capabilities of an animal or a species, or of the sentimentality of porpoise trainers, but of the enormous potential of interactive training as a window into animal behavior *and* potentially into animal consciousness.

Conclusion

Traditional animal training can also develop a situation of rapport and communication between trainer and subject. Traditional training, however, of dogs or horses, say, requires the patient acquisition of physical skills, sometimes at considerable risk. Just learning to ride a horse involves more time and physical effort than most people care to spend, and that is nothing compared to the physical skills and risks involved in training a horse. Thus the "glimpses through the window" afforded to the traditional animal trainer are not available to most people; and those who are both traditional trainers and convincing communicators are few.

Here, slightly paraphrased, is a statement from a professional writer who is also a trainer:

"These are beautiful, marvelous creatures, whose responses and instincts work on a plane as different from humans as water and oil .... Insight into their senses and consciousness is like a half-opened door or a half-learned language; our comprehension is maddeningly balked by not having the right sorts of hearing, or sense of touch; or maybe good enough telepathy. The feeling of oneness I have sometimes had with them has been their gift to an inferior being; but maybe my passion to [find out what we can accomplish together] has been my gift to them." (Francis, 1976)

This paragraph was not written by a dolphin trainer, but by Dick Francis, a horse trainer and steeplechase jockey. The oneness he speaks of is the learned interaction of horse and rider in a race. It's a communication not available to many, and not particularly accessible to research. However, reinforcement training brings this particular window into the house of science. As the philosopher Gregory Bateson said, "Operant conditioning is a method of communication with an alien species" (Pryor, 1975). It is not merely a way of communicating our wishes to an animal, but a two-way system. It is, in fact, a game, rigorous in rules but admitting of spontaneity. We should not be misled by the effects of this system into thinking that dolphins are somehow more "intelligent" than they are, nor that all other animals are necessarily less. Instead we should perhaps give more serious attention to the possibilities of the training context as an investigative tool in the study of animal awareness and cognition.

References

Defran, R. H., and Pryor, K. (1980). Social behavior and training of eleven species of cetaceans in captivity. L. Herman (Ed.), In *Cetacean Behavior: Mechanisms and Functions*. Wiley-Interscience: New York.

Francis, D. (1979). *Whip Hand*. Harper & Row: New York.

Lorenz, K. (1975), Foreword. In K. Pryor *Lads before the Wind: Adventures in Porpoise Training*. Harper & Row. 1987, Sunshine Books: North Bend, WA.

Pryor, K. W. (1974). Learning and behavior in whales and porpoises. *Naturwissenschaften*, 60,137-143.

Pryor, K. W. (1975). *Lads Before the Wind: Adventures in Porpoise Training*. Harper & Row: New York; 1987, Sunshine Books, WA.

Pryor, K. W. (1981a). The rhino likes violets. *Psychology Today*, April, 92-98.

Pryor, K. W. (1981b). Why porpoise trainers are not dolphin lovers: Real and false communication in the operant setting. *Annals of the New York Academy of Sciences*, 304, 137-143.

Pryor, K. (1984). *Don't Shoot the Dog*. Simon & Schuster: New York.

Pryor, K. W., Haag, R., and O'Reilly, J. (1969). The creative porpoise: Training for novel behavior. *The Journal of Experimental Analysis of Behavior, 12*, 653-66 I.

Turner, R. N. (1964). Methodological problems in the study of behavior. In W. N. Tavolga (Ed.), *Marine bio-acoustics*. Oxford: Pergamon Press.

Schusterman, R. (1980). Behavioral methodology in echolocation by marine mammals. In R. G. Busnel & J. F. Fish (Eds.), *Animal Sonar Systems*. New York: Plenum.

In conference...

Once again I was trying to draw people's attention to the usefulness and potential usefulness of operant conditioning in studying just such slippery matters as cognition. Nobody was much interested, as far as I could tell. Once, when some particularly egregious overinterpretation of dolphin behavior crossed the conference table, I pointed out how such behavior might easily arise due to reinforcement contingencies. A brain physiologist named Harry Jerison bristled.

"That's B.F. Skinner stuff," he said. "That's completely out of fashion, you'll never get a grant with those ideas!" What a weird threat, I thought; I don't need grants, Harry. But I shut up. Maybe this work would have to wait a generation.

One other interesting thing happened at this conference. Three young woman biologists cornered me with a mutually arrived-at question. All three had their doctorates, good jobs, and interesting research. What they wanted to know was: since I had a) raised a family and b) achieved some modest recognition in a scientific field — which was more important to me, now?

That took no thought: I at once said I'd give up everything I'd ever done and every dime I'd ever earned before I gave up Ted, Michael, and Gale. Hmm, they said.

And since then? One of the three married a non-scientist and now has several children. She also became a professor, has edited several scientific books, authored many papers, chaired international conferences, continues to write and do research, and is currently the president of an international scientific society.

The second, I gather, divorced her husband when he began to object to her dedication to her research. She is childless, a professor with many students and a very busy research lab, and has become world-famous for her discoveries and research.

The third decided to do it all on her own, by remaining a scientist while also becoming a single mother. However when the baby arrived she fell madly in love with the baby *and* with the baby's father, married him, quit her research position, and has as far as I know been a happy at-home wife and mother ever since.

The Marine Mammal Commission...

North Bend is definitely a dolphin-free community. The Cognition conference was done and my paper was finished. Once more I was sure my work with dolphins was over and done with. Wrong. The government came after me.

At the time, I found the experience frustrating and indeed sometimes infuriating. It took me a while to see the funny side of it. Julian Bach loved this piece and circulated it to ten magazines, from *Ms.* to *Newsweek*. Everybody thought it was funny. Everybody wanted to see it in print—but not in their publication, if you don't mind.

This piece and the tale in Chapter Nineteen are the only articles in this collection that have not been previously published.

The Marine Mammal Commission, and its board of scientific advisors, in full session. Head Commissioner Bill Evans is in the middle, with me on his left, the other commissioner Bob Elsner on his right, and Director John Twiss next to him.

CHAPTER FIFTEEN

When the President Appointed Me

by Karen Pryor

In November of 1984 President Reagan, or rather, a faceless organization called The White House, appointed me as a commissioner on the Marine Mammal Commission. The Marine Mammal Commission is a federal agency which oversees the safety and well-being of American marine mammals, from the biggest blue whale in the Bering Straits to the smallest sea lion pup in the Central Park Zoo. The Marine Mammal Commission is itself probably the smallest agency in the Federal government, with a budget of less than a million dollars a year, a staff of twelve, three part-time commissioners who meet once a year and make policy, and a board of scientific advisors.

Appointing Marine Mammal Commissioners was not high on the White House list of urgent matters. When I was nominated two positions on the Commission had been sitting empty for a year or more. I found out I was nominated when the Marine Mammal Commission Chairman, Bill Evans, the only existing commissioner at the time, called me up and told me so.

Bill Evans and I have both been involved in dolphin research and have known each other for years. But when he asked me if I'd like to be on the Marine Mammal Commission I was surprised. I thought I was probably qualified, but surely there were

239

candidates available with much more status. Who put me up for this job?

Later Bill gallantly implied that he himself had recommended me, but my impression at the time was that he was just as mystified as I was. "You must have some important friends in Washington," he said. Who? My college roommate? My Aunt Dorothy? In fact I have never learned who put my name on the list; and I suspect now that my leading attraction to The White House was that I was suitable and a woman.

You would think The White House nominates someone for the Commission, the person says yes, Congress says oh, why not, and the person becomes an appointee and starts deciding stuff, right? No. First came a questionnaire from the Senate. They already had my resumé, since Bill Evans had told me to send it in; but now they wanted much more detail, including an essay on why I thought I would be a good commissioner. I swallowed my self-respect and created the required puffery and mailed it.

Then came a request for information from the F.B.I. They were going to do a full-scale investigation of me. What they wanted was the names of thirty people who know me well in North Bend, the town near Seattle where I live. I had recently remarried, and had moved from New York to North Bend just a few months earlier. I told them I couldn't think of five people in North Bend who would even recognize me on the street. If they wanted thirty names they'd have to settle for people in New York. All right they said, give us what you can in both places; so I made two lists.

The F.B.I. went around and interviewed the North Bend list — the postmistress, my secretary, and a few others. They all said No, they'd never seen me drunk, No, I'd never passed a bad check, No, I had no criminal record as far as they knew. The F.B.I. visited everyone on the New York list, too, paying particular attention to the doormen in my old apartment building; but they still weren't satisfied. The local Seattle agent finally threw caution to the winds and came to our house to see for himself what I was up to. He was a young man of Chinese extraction. I liked him. When he came to understand that I am a writer he bought a copy of my most recent book and had me autograph it to his wife.

Then The White House sent me the government's Financial Disclosure Form, Form 278, a bulky pad of legal-sized pages, arranged horizontally, printed in blue. On this form you are supposed to explain every source of income you or your spouse have earned in the past year. Also you must list and give a value to every piece of property that either of you own, other than your house and your clothes. If you bought or sold anything in the past year, from stocks and bonds to one copy of your last book, you have to tell all about that, so The White House can see if you took advantage of your government position to do so; and if you took any lecture fees or other gifts or honoraria you have to say from whom, and how much.

The instructions alone filled many pages. I found them both complicated and oddly inappropriate. The instructions addressed a reporting individual—"You"—who was implicitly male, salaried, propertied, and a businessman, with a spouse who was none of the above. The single example of spousal earnings in the instruction described a "practicing psychologist" (why not just "psychologist?") who earned $10,500 a year—not much of a practice. The sort of wifely, poorly paid, part-time job spouses of presidential appointees were expected to have.

This was the form that got Geraldine Ferraro in trouble, and I could see why. Filling it out for myself was cumbersome; filling it out for my husband Jon, whose business affairs are much more extensive than mine, was nearly impossible, given the complex instructions. For example it took many hours to resurrect the details we were required to report concerning Jon's speaking dates for the previous year. We knew what the Richmond Women's Club, say, had paid Jon to be their luncheon speaker, because we'd told that to the I.R.S. But what was the value of the Club lunch? You were supposed to report free meals. And if Jon spent the night with my Uncle Jimmy and Aunt Margaret, who live in Richmond, was that a reportable "gift of lodging?"

Filling out Form 278 took two full weeks of work. Nobody was paying me for that, either. And one could not just turn it over to an accountant; what would the accountant know about, say, Richmond and Uncle Jimmy? A horrid job.

About a month after I sent in that first 278, The White House called and chewed me out. First, I had filled the forms out by hand. Wrong. "This is going to the *Senate*," the man said oppressively. I was amused at this glimpse of The White House brushing the crumbs from its vest for the Senate, and I laughed. Bad. The man was cross now. He said irritably that furthermore I was not supposed to number the many pages of my submittal where I saw fit, but *in the boxes provided* for page numbers. I guess I failed to respond with sufficient chagrin, because then The White House started really scolding me, accusing me of "trying to get away with something," and threatening me with the law.

I pointed out that the forms were very complicated; that I was doing the best I could; and that I hadn't asked for this job, anyway. The man on the phone remembered his manners. He needed woman appointees, I suppose. He explained more courteously, if not cordially, what needed correcting, and I agreed to type the corrected version. I took mental revenge by envisioning this representative of The White House as being blond, hard-eyed, expensively dressed, and just the teeniest bit overweight.

While various government agencies mulled over my completed 278 I enjoyed a nice three-month hiatus from the business of being a nominee. Then I got one more angry phone call, this time, I think, from the C.I.A. An unpleasant male voice asked me to identify myself, and then said "It's about your resumé. There's a four-year gap in your resumé. You'll have to explain that."

"There is not!" I said hotly; I know my resumé well, and it's quite complete.

"Oh?" drawled the voice, in a "gotcha" tone. "You graduated from Cornell in 1954, right?"

"Right."

"And then in 1958 you started going to graduate school at the University of Hawaii, right?"

"Right."

"That leaves four years unaccounted for," he said triumphantly. Then he barked, "Where were you and what were you doing in those four years?"

I was flabbergasted. I bit back an impulse to say I was behind the Iron Curtain learning Chinese. Instead I explained.

"If you look a little further down the first page of that resumé, you will see that I got married in 1954, and had three children in the next five years. During that four-year 'gap,' as you call it, I was at home, taking care of infants, and usually either pregnant or lactating. Or both."

Interesting: I'd never *heard* someone blush over the phone before. But I wondered. How come I get to go through all this—and the procedure took many months, all told—while any number of bankers and lawyers have become presidential appointees in a matter of days or weeks? Were their resumés more plausible? How did they fill out their 278s?

Eventually the investigation was complete, and I became a Commissioner. I got a very large document from The White House, suitable for framing if you had a big wall, beginning "Know all men by these presents..." and signed "Ronald Reagan" at the bottom in a clear, almost childish hand. It was still not official, because the Senate had to approve my appointment, and Marine Mammal Commissioners were not high on the Senate's urgent list, either. But I was allowed to start working without their go-ahead. Eventually the Senate summoned me to a subcommittee hearing in Washington, and in five minutes of formalities approved my appointment. I had not expected controversy. Still, I did my hair carefully and wore new clothes.

Most of what I did for the Commission I did at home, reading reports and proposals and commenting on them over the phone. I thought the work of the Marine Mammal Commission was valuable. The staff was dedicated and so was the scientific advisory committee. I learned a lot from them all. I felt quite dedicated myself.

After I'd served about eighteen months another missive from The White House came to my house, consisting of several pages of advice on how to be a good and tactful appointee in your new position. Alas, it came too late. Most of the things one was advised against doing I had already at least tried. Studying the document I decided that the person who followed all this sound counsel would be, in the eyes of a civil service staff, a perfect appointee: one who did nothing at all.

However I expect I made a contribution during the three years that I served. There were areas where I did have expertise. Sometimes a permit holder or a research organization found my suggestions useful. I know I accomplished one thing: during my tenure, documents issuing from the Commission offices were no longer riddled with split infinitives.

One day the Commission's Executive Director, John Twiss, phoned me to say a new commissioner had been appointed, and I'd been replaced. The annual meeting was a week off and a continent away. Now someone else would sit on the dais for five days instead of me. I canceled my plane reservations. I thankfully drove an entire stationwagon load of Marine Mammal Commission papers to the dump.

There was no official notice of termination, nor expression of gratitude for my services, from The White House or anyone else. However, like a retired general or ambassador I was entitled to keep my title, and could insist on being introduced as Commissioner and having my mail addressed to The Honorable Karen Pryor if I wished.

The Commission and its multitudinous courier-delivered documents and reports disappeared from my life like a turned-off television. However, about a year after my duties were over, I got a letter from the Commission informing me that I was required to fill out one more form: a "termination" Form 278. This time the form was printed in green ink instead of blue. This time I was much more experienced; filling out the 278 took only two days.

The Marine Mammal Protection Act...

The Marine Mammal Protection Act is a remarkable piece of legislation which has had a powerful impact on our national environmental policy, not just in conservation of marine mammals, but of the oceans in general. The Marine Mammal Commission, which oversees the management of the Act, has been extraordinarily effective, due largely, in my opinion, to the skills of the director, John Twiss, who for decades now has guided his staff, his scientific board, and his ever-changing commissioners as they juggled the conflicting needs of science, the environmental community, other government agencies, and the law itself. Guidance and input from the MMC has helped to set *effective* policies and programs in place again and again.

My duties as a Commissioner included reading every permit request and research report, which gave me a detailed overview of current marine mammal research. It was fun reading about people landing helicopters on tippy pieces of sea ice to put radio collars on anesthetized polar bears; or people watching over the safety of baby monk seals on sun-blasted beaches in French Frigate Shoals.

It was also fascinating, for those three years, to watch the threads of problems and solutions weaving together in the papers that crossed my desk. Here came an ingenious way to collect convincing data in Florida, so that the Floridians themselves developed programs to protect the manatees—and with them, whole chunks of fragile coastal ecosystems. Another program surfaced, developed person by person and bit by bit, to reduce sea otter mortality in drift nets off California, at the same time eliminating a horrendous level of sea bird mortality. A world-wide annual beach survey, conceived of and carried out by amateurs with seed money and organizational support from the Commission, produced such graphic evidence of the abundance of manmade ocean trash that it led to new international laws prohibiting all ships everywhere from dumping garbage at sea.

I liked the annual meetings, where one had a chance to meet a lot of people and ask questions. I didn't like the male chauvinism I tripped over now and then, nor the hidden resentments and surprise attacks that are a natural part of any bureaucracy. As I said in this piece, I know I helped some people, and solved some problems. I was glad to have served in the Government. I do hope I won't ever have to do it again.

Part Four

North Bend

Mountain View
1985 to now

Dolphin Societies: the creation of a tome...

Jon and I went house hunting. We had a joint list—land facing south for sun and warmth, an easy drive to the airport, and so on. We had individual lists, too. On the bottom of Jon's list— desirable but not crucial—was that the house should be in terrain wild enough so that elk would graze on our lawn. On the bottom of my list—desirable but not crucial—was cable TV.

We soon realized we might never find a prebuilt house that suited, mostly because the rooms we would need for offices were too small. So we bought a piece of land, five acres sloping south, forty-five minutes from SeaTac airport, and just two miles from where we were renting. Jon felled enough trees to make room for a house and a garden. We found a friendly contractor and a low-ego architect who understood weather and sun. We built a simple house with a big basement, wood stove heating, and four bedrooms: one for us, one for family and guests, one for Jon's office, and one for mine.

We were on the edge of a protected forest. The elk came at once. Jon had to put up an electric fence around the garden after a large cow elk rudely ate all my narcissus, even though I was jumping up and down and banging on the window at the time. And although the house is at the end of a mile of dirt road, six miles from town, we have fifty channels of cable TV.

My new office was the best writing space I have ever had. The first book I finished in it was—sigh—about dolphins. I had been dickering for years, off and on, with George Narita, an editor at a textbook publishing house in New Jersey, about a possible book on dolphin behavior. In New York we had always met over an excellent lunch. I liked the free meals, but the book Narita had in mind looked to me like a lot of work for no money. At first I wasn't interested.

Now I realized it might be a way to get my tuna-porpoise stuff published. Narita was in Seattle on business. We met for lunch. We came to an agreement: The book would contain the work Ingrid and I had done on wild spotted dolphins, as well as some fascinating studies a Russian scientist had sent me on dolphin hunting behavior, and perhaps one or two more papers by others who were studying dolphins in the wild. I would write my part and be the editor for the rest. We shook hands on the plan. George went back to New Jersey.

Then he phoned me. His boss, the editor-in-chief, refused to publish the book unless it had a co-editor with a bigger name than mine: Ken Norris, for example. I was miffed, but I saw the point, and phoned Ken to see if he was interested. Ken was delighted; he had several students and post-docs whose work would fit into such a book. He didn't however have a great deal of time to put into the project, so he would do it only if I remained the senior editor.

I conveyed this information to Narita. In due course a contract arrived. Lo, Ken's name was first. The publisher was offering us an ultimatum, in effect: Norris is senior editor, or no contract.

Ken was furious, bless his heart. "We'll find another publisher." We? Okay, I'll try.

I happened to know the name of an editor at the University of Chicago Press. I called her. She was not able to take on the book but she suggested someone at the University of California Press. That editor, Betty Ann Kevles, jumped at our idea. Ken was on the University of California faculty, and they had already published one book he'd edited. They would be delighted to have another, and they wouldn't object to my being the editor in charge. So in two phone calls we, indeed, had found another and more prestigious publisher, who would furthermore give us a bit of money, and no doubt a much handsomer book. I sent the unsigned contract back to Narita—that was the end of the free lunches, of course—and got to work.

With Ken aboard we were able to attract an additional dozen scientific papers by various contributors, besides the Russian work and my research (Chapter 9 in this book.) We decided that the book should also include some informal essays by one or the other or both of us. The essays would set the stage for some of the research topics, and also give us room to talk about what we thought was important, and why.

Here are three of those essays. The first one preceded a paper on dolphin sonar research. The second introduced a group of papers on laboratory studies, and the third, by both of us, commented on a paper that showed that female pilot whales, like female humans, can live on for decades after their reproductive years are over. The authors quite correctly refused to speculate about the implications of these findings but Ken and I considered that we were free not only to speculate but to bicker.

DOLPHIN SOCIETIES

Discoveries and Puzzles

Edited by Karen Pryor
and Kenneth S. Norris

CHAPTER SIXTEEN

Three Essays from *Dolphin Societies: Discoveries and Puzzles*

I. The Domestic Dolphin

by Karen Pryor[1]

Whenever we humans have moved into a new habitat, we have tamed and made use of animals living there already, animals whose skills in that environment exceed our own: pigs in the jungle, camels in the desert, Himalayan yaks. Some of these domesticated species, sheep, for example, have been so changed by selective breeding that similar species no longer exist in the wild. Other working animals—the falcon, the elephant—are unchanged and, in fact, are sometimes still captured from the wild and then trained to perform work for us.

Metaphorically, domestication is a trade-off. An animal gives up its freedom and wild companions and contributes produce or work of some sort; in return, it is fed and kept safe from predators, thus escaping the two biggest problems of life in the wild, going hungry and getting eaten. Many species have proved quite willing to make this bargain, and the bottlenose dolphin,

[1]Reprinted with permission from *Dolphin Societies: Discoveries and Puzzles*, K. Pryor and K.S. Norris, Eds., University of California Press, 1991.

in my experience, is one of them. I have even seen the trade-off acted out: for some months, at the Oceanic Institute in Hawaii, we kept a pair of bottlenose dolphins in a pen next to a pier in the ocean, a pen they could jump in and out of at will. They spent most of the day loose, playing at the bows of boats coming in and out of the little harbor, but they spent the nights in the pen, jumping back in at 5:00 P.M. when a trainer showed up with their suppers. And they were once seen to jump hastily into their pen when a large hammerhead shark cruised under the pier.

Living in an environment that to us is so alien, the dolphin can perform tasks that we, even with all our technology, find difficult. The dolphin, for example, is superb at finding lost objects underwater. We taught one of our free-swimming Institute dolphins to look for objects in the waters around the pier and report them to us. Our criterion was "anything man-made and bigger than a breadbox." I do not know how the dolphin defined that, but he soon found engine blocks, a movie camera, quite a lot of fishing equipment, and a World War II airplane.

And apparently the animal enjoyed being asked to do this. Domestication may require an animal to give up the extensive social contact of a large wild group, but working animals, at least, gain the benefit of interesting things to do (gun dogs and cutting horses, for example, appear to be fascinated and exhilarated by their work.) Whatever we may think of the merits of what dolphins do in oceanarium shows, for the animals, it can be challenging; I have seen a dolphin, striving to master an athletically difficult trick, actually refuse to eat its "reward" fish until it got the stunt right. When the U.S. Navy released the news that it was using dolphins to search for mines in the Persian Gulf, a reporter asked me if I thought the dolphins would find the work arduous or unpleasant. Knowing the character of the animals and the skills of the Navy trainers, I could answer instantly, "Are you kidding? They love it."

It has been suggested in the press that dolphins could be used to sabotage ships; I regard this as unrealistic, if only because the highly streamlined dolphin cannot carry much of a payload. Dolphins could be used, however, to detect the presence of any underwater activity; for example, they could be used to notify swimmers of the presence of sharks. And the echolocation skills have real potential; dolphins would be the partners of choice in searching shallow Caribbean waters for a wrecked treasure ship buried in the sand.

The U.S. Marine Mammal Protection Act prohibits the use of dolphins for any such commercial purpose. Under this carefully administered federal law, dolphins may only be kept for public display, research, or, in the case of the Navy, national defense. And a working partnership with dolphins is not something to be entered into lightly. Dolphins are extremely expensive to maintain. They need a lot of food and room and care. A working dolphin requires a full-time trainer, and not just anyone can be a good trainer. Veterinary supervision alone calls for enormous expertise. But we have developed this expertise. Also we are beginning to breed dolphins successfully in captivity. The dolphin, primarily the bottlenose dolphin, may well prove to be the newest large animal in our history to accept domestication.

II. Mortal Remains: Studying Dead Animals

Karen Pryor

Queen Elizabeth I of England loved to eat dolphin meat. I can't think why; to me it tastes like steak fried in cod liver oil.[2] Elizabeth decreed that any dolphin or porpoise corpse that washed up on shore was "The Queen's Fishe" and had to be sent to the palace cooks at once.

The queen passed on, but the decree remained; in due course, the British Museum became the repository for dolphin remains, whether from the British Isles or elsewhere, thereby acquiring one of the world's greatest collections of cetacean skeletons. From this trove, a series of British Museum scientists defined our basic understanding of the species and distributions of small cetaceans.

[2]Elizabeth's choice should not be confused with mahimahi, or dolphin-fish, commonly served in restaurants, which is not a mammal but a white-fleshed, saltwater fish, *Coryphaena* spp., which tastes like a snapper or a cod.

Meanwhile, the whaling industry of the eighteenth and nineteenth centuries provided data about large cetaceans—where they were caught, what kinds were caught, their measurements. And until very recently, all we knew about most cetaceans was the location of death and the measurements of their carcasses and bones.

This told us very little about behavior. For example, in 1965, Sea Life Park was the first oceanarium to capture a pygmy killer whale *(Feresa attenuata)*, a strange little black animal with white lips, like a clown. It was such a rare specimen that Ken Norris flew out from California just to measure it. Museum data could tell us what species it was and where it had been seen before; but nothing warned us that in behavior it was more like a wolf than a normal dolphin, that it was going to growl and snap like a canid and would not hesitate to attack people and other cetaceans.

And yet, behavioral information can be deduced from dead data, from bones and teeth, ovaries and stomach contents. It is only necessary to ask the right questions. Helene Marsh and Toshio Kasuya took advantage of the Japanese onshore fishery for small cetaceans to study pilot whales. Being able to look at a whole school simultaneously made it possible to age and sex every animal and thus see the structure of the school; looking at ovaries showed the reproductive status of each female. But it seems to me it took a leap of the imagination to perform the simple test for milk sugar on the stomach contents of *all* animals and thus find out that females may nurse their young up to seventeen *years* and that lactation may have unusual bonding functions in pilot whale society.

One of the most impressive collections of dolphin remains in the world occupies the basement of the Southwest Fisheries Center in La Jolla, California. Here, for over two decades, the National Marine Fisheries Service (NMFS, pronounced "nymphs") has been amassing specimens collected from tuna vessels engaged in purse seining for tuna in association with dolphins in the eastern tropical Pacific: the so-called tuna-porpoise fishery. The procedure involves locating and encircling dolphin schools that are often accompanied by tuna and then releasing the dolphins.

Dolphin mortality in some years was enormous. Scientists at the Southwest Fisheries Center and elsewhere expended major efforts both to mitigate the mortality and to understand the dolphin populations and the effect of the fishing. These efforts were, on the whole, successful; cooperative research with the fishing industry resulted in improvements that reduced dolphin mortality from over 100,000 a year in the early 1970s to under 14,000 in 1986. (Unfortunately, improvements in the U.S. fleet have recently been offset by mortality caused by new and increasing foreign fleets.)

During the course of this research, government scientists and observers on hundreds of ship voyages, across a million square miles of ocean, collected data and samples of anatomical material from specimens incidentally killed in the nets. In the basement of the Southwest Fisheries Center, the library stacks holding the resulting collections reach in shadowed corridors from floor to ceiling, wall to wall, and one end of the building to the other. The shelves are crowded with jars of uteri and stomachs; jars of teeth and jawbones; books full of stained slides of cross sections of testes; racks and racks of bones and skulls. A conservative estimate is that the collection includes samples of over 22,000 spinner and spotted dolphins.

Every specimen is precisely labeled—sex, size, when and where it was taken, and much more. The intangibles that cannot be pickled in formalin, such as color patterns (a clue to population distributions), are stored in computer data bases and also on paper, in carefully organized library binders, in other rooms upstairs. Here one can locate the original, grimy, water-stained work sheet, filled out on shipboard by one of hundreds of data collectors, for every dolphin. And the Southwest Fisheries Center houses yet another enormous collection of data resulting from this fishery: the computer data on thousands of sets of the net by boats in the U.S. fleet, accumulated by NMFS and by the InterAmerican Tropical Tuna Commission (IATTC), which for many years has overseen the conservation and management of the tuna themselves.

A primary organizer of this enormous collection has been NMFS biologist William Perrin. The methodical studies by Perrin and his associates of these thousands of anatomical specimens have themselves provided a vast quantity of data for other scientists to work on (it is informative to glance at the references in this book to see how often Perrin's work is cited).

The NMFS and IATTC scientists have done much to define the geographic distribution of spinner and spotted dolphins, to depict the apparent division of these populations of many millions of animals into separate stocks, and to identify their growth rates and reproductive cycles, all crucial information for making management decisions and protecting the population's survival. Now other researchers are beginning to tease behavioral information out of this mass of samples and data. For example, Southwest Fisheries Center scientist Aleta Hohn and her associates performed extensive statistical analyses of computerized data on the sizes of encircled schools, compared to the sex and maturity of animals taken in the same sets. They have been able to show, among other things, that spotted dolphins have two different kinds of schools: breeding schools, such as those described by myself and Shallenberger, and small schools of immature males that spend most of their time living among large aggregations of spinners. This arrangement, which I find amazing, would have been very hard to pin-point by underwater observation, since the fishermen do not encircle large aggregations of spinners because they are seldom accompanied by tuna; but it immediately made sense of occasional anecdotal reports, from fishermen and government observers, of "a few little spotters" among big spinner schools.

Two chapters in this book [*Dolphin Societies:* Ed.] describe behavioral information gleaned from the tuna fishery sampling and data collections: Michael Scott and Wayne Perryman describe what they have learned about social behavior from the aerial photographs taken in population survey studies. Albert Myrick tells us how he and others unraveled some interesting mysteries from those jars of teeth down in the basement. To me, these contributions demonstrate the ultimate value of what sometimes seems like the dustiest and most useless part of biology: museum collections, the warehousing of specimens, the laborious filling out of labels, the minute measurements of taxonomy. The dolphin teeth Myrick used had been collected over the years not in the certainty but only in the hope that someone might be able to use them all. The Southwest Fisheries Center's donations of material to other museums and its own present collection of interrelated specimens and data derive from a depressing loss of life, to be sure, but it constitutes an unequaled research tool. We can only guess at what questions will be asked of it in the future and what new understandings may be acquired, which in turn can be used, in fact, to save the dolphins.

III. Some Thoughts on Grandmothers, Part I

by Kenneth S. Norris

In recent years, it has emerged that the social patterns of the various whales and dolphins are not all alike. They range from the very fluid schools of spinner dolphins, in which school membership changes substantially from day to day, drawing from a population of as many as one thousand dolphins, to the very rigid pods of killer whales that seem to consist of exactly the same members, apparently groups of mothers and offspring, for years on end.

Now comes the news, from the work of Toshio Kasuya and Helene Marsh, that pilot whale schools, which include family units, are different in another way. They contain large cadres of postreproductive females, including some that are more than a decade older than the age of last reproduction for the species. And some of these females are still lactating. Why?

Marsh and Kasuya suggest that a postreproductive female might continue to let her last calf nurse for many years, in some cases until it reaches adulthood. The fact that some old females are still nursing, fourteen years past their last pregnancy, could thus be an artifact of failure to wean. Still, it seems anomalous that only the last calf of a whale should receive such preferential treatment.

And why so many postreproductive females? Normally, each member of a biological population has important duties to perform in the society of which it is a part. I do not know of another animal that commits a substantial percentage to an age class with nothing to do (except our own). Does the postreproductive pilot whale female serve some important social function, one that could be supported by natural selection and one that is not carried out by the other whales in a school?

One possibility might be that postreproductive females nurse the calves of others. Pilot whales are diving animals that apparently feed at considerable depths (Navy scientists have been able to train pilot whales to dive on command deeper than two thousand feet). One wonders if such a species requires a cadre of school members who can tend nursing young while others, including nursing mothers, are feeding deep beneath the surface. If so, postreproductive females capable of providing "milk rewards" to calves incapable of the dives of adults might be a crucial part of pilot whale society.

Marsh and Kasuya point out that there is little evidence for fostering (nursing offspring other than your own) in cetaceans but ample evidence of alloparenting (providing other types of care for young other than your own). It is suggestive that the only other odontocete known to have significant numbers of postreproductive females in its societies is the deep-diving sperm whale.

If this scenario proves to be true, it might be found more widely among diving species, such as the various beaked whales. No one yet knows the answers to the intriguing questions raised by this work.

Some Thoughts on Grandmothers: Part II

by Karen Pryor

So the only use for postreproductive females is babysitting? I suggest that the role of postreproductive females in pilot whale schools may be as a repository of cultural information, such as the whereabouts of feeding grounds.

Pilot whales and people are not alone in their production of old ladies. Postreproductive females, often surviving to a grand old age, are commonplace in several terrestrial mammals, including horses and cattle (as many farmers can testify) and elephants. In some of these species, mature males join the female groups only temporarily, for breeding. In all of them, a dominant male may be replaced by a rival at any time. If long-term experience is necessary, for example to learn and remember the terrain beneath your feet or fins, then continuity of individuals in the group is vital: and older females can provide it.

The current evidence suggests to me that pilot whales, at least in New England and California waters, do not cruise at random, finding food where they can, but migrate along the coasts feeding on squid by diving in particular canyons along the edge of the continental shelf (and perhaps on seamounts, as well). Random 2,000-foot dives in the wrong spot would be very expensive, energetically. Locating food, year-round, might be at least partly a function of long-term memory of the oldest animals, comparable to the need of wild horses, cattle, and elephants to remember migratory routes and the location of water holes.

While extended lactation certainly plays some role, not yet clear, in pilot whale society, not all the old females lactate; I suggest their principal biological contribution might be to learn, remember, and transmit what pilot whales need to know.

A useful contribution...

They say that if a job turns out to be much, much more difficult than you foresaw, and to take much longer than you planned, then you are probably doing it right. When Ken and I first sat down together to outline the book, we thought *Dolphin Societies* would take a year and a half to put together. It took seven years, including various delays at the University of California Press.

It was a handsome book. It was even quite readable. I learned a lot about editing as I progressed. Each paper was eventually quite clear and concise, with no statistics designed to impress rather than inform, which Norris calls "flute music." Some of the authors may never speak to me again, but others very nicely said thank you. In completing my own research paper I received a great deal of guidance, admonishment, and instruction from Ken and from William Perrin, who is the National Marine Fisheries Service's head scientist on dolphins in the tuna fishery. If I had been formally submitting the work toward a Ph.D. I could not have asked for a finer thesis committee.

Dolphin Societies: Discoveries and Puzzles was well received and well reviewed. *Science* magazine not only praised it but republished the frontispiece, an old photograph of me and Ken, giggling while repairing a porpoise harness on the deck of a boat somewhere off Hawaii. This pleasantly unsolemn picture had been taken, and given to me, twenty years earlier by a *Life* magazine photographer. I had hung onto it all that time, through five or six moves, feeling sure I would have a use for it some day.

The book was also many hundreds of pages long, unavoidably crammed with tables, diagrams, and pages of references. One doesn't expect a book of that nature to sell more than a few hundred copies, but in fact it sold well and continues to sell. The papers in it, including my own, are being cited by others in their scientific papers, which is one mark of whether or not one has made a useful contribution. Our Russian contributor, V.M. Bel'kovich, was delighted to be published in the U.S.; he returned the favor by translating *Lads Before the Wind* and arranging for its publication in the Soviet Union—where it sold 200,000 copies.

And, by the way, Ken's far-fetched notion of elderly babysitter pilot whales giving milk rewards for calves may not be wrong. Norris is famous in the marine mammal community for imaginative speculations that later prove to be true: that dolphins hear through their jaws, is one; that they can stun fish with concentrated sonar blasts, is another. Now some research recently undertaken by oceanarium trainers and scientists indicates that not only can grandmothers provide milk to dolphin calves—so can sisters, and other females, even if they have not yet had a calf themselves, something that happens in no other mammalian group. As far as I know, as Dr. Perrin would caution me to add.

The final cover of "Nursing Your Baby."

Revising Nursing Your Baby...

The next book I finished in my new office in our new house was also a collaboration.

In the 1950s, when I was having my family, I had researched and written a book on breastfeeding, called *Nursing Your Baby*. I had discovered from my own experience that breastfeeding was at least in part a learned skill; and the medical customs of the time not only didn't help mothers and babies learn, but actively interfered with the process. I wrote a book presenting the facts in a useful way, so readers could nurse their babies in spite of the bad advice they might be given. My father's literary agent, Harold Ober, sold the book to Harper & Row for a $700 advance.

Over the next two decades, *Nursing Your Baby* sold about 1.5 million copies in a Simon & Schuster paperback. Now, however, it was being displaced on the shelves by more recent books on breastfeeding. I got a call from an editor at Simon & Schuster who had herself breastfed twins with the help of my book: would I consider doing a revision?

The book was indisputably dated. When it was first published, in 1963, all doctors were male, all mothers were called "girls," (many of us actually were still in our teens when we married and had our first babies), and practices which are common nowadays, such as combining working and nursing, were unheard of.

I was working on other things now, and completely out of touch with the subject of lactation. Also, understandably, I was no longer personally very interested in the topic. I discussed the matter with friends and family. My daughter Gale, who was expecting her first child, had a solution. We could do it together. Gale would update the book, taking out all the sexism and anachronisms, both of which were invisible to me; and I would update the medical research.

It turned out to be a big job, of course. By the time we signed our contract Gale and her architect husband, Karl Leabo, who were living in Boston, had produced a baby boy, and Gale also had a full-time job at Little, Brown, a publisher. She had to write from 5 to 6 AM before the baby woke and she and Karl got ready to go to their offices. I was working on *Dolphin Societies* at the same time, *and* on a collection of my father's fishing stories for Nick Lyons Press in New York. I had the horrendous experience of having two sets of galley proofs arrive in the same UPS delivery, a nightmare perhaps only another writer can really appreciate.

But we did it. Gale wrote a competely new chapter on working and nursing, new practical chapters, and several new sections. She also did some of the medical research. I wrote a new chapter on the nature of human milk. (On this topic there was fascinating new research: human milk is literally alive, like blood, composed to a startling degree of living cells which go right to work in the baby.)

I have always been interested in the widespread conviction that humans are "above" all those "instincts" animals supposedly are slaves to, when actually we are rich in species-wide innate behavior; and it shows up especially in parental behavior. The breastfeeding relationship is a vivid expression of the combination of innate behavior, passed on by genes, and learned behavior, acquired through experience and/or passed on by culture. Thanks to new research, we were able to beef up considerably the chapters in *Nursing Your Baby* on innate behavior in humans. Here's a sample.

CHAPTER SEVENTEEN

Parents and Innate Behavior. Chapter Six from *Nursing Your Baby, Updated for the '90s.*

by Karen Pryor and Gale Pryor[1]

Instinct and the new insecurity

In 1850, a new mother learning to take care other first baby might have felt nervous, but she was bolstered by the firm conviction that whatever she did was right. Only a mother knew what to do for her infant, and she—by the grace of God, having become a mother—would be able to feed and care for her infant, thanks to her "mother instinct." Today, however, parents feel a distinct insecurity about child-rearing in general, as shown by the proliferation of parenting advice from columns, books, magazines, talk shows, and famous experts. The more experts, the more confusion. Today, many parents are uneasy about the job. Parenting authorities (who, after all, see and address themselves to the most confused of us) seem to take for granted that the primary parental emotion is not affection, or satisfaction, or enjoyment, but "inadequacy." What ever happened to mother instinct?

We are coming to understand that instinct is not a blind, inflexible force but a series of nudges, of small reflexive responses

[1]Reprinted with permission from: *Nursing Your Baby Updated for the '90s* by Karen Pryor and Gale Pryor, 1991. Simon and Schuster Pocketbooks, N.Y.

to internal or external stimuli that, added together, tend to produce certain patterns of behavior. There is room for lots of variation, however. Innate behavior does not operate mechanically in every animal, every time; even ants have been found to display individuality in their behavior. It is only by long and careful observation of many individuals that the patterns of innate behavior can be seen.

We know now that unrestricted breastfeeding elicits and promotes appropriate mothering behavior. So it is perplexing to read the current medical research literature in which breastfeeding is seen as an *outcome* of a mother's nurturing feelings when it is in fact a cause. The psychological literature is even more astonishing. Whole schools of thought and research on parent-child "attachment" have arisen in which breastfeeding is completely ignored. A recent monograph titled "Growing Points of Attachment Theory and Research," supposedly a review of all significant new research on parent-child attachment, includes not one reference on breastfeeding. It's as if one were to study the marriage bond without considering sex.

Learned and innate mothering

It seems infuriating that humans, with all their advantages of brainpower, face the care of an infant with minimal instructions from Mother Nature, while any cat or cow or rabbit has the genetic programming to raise fine babies, knowing exactly what to do from start to finish. But is that really true? Do animals have a real advantage over us? The truth is that with animals, as with people, experience is a factor in successful mothering.

Every person who has raised horses or dogs or any other animal knows that mammal mothers do not do a perfect job the first time. Some horses are so nervous with their first foal that they must be restrained by force before they will let it nurse. Laboratory rats may lose some or all of their first litter through inexperience—letting the babies get chilled, or go hungry too long or stray from the nest.

Many dogs are quite incompetent with their first litter. When puppies are born, they, like other animal babies, move toward the nearest large object; when their noses make contact with fur, they grope around until they eventually find the nipples. An inexperienced female may get up and down a lot at first, giving her babies no chance to start sucking, As one kennel owner put it, "It looks as though the bitch is *puzzled*. There they are, ten babies, and she thinks she ought to do something about them, but she isn't sure what. Finally she gives up, and lies down to rest—and it happens."

Experimenters have found that animals have a chance to practice some aspects of baby care before the babies arrive. If a female rat is made to wear a collar throughout life, so that she cannot reach her body and never has a chance to lick herself, she does not know how to lick her babies as they are born. Then they have a hard time functioning normally and making contact with her; generally they do not survive. If a rat is deprived of the experience of carrying things in her mouth, she will not know how to build a proper nest, nor how to retrieve her babies if they stray. It is possible that some house cats arrive at maturity without good carrying experience. A new mother cat, for all her aplomb, may not know how to pick up a kitten. She may spend half an hour taking it by a paw, by the nose, by the tail, before she discovers the scruff-of-the-neck hold. The cat that has had a chance to hunt and kill and carry mice will pick up a kitten properly on the first try.

Observation can be important, too. A chimpanzee that was reared in the London Zoo and had never seen a baby of her own species was so horrified at the sudden appearance of her first baby in her hitherto private cage that she leapt backward with a shriek of terror, and could never thereafter be persuaded to have anything to do with it. Her second, born a year later, she accepted only after her friend the keeper demonstrated its harmlessness and showed her how to hold it. Gorillas are even more susceptible to problems of inexperience. For many years, gorillas born in captivity had to be taken from their mothers and hand-raised if they were to survive. Zoos have now learned that captive gorillas should be kept in compatible groups instead of alone or in pairs. In these colonies, when a young and inexperienced female gives birth, older females not only watch her and the baby, but tend to coach or reprimand her if she does something hazardous, such as holding the baby by one limb or upside down. One zoo had success in breeding a solitary female gorilla when a keeper persuaded a woman friend to bring her nursing baby to the zoo after hours and breastfeed in the aisle of the gorilla house, so the pregnant female could see how it was done. The gorilla watched with every evidence of interest, and was indeed able to feed and raise her own baby when it arrived.

The bonding period

Marshall Klaus, M.D., and John Kennell, M.D., were the first, in 1972, to publish research demonstrating the existence of a special period, in humans, for mother-infant bonding. Scientists knew that such periods existed in animals. In 1935, ethologist Konrad Lorenz, M.D., had demonstrated in geese a phenomenon known as imprinting, in which the newly hatched bird recognizes as its parent whatever it sees and hears on first hatching, whether that is an adult goose or a professor making gooselike honks. The subtle detail was that imprinting can occur only in a brief, critical period after hatching; subsequently, the gosling can never learn to recognize or follow a parent or parent substitute. Helen Blauvelt, Ph.D., demonstrated the existence of a similar critical period in goats. Ordinarily, right after the birth of a kid, the mother smells and licks it, lets it nurse, and from then on recognizes this infant as her own, and will accept no other. This instant formation of attachment is called bonding. If the mother, however, is separated from her offspring immediately after birth for as short a period as one hour, she may never accept it; the critical period has passed.

Obviously, matters are not as critical with humans; we are often (and in the past were routinely) unconscious or separated from our babies at birth, and yet we accept and love them. We can bond to adopted babies and to older children as well. But Klaus and his associates began to look closely at what happens when mothers and babies are not separated at birth. They compared a group of women who first saw and held their babies briefly six to twelve hours after birth to a group of women who were given their babies, nude, to hold (and breastfeed, if they liked) for an hour, soon after birth. A month later, a year later, even *two* years later, the "early contact" mothers behaved differently from the separated mothers toward their babies, fondling them more, holding them more, comforting them more in the doctor's office, and giving them fewer orders and instructions. This study, and work that followed, demonstrated a sensitive period in humans. And it became obvious that mothers in a hospital setting were being denied an interaction that the 1850s mother, whose children were born at home, experienced as a matter of course.

Other researchers have also investigated this phenomenon; the studies have come up with some surprisingly uniform results. Mothers who get some time with their newborns in the first hour of life, *and* have long and frequent contact with them thereafter, show long-term differences in behavior from mothers who are separated for hours and then restricted to six or eight twenty-minute feedings a day, the standard-care hospital routine. Furthermore, the babies of early-contact mothers laugh and smile more and cry less than those of delayed-contact mothers. One study of more than three hundred mothers examined parenting disorders: seventeen months after birth, ten of the delayed-contact, standard-care children had experienced abuse or neglect vs. two of the early-contact group. One study found that the effect of early and extra contact with their newborns was greatest on women who had "low social support." These differences were measurable whether or not the mothers were breastfeeding.

Among those mothers who were breastfeeding, the long-term patterns also showed differences. Mothers who had early contact were about three times more likely still to be breastfeeding when the baby was two months old than were hospital-routine mothers. Early-contact mothers on the average also continued breastfeeding for more months than the control-group mothers, and touched and looked at their babies more during feedings. And at twelve months, the babies of early-contact mothers weighed more.

The "bonding" evidence seems to be catching on. To quote T. Berry Brazelton, M.D., Harvard Medical School pediatrician, '"One marvelous effect of Klaus and Kennell's elegant research has been that most hospitals are sensitized to the fact that they must change to be most effective for new parents." Now, many hospitals are routinely giving mothers —and fathers, too—a quiet hour immediately after birth in which to play with and get to know their baby. Many medical care givers also now delay giving the baby the legally required disease-preventing silver nitrate eyedrops (which sting) until after the first hour, so the baby can keep his eyes open and see his parents' smitten faces.

Innate tendencies in new mothers

One need not conjure up elaborate explanations to understand at least partly why contact in the hour of birth can have critical and long-term effects. The completion of the birth process is a tremendous thrill and relief in itself. Parents' emotions are heightened already by the dramatic birth experience; they begin a series of interactions with the baby, who is also wide-awake and responsive in this hour, in a flood of euphoric feelings. It is the perfect setup for love at first sight.

The standard-care mother, on the other hand, may meet her baby, a wrapped-up, somnolent stranger, a day or more after the birth, when triumphant feelings are long gone, a sore bottom remains, and she has been worrying for hours about whether the baby is normal or even breathing. The father may see the baby at first only through the glass window of the nursery. In the first case, the baby is a powerful reinforcer of nurturing behavior; in the second, a neutral or even a negative presence.

Parents, of course, can become attached to their children without this instantaneous experience, just as one can fall in love at any time during a relationship; happiness does not require love at first sight. Mothers and fathers come equipped with many innate tendencies that help to bridge the distance and to form an attachment to the newcomer, whenever the opportunity finally arises. For example, in light of the evidence that babies are soothed by a sound simulating the maternal heartbeat, researcher I. Salk made a startling observation in 1960. Out of 287 newly delivered mothers the great majority, regardless of past experience or right- and left-handedness, held their babies on the left side, over the heart. This observation has proved to be so sound that care providers can use it diagnostically. The mother who does *not* hold her new baby on the left (like the mother who does not look at her baby while discussing it) may be at risk for what are called parenting disorders: child neglect or abuse.

Another example is the almost irresistible tendency mothers have to unwrap their new baby and look at it all over when it is first brought from the nursery. If the nurses, in the interests of protecting the baby from exposure to germs, are particularly fierce about not permitting this, the mother my do it secretively, and try to wrap the baby up again exactly as it was. But do it she will, with the inevitability with which a little girl of two or three will strip the clothes off a new doll.

Many of the ways we touch babies have innate components. If a newborn is lying on its back, mothers tend to put a hand flat on the baby's chest, middle finger aimed at the. baby's chin, and rock it slightly, in a gentle, rousing gesture. Holding the baby vertically against the shoulder and patting it between the shoulder blades is also a mildly stimulating or rousing behavior. A new mother tends to orient herself so that the baby is looking straight at her, and their heads are angled the same way, or face to face; researchers call this position *en face*. Mothers of preterm babies in incubators may bend over to put themselves *en face* to the baby lying on its side.

It's common for a new mother to place the baby in her lap, facing up, and spend long periods—many minutes, even hours—face to face, looking into the baby's eyes, talking, and touching the baby. One lactation consultant who works with many single teenage mothers teaches them to breastfeed in the so-called "football" hold, with the baby under one arm, looking up, so that the baby's eyes look straight into the mother's. This position tends to make the mother laugh, talk, and play with her baby, bolstering her sense of attachment, a crucial benefit in an environment where infant neglect can be a real risk.

Fathers and innate behavior

Fathers exhibit innate behavior in many of the same ways mothers do. Fathers, like mothers, respond to infant vocalizing by vocalizing themselves. Both tend to begin contact with a new baby by touching the arms and legs, then by touching the body with the fingertips, then with the whole hand (men then tend to stroke the baby with the back of the fingers, which women do not). Men also tend to regard the baby *en face* and will twist themselves around to do so, if the baby is lying down, and they make regular and continuing eye contact.

Men are also susceptible to instant bonding to an infant at birth (although, of course, like women, they can also develop equally strong bonds through later exposure). In many hospitals, it has become customary to use the father as a labor coach and companion and to let him be present at delivery. The hour of birth can be an emotionally intense period for fathers. Yale University psychiatrist Kyle Pruett, M.D., in his book *The Nurturing Father,* quotes a man who had been present for his daughter's birth: "... she opened her eyes and looked at *me—right at me...* Perfect! Just perfect!... the doc cut the cord and put her on my wife's belly, and I touched her. I was sort of afraid because she was so small and soft... but she opened her eyes again when I touched her—like she liked it! A shiver went up my back." Dr. Pruett comments, "What a lucky little girl and mother. There appears to be no turning back from such experiences. This father seems hooked for good." With men, as with women, nurturing behavior, once elicited, flourishes.

Irinaus Eibl-Eibesfeldt, in his landmark book *Human Ethology,* looks at human behavior as it occurs in the natural setting in preliterate cultures. His studies show that even in the most warlike tribes it is not considered unmanly for a warrior to play with an infant; men as well as women spend a lot of time with babies and toddlers, and find them amusing. Fathers share food with babies and toddlers, cuddle, fondle, and kiss them, respond to them in sensible and competent ways, and feel and display affection from the first days on. Studies have been made, also, of middle-class American fathers who take a strongly nurturing role with their babies and small children. Interestingly, both sons and daughters of these nurturing fathers tend to exhibit high levels of nurturing behavior (toward pets and smaller children, for example) themselves.

There are differences, however, between the ways in which men and women interact with babies that are consistent across cultures, whether the parents are primitive Eipos in New Guinea or upper-middle-class Americans. Fathers play with babies more often than mothers, but clean them far less; mothers feeding toddlers, for example, are far more likely than fathers to wipe the baby's face and hands during the process. If a baby chokes, coughs, sneezes, or starts crying, the father is apt to draw back and wait for order to restore itself, while the mother is more apt to intervene. And fathers interact with babies far more actively than mothers, initiating games and motor activity as mothers never do. Fathers are much more likely than mothers to hold babies high in the air, shake them, spin around with them, and, as they grow older, engage in roughhousing and physical scuffles. Babies learn to expect this; as early as eight weeks, an awake and alert baby will respond to the father's approach with hunched shoulders and evident excitement. The world over, mommies are a comfort, and take care of you, but daddies are fun!

Baby talk

One phenomenon in parenting that is hard to explain without reference to innate behavior is baby talk. Every mother and father in the world—every grandparent, too—speaks two languages: their own language, be it English, German, Russian, Tagalog, or Yanomami, and baby talk. Baby talk has absolutely universal characteristics: it is high-pitched, singsong, repetitive, and often ends sentences with a rising tone: "Are you a pretty baby? Hmm? Pretty baby?" It is also apt to contain diminutives, slips or elisions, and grammatical errors, as if a small child were speaking. "Is ums a pwetty baby?"

Like all innate behaviors, baby talk has purpose and value. Babies hear high-pitched sounds more easily than low-pitched tones; and both men and women raise their voices just about an octave when they talk to babies. Repetitions and questioning probably help babies to focus on the sounds more easily than they can on sounds in many-worded sentences; baby talk is actually a prelude to the way we talk to toddlers—"See the doggie? Look, there's a doggie. Can you say doggie?"—and part of the path of learning language. And perhaps most important, baby talk signals to the baby that this voice is directed at *him*. Out of the sea of voices around him, even a small baby knows, from the tone and tempo, when he personally is being addressed, and should respond. This awareness does not depend on eye contact: a three-month-old can be made to laugh and wriggle by the sound of a grandmother's voice speaking baby talk on the telephone. Baby talk, in fact, is a powerful behavior for looping even very small babies into the social circle.

In the 1930s and 1940s, with the advent of "scientific" child rearing, baby talk was denigrated, even forbidden. It was "silly;" it was thought to set the baby a bad example; mothers were told, "Don't talk like that, the baby will never learn to talk properly!" The prejudice continues; in 1990, a syndicated newspaper cartoonist devoted several strips to the amusement afforded by father and grandfather secretly giving way to forbidden baby talk whenever they were alone with the baby. In fact, the almost irresistible strength of the urge to coax response from a baby in this "undignified" manner is evidence for the innate nature of the behavior.

Baby talk surfaces again in adult life during courtship and in affectionate exchange between lovers. Similar infantile exchanges are common in many species of birds and animals during courtship. In house sparrows, for instance, when a pair is being formed, the female chirps and flutters her wings like a begging chick, and the male offers food. While lovers might be embarrassed to have their pet names and baby talk broadcast in public, this undignified behavior is by no means trivial; the use of baby talk, signaling intimacy and dependency, is quite appropriate to courtship and pair bonding.

Adult responses to baby signals

Regardless of presence or absence of early bonding experiences, we grow attached to babies; and to facilitate this hold on adult emotions, babies have a large armory of attributes that function as social signals for eliciting attachment. All animals give and receive social signals, with ears, tail, posture, vocalizations: "Get off my hunting ground!" "Don't hurt me, I'm a harmless subordinate." "Look out! Danger!" "Hey, I found something to eat!" "Shall we dance?" Konrad Lorenz called this kind of signal a "social releaser," a stimulus automatically supplied by one animal that triggers or releases a specific mood or emotion, often leading to action, on the part of other animals in the same species.

A social releaser can be a sound, such as the wailing cry given by a chicken when a hawk passes overhead, making every chicken within earshot run for cover. It can be a scent—the odor of the urine of a female fox, mink, or dog in heat that arouses mating behavior in the male. It can be a gesture—the way a puppy rolls on its back, exposing its vulnerable throat and belly, to plead for mercy. It can be a pattern, such as black or white markings on the tails of many birds, or the phosphorescent array of lights on the sides of some deep-sea fishes, conveying the message to others of the species, "Come with me, we are the same kind."

Human babies automatically present many social releasing stimuli, to which all other humans are programmed to respond. Lorenz pointed out that the whole appearance of a human baby is a social releaser. For basic anatomical reasons, babies are born with disproportionately large heads, bulging foreheads, and large eyes, compared to adults. The very features that adapt the baby for breastfeeding—the fat pads that round the cheeks, the short nose and chin, the small mouth with elevated upper lip—also contribute to a characteristic look that makes us say, "Oh, how cute!" whether we are male or female, old or young, and whether the possessor of these attributes is a baby human, calf, raccoon, or even a duckling.

Soft cuddly contours and very short limbs complete the picture that seems to us innately adorable; this combination of characteristics may he seen in dolls, stuffed animals, and many cartoon characters. Think of Mickey Mouse, or Alvin the Chipmunk, or Bambi: big head, big eyes, button nose, no chin, short legs and arms, tubby tummy—all baby signs. At least two well-known artists have built careers on painting pictures of children and adults that are appealing solely because the eyes are about five times normal size, triggering the "cute" response.

Interestingly, human babies are not born with this full display of "cuteness" but develop it from about eight weeks on; people unfamiliar with newborns are sometimes taken aback by their appearance. The newborn, perhaps, has enough other things going for it to appeal to the crucial people, its parents. Only as the baby grows older does it need to be able to promote affection and forestall aggression from all the other people in the community, no matter what age and sex.

Social releaser stimuli often consist of behavior. The baby's grasp reflex, besides helping him hang on to the mother, serves as a social releaser. At the Yerkes Laboratory in Florida, where chimpanzees have been carefully raised and studied for years, it has been noted that a female that has just given birth is apparently very impressed when her baby reaches out with its little hands and takes hold of her. It is this touch of hands that tells her the baby is one of her own kind. In humans, touching of hands conveys friendship in a simple, universal—and therefore instinctive—way. The firm, responsive way a newborn baby grasps one's finger is a moving experience for both parents. It triggers affectionate behavior.

One easily observed social stimulus presented by all young animals is the infant distress call. This is the cheep, cheep, cheep of a hungry chick, the earsplitting ki-yi-yi of a puppy caught in a fence, the bawling of a strayed calf, the wail of a newborn child. The infant distress call is usually loud, rhythmic, and distinctive. It is not easily ignored. All animals, including humans, react to the distress call of their own species by exhibiting anxiety and distress of their own. As Benjamin Spock, M.D., has said, "The cry of a young baby is like no other sound. It makes parents want to come to the rescue—fast!" It does indeed. It also makes unrelated people highly irritated, adding social pressure to a parent's desire to stop the noise. That is what a distress call is meant to do: to get on your nerves, to make you feel distracted and upset until you can put a stop to it.

An interesting social releaser in very small babies is sound other than crying. From the first weeks of life, breastfed babies murmur as they nurse. Little coos and hums that seem to express pleasure and relaxation can be heard throughout the feeding. A toddler may make the same little singing sounds when he is happily playing by himself, and one can hear the same class of sound—little sighs and murmurs of comfort—from an adult who is enjoying, for example, a good back rub. Richard Applebaum, M.D., points out that bottle-fed babies do not vocalize during feeding, or, if they do, that the sound is apt to be sputtering and grunting rather than cooing, melodious murmuring. Furthermore, a breastfed baby who is switched to the bottle will stop cooing within a few feedings. If she is switched back to the breast, the vocalizing begins again. Probably the artificial configuration of mouth and throat during bottle-feeding hampers the baby's ability to vocalize and eat at the same time. Possibly, however, the baby does not feel the same sublime enjoyment at the bottle as she did at the breast, and so has no emotions of comfort and pleasure to be expressed in pleasant sighs and murmurs. Certainly the nursing baby's little song is received by the mother as a message of comfort, contentment, and love, even if she is not consciously aware of it, and thus serves to strengthen the nursing bond.

Smiling is a social releaser. A newborn baby, when his stomach is full, often smiles—a fleeting grimace—as he falls asleep. While the baby is still very small, four to eight weeks old, this smile of satiety becomes a true social smile. At first, the releasing stimulus for this smile is a pair of human eyes. When the baby sees you looking at him, he smiles. Smiling as he catches your eye is a very valuable instinctive response, and it in turn acts as a releaser for social behavior from the parent, or indeed from almost any human, even another child or a grouchy old man; in fact, siblings and grandparents are often especially elated when smiled at by their baby relatives.

Pheromones

One special class of social releasers is scent. Scents used as social signals in lower animals are called pheromones. In insects, these scents are single compounds giving single messages; in mammals, both the compounds and the messages are more complex, but the phenomenon of scent-triggered behavior is very widespread. Dogs, for instance, use scents to mark their territories and advertise their own presence, and recognize instantly the odor of a female in season. We humans are less aware of our pheromone-like messages—in fact, in crowded cities, we do all we can to erase them, with cosmetics, bathing, deodorants, and laundering. Still, you may have noticed "good" scent markers—the enjoyable scent of the room or the clothes of a much-loved person—and "bad" scent markers, such as the sharp, sour smell of a shirt you wore to a frightening interview.

Scent signals are particularly profuse in the crucial area of reproductive behavior, even when we are not consciously aware of them. Researchers have found that when women of reproductive age live together as roommates or house mates, after a few months their menstrual cycles fall into synchrony; the evolutionary advantage of having your period at the same time as everyone else is not obvious, but the phenomenon is easy to demonstrate, and unconsciously recognized scent signals appear to be the mechanism. Women who live in close association with a man tend to reach menopause later than single women, not, the researchers say, because of sexual relations but of exposure to male body scent. In both sexes, pubic hair and underarm hair are scent traps, concentrating these reproduction-related messages; we recognize that a woman clasping her hands behind her head is in a provocative pose but we don't usually stop to think that she is also sending a scent message.

The fact that the nursing baby smells good is probably more important than we think; it is not just that smelling nice reinforces close contact from adults. Some working mothers who must pump their milk while they are away from home find that the letdown reflex can be triggered by smelling a nightie the baby has worn. Nursing babies put down to sleep in a crib drop off more easily if they are lying on a nightgown the mother has worn. These old, old signals of scent appear to be crucial in every stage of the reproductive cycle; lactation and care-giving behavior are certainly among them.

Kinship

All of the releasing stimuli presented by babies send the same messages to all related humans, not just mothers and fathers. The intensity of the response one feels increases with familiarity, of course; one's own child becomes heart-wrenchingly adorable, while the children of strangers are merely cute. However, if people are hard-wired to like babies, how can one explain cruelty to children? Distorted behavior can arise from disruption of an individual's development, of course, or to individual pathology; and it may also be that humans, like other social animals, tend to favor known kin over unrelated people.

In recognizing relatives, personal experience may be augmented by the nonverbal behavior and attitudes of others. For example, if you are a member of a large family that goes in for reunions, you will be well-acquainted with the phenomenon that children who are cousins, meeting for the first time, may take to each other and start playing together more rapidly than they would with any new schoolmate. Babies and small children can form close relationships with grandparents and aunts and uncles, climbing all over them with the confidence of ownership from the first meeting, when they ordinarily would flee from a stranger. Adults may find themselves bonding strongly to a distant and seldom-seen niece or grandson, in a way they might never do to a neighbor's child. Intellectual awareness of the relationship plays a part, to be sure; but the genes murmur strongly in the background: kinfolk are more important than strangers.

The absence of kinship, in contrast, can disrupt parenting or care-giving behavior; an unrelated child may be seen as a liability or even a competitor. European and U.S. folklore abounds in wicked stepmothers who are good to their own children but mistreat their stepchildren. Cruel stepfathers do not show up as often in legend, but they are not infrequently found in real life. As the newspapers and police blotter testify, no one is more likely to abuse an infant than the mother's "boyfriend"—a male resident of the house who is not the infant's father. Perhaps the innate anxiety aroused by a crying infant causes anger in an adult who has no parenting skills and in whom the absence of kinship takes off the brakes. A more subtle mechanism may be at work, as well; in many mammalian species, including lions, horses, and quite a few primates, a new dominant male moving into a group of females is highly likely to kill or try to kill any present young (which have been sired by some previous male) and replace them with his own. Humans usually control such antisocial behavior, but the genetic incentive is still there.

Breastfeeding—the great teacher

Both on the inborn and the learned levels, breastfeeding teaches new mothers what good mothering is. The innate needs and urges of the mother are met by breastfeeding. The frequent close bodily contact reassures mother as well as child—we all need hugs and cuddling, and babies can give this comfort as well as get it. Breastfeeding requires and creates attentiveness to and interest in the baby's moods and signals. The baby becomes easier for the nursing mother to understand; the comfortable interaction in a well-established lactation builds up a mutual communication, not dependent on words, that lasts long beyond weaning.

The hormones of lactation have a powerful effect on behavior. If prolactin is injected into male rats, they will retrieve baby rats and lick them. In humans, men as well as women have prolactin in their systems; researchers have found that prolactin levels increase in men who are nurturing small children. Prolactin levels are high during pregnancy, and in a breastfeeding mother will continue to be high for as long as a year.

The hormone that triggers mothering behavior most powerfully, however, is oxytocin. Dr. Niles Newton and her husband, Michael Newton, M.D., were the pioneering research couple who first demonstrated that humans have a letdown response triggered by oxytocin, and that the release of oxytocin and the letting down of milk could be inhibited by emotional disturbance. (They demonstrated this in a famous experiment, by tying a string to Niles's big toe as she nursed one of their four babies; if Michael, in the next room, unpredictably jerked the string during feelings—an annoying though not painful event— weighings showed that the baby got less milk.)

Oxytocin production can be reduced by emotional disturbance, but the reverse is also true, and very important for the nursing mother. Oxytocin release in itself triggers emotional tranquillity and strong nurturing feelings—and, unlike prolactin, which has a long-term, slow effect, oxytocin works its magic instantaneously. Laboratory animals that have never had litters will exhibit mothering behavior within one minute of receiving a dose of oxytocin directly into the nervous system. No matter what her species, every time a mother's milk lets down, she is being primed on a very fundamental evolutionary level to cuddle and nurture. (Oxytocin is also the hormone of lovemaking, released during sexual climax in both men and women, although twice as much of the hormone is released in women.)

Many mothers are conscious of the soothing, almost euphoric side effects of oxytocin released during breastfeeding; it can be the working mother's daily high point, on reuniting with her child. A nursing mother is also sometimes conscious of how much she loves this particular baby, as the baby is nestled up to the breast; we now know that the flood of oxytocin, as the milk lets down, contributes significantly to that emotion. Niles Newton, now an international authority on the psychophysiology of lactation, points out that the survival of the human race depends on reproduction, and that the continuance of reproductive behavior depends on the "voluntary satisfaction" to be gained from those largely self-initiated behaviors, coitus and breastfeeding. "Sexual intercourse," Niles Newton has said, "is well-known to foster bonding and care-giving behavior, especially if frequently repeated with the same individual." The same, of course, is true of breastfeeding.

Newton has also pointed out that women who practice unrestricted breastfeeding become physically different from bottle-feeding mothers, not only in hormonal levels, but in galvanic skin response (they are calmer), heart rate (which alters, as the baby cries or is soothed, strikingly more than the heart rate of bottle-feeders), and thermal skin responses, as the mother's breast heats and cools in response to the baby.

If lactation is suppressed, prolactin levels fall abruptly after delivery, and breastfeeding's multiple daily flushes of oxytocin don't occur at all. This hormonal "crash" may be a major factor (in addition to separation from the infant and other loved ones) in immediate postpartum depression, the so-called "baby blues." Not only are all innate urges being frustrated, but the sustaining, love-and-tenderness-inducing hormones are rapidly draining from the system.

The mother who breastfeeds feels this hormonal deprivation much later—on weaning—and much more slowly; as the baby gradually nurses less and less often, the mother's body is weaned from lactation, too. Even so, many women feel some sadness on weaning, especially those who do not plan to have another child. This is not just hormonal; as Newton says, it's only natural: "We *like* to breastfeed."

We are just beginning to see some of the results of changes that have been occurring over the past decades. Long-term studies of cognitive growth, and social and family interactions, as related to duration of breastfeeding are now in progress. Perhaps, as we come to understand more about genetically controlled patterns in humans and the biological advantages of these patterns, we can remove some of the strict rules that our society imposes on such functions as childbirth and child care, and give the natural patterns freedom in which to emerge. Then, one part of the pattern can lead smoothly to another as nature intended. Biologically normal labor can result in appropriate parental responses to the baby; successful early contacts can contribute to bonding and nurturing in both parents; and successful lactation can lead to continued good mothering and healthy and happy children.

Selected references

Bottorff, J.L., 1990. Persistence in breastfeeding: a phenomenological investigation. *J. Adv. Nurs.* 15:201-209.

Brazelton, T.B., 1983. *Infants and Mothers*, rev. ed. Delacort Press/ Lawrence, N.Y.

Bretheron, Inge, and E. Waters, Eds., 1985. *Growing Points of Attachment Theory and Research.* Univ. of Chicago Press.

Cohen, S.P., 1987. High tech — soft touch: breastfeeding issues. *Clin. Perinatol.* 14(1): 187-195.

Eibl-Eibesfeldt, I., 1989. *Human Ethology.* Aldine de Gruyter, N.Y.

Elander, G., and T. Lindberg, 1984. Short mother-infant separation during first week of life influences the duration of breast-feeding. *Acta. Paed. Scand.* 73:237-40.

Goodine, L.A., and P.A. Fried, 1984. Infant feeding practices: Pre- and post-natal factors, affective choice of method and the duration of breastfeeding. *Can. J. Pb. Health,* 75:439-444.

Jelliffe, D.B., and E.F. Jelliffe, Eds., 1978. *Human Milk in the Modern World.* Oxford University Press, Oxford.

Jimenez, M., and N. Newton, 1979. Activity and work during pregnancy and the postpartum: a cross-cultural study of two hundred and two societies. *Am. J. Ob.Gyn.* 135:171-76.

Kemper, K., B. Forsyth, and P. McCarthy, 1989. Jaundice, terminating breast-feeding, and the vulnerable child. *Pediatrics* 84:773-778.

Kemper, K., B. Forsyth, and P. L. McCarthy, 1990. Persistent perceptions of vulnerability following neonatal jaundice. *Am. J. Dis. Child.* 144:238-241.

Kennel, J.H., and M.H. Klaus, 1971. Care of the mother of the high-risk infant. *Clin. Ob. Gyn.* 14:926-54.

Klaus, M. H. and J.H. Kennell, 1982. *Parent-Infant Bonding.* C.V. Mosby Co., St. Louis.

Klaus, M. H., J.H. Kennell, and N. Plumb, 1980. Human maternal behavior at the first contact with her young. *Pediatrics* 46:187.

Lozoff, B., G. M. Brittenham, M.T. Trause, J.H. Kennell, and M.H. Klaus, 1977. The mother-newborn relationship: limits of adaptability. *J. Ped.* 91:1-9.

Millard, A.V., 1990. The place of the clock in pediatric advice: rationales, cultural themes, and impediments to breastfeeding. *Soc. Sci. Med.* 31:211-221.

Modahl, C., and N. Newton, 1979. Mood state difference between breast and bottle-feeding mothers. In: *Emotion and Reproduction: Proceedings of the Serano Symposia,* Vol 20B, L. Carenza and L. Zichella, Eds., Academic Press.

Mori, M., et al., 1990. Oxytocin is the major prolactin releasing factor in the posterior pituitary. *Endocrinology 126*(2) 1009-1013.

Newton, N., 1955. *Maternal Emotions.* Hoeber, Inc. N.Y.

Newton, N., 1971. Psychological differences between breast and bottle feeding. *Am. J. Clin. Nutr.* 24: 993-1004.

Newton, N., 1978. The role of the oxytocin reflexes in three interpersonal reproductive acts: coitus, birth, and breast-feeding. In: *Clinical psychoneuroendocrinology in reproduction: Proceedings of the Serano Symposia,* Carenza, L., P. Panceri, and L. Zichella, Eds., Academic Press, N.Y., p. 411-418.

Newton, N., D. Foshee, and M. Newton, 1966. Experimental inhibition of labor through environmental disturbance. *Ob.Gyn.* 27:371-77.

Newton, N., and C. Modahl, 1989. Oxytocin — psychoactive hormone of love and breast feeding. In: *The Free Woman: Women's Health in the 1990s.* Van Hall, E.V., and W. Everard, Eds. The Parthenon Publishing Group, Park Ridge, N.J.

Parke, R.D., 1979. Perspectives on father-infant interactions. In *The Handbook of Infant Development,* J. D. Osofsky, Ed. John Wiley and Sons, Inc., N.Y.

Pruett, K.D., 1987. *The Nurturing Father.* Warner Books, N.Y.

Raphael, D., 1977. *The Tender Gift: Breastfeeding*. Schocken Books, N.Y.

Rohde, J.E., 1988. Breastfeeding beyond twelve months (letter). *Lancet,* 2:1016. Also Tangermann, R.H., *et al., ibid.*

Taylor, P.M., et al., 1986. Early suckling and prolonged breastfeeding. *Am. J. Dis. Child.* 40:151-54.

Waletzky, L.R., 1979. Husbands' problems with breast-feeding. *Am. J. Orthophyschiat.* 49:349-52.

Waletzky, L.R., 1979. Breastfeeding and weaning: some psychological considerations. *Primary Care,* 6:341-55.

Waletzky, L.R. 1982. The romance and power of breastfeeding. *Breastfeeding Abstracts,* 2:5.

Weisenfeld, A., et al., 1985. Psychophysiological response of breast and bottle-feeding mothers to their infants' signals. *Psychophysiology* 22:79-86.

Whitehead, R.G. 1985. The human weaning process. *Pediatr.,* 75:189-193.

Behavioral photos...

The revising of *Nursing Your Baby* turned out to be a job worth doing. The book regained its nice sales figures. Karl and Gale were able to use the advance toward a down-payment on a house. Gale is now enjoying a fine career as a freelance writer. Parents continue to value the information and, I think, the "voice" in *Nursing Your Baby,* which is now our voice, not just mine. In fact our writing styles turned out to be seamless; there are places in the book where even we cannot tell or remember which one of us wrote that particular passage.

We had one unnerving episode before publication. We had required, in the contract, that we would have approval of the jacket design. This was not vanity, but common sense. When the jacket design arrived, it was attractive, visually, but behaviorally a disaster. There was a mother and a newborn baby on the cover, but the baby was asleep, not nursing; the mother was (horrors!) in a hospital bed with barred sides, and what we could see of her face looked miserable. All the non-verbal implications were appalling: babies don't like to nurse, breastfeeding has to do with sickness and pain, only tiny babies breastfeed, etc. etc.

I was not surprised. Art directors are not paid to think about content, but about color, proportion, placement, and so on; that was why we had insisted on cover design approval. I raised hell, and was told "it was too late to make changes." Hit 'em in the pocketbook, I thought, and said that La Leche League, the nursing mothers' organization, would certainly withdraw their recommendation if they saw this picture. (I don't know if that was true or not, but they would certainly have agreed with us that the picture was all wrong.)

The art director agreed, then, to change the cover; but said that I would have to supply a suitable photograph; and within two weeks. I immediately called a well-known photographer of mothers and babies. She sent me several lovely photos of nursing mothers, in their own livingrooms, in everyday clothes, which I sent to Simon & Schuster. All rejected: too much nudity (you could, in some cases, see part of a breast.)

I knew what S&S wanted; something discreet, and yet professional-looking , i.e. well-composed and in focus. I knew what I wanted: a picture that shows that circle of love, that glowing exchange between mother and baby, expressed in pose, setting, and faces. The trouble with most professional photographs of nursing mothers, however, is that most photographers are male, and the mothers feel self-conscious, and look it. If the pictures by the one woman professional I had located were unacceptable, there was no point in hunting further for a professional source. I decided to take the cover photo myself.

I called a friend who teaches childbirth classes, and got the names of six women who had recently given birth, were attractive-looking, and would be breastfeeding. I called each of the women and explained my aims; they all agreed to pose. I went to their homes and found a pretty place for them to sit, with backlighting from a sunny window. I picked out a shirt or blouse for the mother to wear that would keep her completely covered (in a couple of cases I bought a nice top in colors that would match the book jacket design, and then gave it to my model to keep after the shoot.)

My models were, without exception, intelligent, interesting women with interesting lives. They were also all madly in love with their delightful babies. We had tea and talked. When the baby felt like nursing, I let them settle in, and then quickly took two rolls of film, bracketing exposures and focus. The mothers didn't seem to mind a grandmother fussing around them with a camera, in the slightest.

I took 400 slides in four days. Jon and I looked at the slides, throwing out all that had technical flaws (about half). We threw out all that did not clearly express that glow, or that did not show the mother to advantage. We narrowed the rest down to the six best. Heart in throat, I FedEx'ed them to the art director at Simon & Schuster, two days before the deadline. I enclosed a bill, for the same sum a professional photographer would have charged for a cover shot.

The art director called me. "These are great!" she said. "The only problem I have is deciding which one to choose. But I don't quite understand this bill. There's no name. Where should I send the check?"

I had deliberately made the bill anonymous, lest they dismiss the pictures without looking at them, if they thought they were amateur work. Now, with that problem surmounted, I confessed. "I took them." There was a stunned silence. Yippee. I got the money. And the book jacket looked great.

Roman holiday...

Navy acoustician Jeanette Thomas called me in North Bend and invited me to give a paper in a conference on Cetacean Sensory Systems to be held in Rome, Italy, three years away. I said I didn't know much about sensory systems, cetacean or otherwise, but Jeanette said she needed a good turnout to get funding, and I could always change my mind later. So I accepted. Three years away looked like forever, and besides, the conference was just an idea, at that point.

The three years went by in a blink. Guess what: Jeanette and her European colleague, Ron Kastelein, had not only had created a conference, they had found government travel money for the participants.

The Cetacean Sensory Systems meeting, involving about 200 people, was to be part of a much larger European conference on wildlife. Jeanette asked me to chair a working group, someone else put me on a panel, I gave a poster presentation as well, and thus Jon and I ended up spending about a week in Rome.

I did have something to say that related—sort of—to the topic of dolphin sight, hearing, and other sensory systems. For decades researchers had been interested in dolphin sounds and the role of sound production in communication. To me, however, it seemed that people were overlooking, or forgetting, that dolphin communication is by no means limited to the acoustic mode. This oversight had led, in my opinion, to exaggerated views of the role of dolphin sounds, along with an inadequate understanding of what dolphins actually do "say" to each other using normal mammalian channels such as body English. I particularly wanted to point out the communicative usefulness of a peculiarly cetacean skill, the ability to blow bubbles.

The hundreds of photographs I had taken in the tuna boat nets gave me a fine source of slides. I had used the slides in lectures and publications to illustrate dolphin social groupings. Now I picked a different set out of the same supply and used them to illustrate communicative behavior.

CHAPTER EIGHTEEN

Non-acoustic Communication in Small Cetaceans: Glance, Touch, Position, Gesture, and Bubbles

Karen W. Pryor[1]

Introduction

Behavior enables an animal to interact with and survive in its environment. In cetaceans, as in all other animals, sensory systems exist to serve behavior. Perhaps more than most animals, cetaceans may be said to live in two worlds: their physical universe of air and water, and the social universe of the other dolphins around them. Their sensory systems serve them in both. In the physical universe, sensory systems are used in locomotion, foraging, maintaining physical and physiological equilibrium, and so on. In the social universe, sensory systems are used in communication. In fact, it might be said that all social behavior constitutes communication.

For many years, researchers interested in small cetaceans have concentrated on acoustic communication, partly because it is a conspicuous feature of dolphin behavior, and partly because of the interesting specialization of the dolphin acoustic system for

[1]Reprinted with permission from *Sensory Abilities of Cetaceans: Laboratory and Field Evidence,* J.A. Thomas and R.A. Kastelein, Eds., NATO ASI Life Sciences Series Vol. 191 Plenum Press, NY 1990.

echolocation. Perhaps because of this research emphasis, a common supposition has arisen that the acoustic system is the primary or even the only mode of communication in cetaceans. The assumption has been that life in the water precludes visual and gestural communication (facial expression, for example) and that the acoustic output of dolphins is elaborated, at least partly, due to the necessity of cramming into a single mode the social information that terrestrial mammals convey in many ways.

In fact, in cetaceans as in other mammals all the sensory systems are used in social communication. Chemoreception, the sense of taste and smell in other mammals, has been assumed to be non-existent in dolphins, because dolphins have no olfactory lobe in their brain. Recent work has shown that even chemoreception not only exists, but may play an important role in social communication (Kastelein and Spekreyse, 1990; Kuznetzov, 1989, 1990; Pryor, 1990). And the communication functions of the remaining sensory systems, visual and tactile, are of enormous importance to small cetaceans.

Visual systems

Dolphins were once assumed to have poor eyesight; for example, some early experimenters thought they could only see moving objects. In fact, most species appear to see very well indeed, both above and under water (Herman, 1990; Mass, 1990; Nachtagall, 1986). Cetaceans see monocularly laterally, but have binocular vision downward (and in some species to the rear; Pryor, 1973). In either mode, they readily make eye contact with humans and with each other. This tendency may be the cause of some popular misconceptions about dolphins. In the dolphin, as in many primates, the focus of the eye is obvious; when a dolphin "looks you in the eye" you know it. In cetaceans, however, eye contact is usually brief; the eye does not stare, but quickly moves on. Also, when two cetaceans make eye contact, the dominant animal normally looks away first. In primates, however, like ourselves, dominant animals stare, and submissive individuals break eye contact or look away. Humans, therefore, who are apt to look at dolphins longer than the dolphins look back, tend to feel that the dolphins are "friendly." Their intense and yet seemingly non-threatening eye contact may be a major reason why people develop the feeling that dolphins are in some way human-like or even magical.

Since dolphins literally swim eye-to-eye, and often leap and breathe in unison, they have ample opportunity to communicate with each other by eye contact, both above and under water. Cetaceans convey many intentions and internal states via the eye and surrounding tissues; for example in the killer whale, *Orcinus orca*, the sclerae turn red in aggression. Experienced dolphin trainers can predict behavioral events from eye expression: one can learn to tell when an animal is feeling ill, or when it is about to make mischief, by the look in the eye (Defran and Pryor, 1980). If humans can learn to "read" the dolphin's eye, presumably the dolphins themselves are adept at interpreting each others' visually-signaled information.

Many species of small cetaceans have striking or elaborate color patterns. While such patterns may serve in fish-catching or in predator avoidance they undoubtedly also serve in a social context. Color patterns enable animals to recognize conspecifics. Dramatic or "flashy" color patterns, like the black and white of Dall's porpoise (*Phocoenoides dalli*) may help animals locate each other visually in the open sea or in murky water (Würsig and Kieckhefer, 1990). Individual variations in color patterns, as seen in killer whales, enable humans to identify individuals, and might serve the same function for the whales themselves (Felleman *et al.*, 1990). The Pacific spotted dolphin (*Stenella attenuata*) passes through five different color phases from birth to sexual maturity (Perrin, 1969). In this species, patterns give visual cues to age, status, and social role, as well as to species (Pryor and Shallenberger, 1991). For example, dominant males are marked by conspicuous white jaw tips, which in tropical waters can be seen at 50 m or more: these "white noses" are as much a visual indication of age and status as is the mane of a male lion.

In addition, dolphins can give each other information through visually-perceived gestures and postural displays. An S-shaped body posture is a threat display in the bottlenose dolphin, *Tursiops truncatus* (Tavolga, 1966). In the genus *Stenella* threat displays include halting, spreading the pectoral fins, an S-shaped posture, and nodding or shaking the head with open jaws. Gaping the jaws even slightly (with or without accompanying sound production) is also a common threat display, easily perceived visually at close range. Gestures and postural displays also may be affiliative behavior; in the genus *Stenella* a greeting gesture consists of tilting sidewise to flash the white or light belly at another animal (Norris *et al.*, 1985).

Leaps and aerial actions of some species of dolphins also may serve as visual displays with a communicative function. Different species leap in different ways; for example spinner dolphins (*Stenella longirostris*) popularly are named for their exotic and species-specific rotating leap. Specific leaps also can be related to specific internal states: in many species breaches and headslaps can sometimes be correlated with excitement and aggression (Defran and Pryor, 1980); and spotted and spinner dolphins, pursued in the process of purse-seining for tuna, exhibit an unusual vertical leap when released from the net or upon evading pursuit, that indicates successful escape (Norris et al., 1985; Pryor and Kang, 1980.)

It has been argued that such displays are not visible to other dolphins, since they are likely to be under water most of the time and unable to see through the water surface except directly overhead; and therefore, any social information in leaps or other surface activity is probably contained in the splashing or slapping noises accompanying the activity. The accompanying noises certainly play a part in the communicative value of some aerial behavior. Dolphins however often leap simultaneously or in groups, and can see above water whenever they surface to breathe. It seems likely that the panoply of highly stereotyped aerial displays exhibited by many species do serve as visual signals which are perceived in fleeting glimpses while above the water. Such signals could communicate, perhaps at considerable distance, what species is present and what, to some extent, is going on.

Bubbling

Stereotyped patterns of bubble production constitute a mode of communication in dolphins which is not available to terrestrial animals (Pryor, 1973; Pryor, 1986; Pryor and Kang, 1982). Bubble formations, barely noticeable above the surface, are conspicuous under water both visually and to echolocation. Perhaps the commonest type of bubble display in small cetaceans is the whistle-trail, in which a stream of bubbles is emitted from the blowhole in synchrony with an audible whistle. Dolphins do not need to emit air when they whistle; the bubbles seem to be "added for emphasis." If the whistle is interrupted, the bubble stream will be interrupted too (Fig. 1).

Fig. 1. A juvenile Pacific spotted dolphin emits a trail of bubbles in two sections, accompanying an interrupted whistle sound.

Whistle-trails often are emitted during social interactions and may serve to demarcate the signaling individual. Whistle-trails are produced most abundantly in species which occur in aggregations of hundreds of animals, such as the spinner dolphin. A dolphin which is surprised by an unfamiliar sight or sound may release a sphere of bubbles under water, a "query balloon." Spheres may also be released during play. Released bubbles may themselves be used as toys. During underwater observations within the purse seine net of a tuna vessel, Pacific spotted dolphins were seen releasing torus formations during dominance disputes (Pryor and Kang, 1980). A young adult male engaged in an aggressive interaction with an older male was observed to leap in the air and fall back, creating a large cloud of bubbles on re-entry, and then to escape his opponent behind this "smoke screen." Future underwater observations may reveal other types and functions of bubble displays.

Some aerial displays create almost no bubbles or splash above water, while others produce a lot of spray. Against the dark surface of the ocean, spray produced by surface activity heightens the visibility of many sorts of aerial behavior, and may increase the utility of these actions for visual communication.

Tactile senses

The skin of small cetaceans is well innervated and extremely sensitive. Most species seem to enjoy being touched; acclimated captive bottlenose dolphins can be trained using touch alone as a reinforcement (Defran and Pryor, 1980). Dolphins frequently touch each other. They may stroke or pat each other with pectoral fins, flukes, or rostrum, rub bodies, or swim with fins or bodies in physical contact. Touching is common between females and young, among groups of juveniles, and between males and females.

Tactile contact in small cetaceans also may be aggressive. Tooth-raking occurs in many species: one animal draws the open jaws across another animal's body or extremities, often leaving parallel lines or even drawing blood. In aggressive encounters mates may strike each other with the fins or flukes or ram an adversary head-on.

Positioning

The tactile sense is undoubtedly important to cetaceans in judging water flow and movement, and maintaining position in the water. Dolphins are remarkably stable in the water: a captive dolphin can, if it wishes, render itself virtually immobile in the water, so resistant to a human's push or pull that it seems like a rock set in concrete. The combination of mechanoreception and fine-tuned muscular control enables dolphins to coast in the pressure-wave of the bows of travelling ships, and to travel in storm waves.

Dolphins also may use mechanoreception to coordinate movements with each other. Unison swimming and synchronicity of movement is a conspicuous feature of cetacean behavior. Closely associated individuals often exhibit unison behavior, such as simultaneous respiration and matched leaps or breaching. Unison behavior, in fact, is in itself a statement of relationship. Mechanoreception, particularly pressure sensitivity, may enable dolphins both to perceive and give signals relating to movement, facilitating their ability to synchronize even complex patterns of activity (Fig. 2).

In the eastern tropical Pacific a group of spinner dolphins (Stenella longirostris) leap in unison during rapid travel. [Note: at least two of these are mature males, as evidenced by the enlarged post-anal keels. KP]

Dominance hierarchies are a major feature of cetacean behavior both in captivity and in the wild. Relative dominance can be signaled by position; dominant animals or groups may be slightly ahead of those nearby, or above other groups, or separated from others by wide inter-animal distances. Dominant animals displace others as they pass among them. Small inter-animal distances (a body-width or less) can indicate close or long-term association, and are typical of females and young, juvenile bands, and sometimes adult male pairs and bands. Mechanoreception of water pressure and movement may be vital in the maintenance of inter-animal distance, especially at night, in murky water or at great depths, in a society where the relative position between animals has important social consequences and functions.

It is not unusual for some species of dolphins to travel in silence; killer whales in Puget Sound, for example, neither echolocate nor whistle when hunting seals (Felleman *et al.*, 1990), and bottlenose dolphins are often quiet while traveling. If vision, also, is limited during periods of silence, tactile senses then may help to fill the information gap, providing the sensory input necessary to coordinate behavior, signal intentions, and maintain group structure, in the demanding physical universe of a totally aquatic life.

References

Defran, R. H., and Pryor, K., 1980. The behavior and training of cetaceans in captivity, in: *Cetacean Behavior: Mechanisms and Functions*, L. Herman, ed. Wiley-Interscience, N.Y.

Felleman, F., Heimlich-Boran, J. and Osborne, R., 1991. The feeding ecology of killer whales (*Orcinus orca*) in the Pacific Northwest, in: *Dolphin Societies: Discoveries and Puzzles*, K. Pryor and K. S. Norris, Eds., University of California Press, Berkeley.

Herman, L., 1990. Visual performance in the bottlenosed dolphin (*Tursiops truncatus*), in: *Sensory Methods of Cetaceans: Laboratory and Field Evidence*, J. A. Thomas and R. A. Kastelein, eds., Plenum Press, N.Y.

Kastelein, R., 1990. Marginal papillae on the tongue of harbor porpoises and bottlenose dolphins., in: *Sensory Methods of Cetaceans: Laboratory and Field Evidence,* J. A. Thomas and R. A. Kastelein, Eds., Plenum Press, N.Y.

Kastelein, R. A., and Dubbeldam, J. L., 1990. Marginal papillae on the tongues of the harbor porpoise (*Phocoena phocoena*), bottlenose dolphin (*Tursiops truncatus*) and Commerson's dolphins (*Cephalorhynchus commersonii*). *Aquatic Mammals* 15:4.

Kastelein, R., and Spekreyse H., 1990. The anatomical characteristics of the eyes of a young and an adult harbor porpoise, in *Sensory Methods of Cetaceans: Laboratory and Field Evidence,* J. A. Thomas and R. A. Kastelein, Eds., Plenum Press, N.Y.

Kuznetzov, V.B., 1989. Chemoreception and communication in dolphins, in: *Abstracts,* Fifth International Theriological Congress, August 22-30. Rome, Italy.

Kuznetzov, V.B., 1990. Chemical sense in dolphins: quasiolfaction, in: *Sensory Methods of Cetaceans: Laboratory and Field Evidence,* J. Thomas and R. Kastelein, Eds., Plenum Press, N.Y.

Mass, A. M., 1990. The best vision areas in the retina of some cetaceans, in: *Sensory Methods of Cetaceans: Laboratory and Field Evidence,* J. A. Thomas and R. A. Kastelein, eds., Plenum Press, N.Y.

Nachtagall, P. E., 1986. Vision, audition and chemoreception in dolphins and other marine mammals, in: *Dolphin Cognition and Behavior: A Comparative Approach,* R. J. Schusterman, J. A. Thomas, and F. C. Wood, Eds., Lawrence Erlbaum Associates, Hillsdale, N.J.

Norris, K. S., Würsig, B., Wells, R., Würsig, M., Brownlee, S., Johnson, C., and Solow, J., 1985. *The Behavior of the Hawaiian Spinner Dolphin, Stenella longirostris,* National Marine Fisheries Service Southwest Fisheries Center Administrative Bulletin LJ-85-06C, La Jolla, CA.

Perrin, W., 1969. Color pattern of the eastern Pacific spotted porpoise, *Stenella graffmani* Lonnberg, *Zoologica,* 54:12.

Pryor, K., 1973. Behavior and learning in porpoises and whales, *Naturwissenschaften* 80:4.

Pryor, K., 1986. Non-acoustic communicative behavior of the great whales: origins, comparisons, and implications for management, in: Report of the International Whaling Commission, Special Issue 8, 89-90.

Pryor, K., 1989. Report of the working group on non-acoustic sensory systems, in: *Sensory Methods of Cetaceans: Laboratory and Field Evidence,* J. A. Thomas and R. A. Kastelein, Eds., Plenum Press, N.Y.

Pryor, K., and Kang, I., 1980. School structure and social behavior in pelagic porpoises (*Stenella attenuata* and *Stenella longirostris*) during purse seining for tuna, NMFS SW Fish. Cent. Rept. LJ-80-11C, La Jolla, CA.

Pryor, K., and Shallenberger, I. K., 1991. Social structure in spotted dolphins (*Stenella attenuata*) in the tuna purse seine fishery in the eastern tropical Pacific, in: *Dolphin Societies, Discoveries and Puzzles,* K. Pryor and K. S. Norris, Eds., University of California Press, Berkeley.

Tavolga, M., 1966. Behavior of the bottlenose dolphin (*Tursiops truncatus*): social integration in a captive colony, in: *Whales, Dolphins, and Porpoises,* K. S. Norris, Ed., University of California Press, Berkeley.

Würsig, B., and Kieckhefer, T., 1990. Visual displays for communication in cetaceans, in: *Sensory Methods for Cetaceans: Laboratory and Field Evidence,* J. A. Thomas and R. A. Kastelein, Eds., Plenum Press, N.Y.

To Russia, with love...

Jeanette and Ron's biggest coup was arranging for the participation of about two dozen distinguished Russian marine mammal scientists. Many of the American and Russian scientists knew each other from their papers, only, and were thrilled to be able to sit down and actually talk. Many of the Russians had never been out of the country before. Some had traveled two days and nights, sitting up on a train, to reach Rome.

Most had come with no Western money, a fact a group of us discovered when Vladimir Kuznetzov, sitting with us in the hotel bar, pulled his dinner out of a satchel and offered to share it: a loaf of black bread and a bottle of very strong vodka ("Is NOT for LADIES" he warned me.) Kuznetzov informed us that his supplies for ten days consisted of just that: bread and vodka. From then on we Americans stuffed the Russians with Rome's pizza and pasta and wine, when we could; and sent care packages back to their dormitory.

Some of the Russians had brought their Russian editions of *Lads* for me to sign. Dr. Alla Mass, a vision specialist and former figure skating champion, brought me the perfect dolphin trainer's present, a whistle in the form of a carved and painted wooden bird. We all made many new friends; in fact two years later Jeanette and Ron put on another very successful conference on cetaceans, this time in Moscow, cementing those friendships even further.

Scientifically, the most exciting news to me was Kuznetzov's work on dolphin chemoreception. Since dolphins (and whales) have no olfactory lobe in the brain, and no tastebuds on the tongue, it has long been assumed they have no sense of taste or smell. Practical experience as a trainer suggests otherwise; you should see how expressively a dolphin can spit out a fish that happens to have a broken vitamin capsule hidden inside it.

Kuznetzov had demonstrated in some simple and elegant experiments that dolphins can taste/smell fish in the water, and, one presumes, can chemically sense other dolphins, including lady dolphins in heat. He had found a special organ in the back of the mouth, a cavity lined with tastebuds, in effect, to explain how this "quasi-olfaction" could occur. Furthermore water that is sampled in that cavity is then blown out the blowhole, which explained a lot to me about the spouts of dolphins, who can apparently exhale lots of water right in your face when they choose. I had often queried experts about this common experience of trainers; it had always been explained away as not really happening ("water vapor..." "a teaspoon of water on the surface of the skin, you just *thought* it seemed like a cupful..." and so on.) But no, it really is a cupful, and it's water the animal was sampling with its pseudo-olfactory organ.

A fascinating little training event occurred at this conference. Many of us had slides accompanying our presentations; and the slide projectionist, an Italian student, did not always respond quickly to verbal instructions in English. A Harvard acoustician, Darlene Ketten, got up to give her presentation, and quickly trained the projectionist to change the slide when she pointed. The first few times she had to tell him, point at him, and look at him as well, but she quickly "disappeared the stimulus" until she could just flick her right hand to make the slides change instantly. Darlene was able to tear through a lot of complex and interesting material about whale earbones in next to no time.

The next speaker had slides too; but he relied on the standard system of saying, "Next slide, please," or "May I have the next one now." These changes of wording didn't help a projectionist with skimpy English. Sometimes the speaker had to ask for the next slide two or three times, which of course brought the tempo of his presentation to a yawn-inducing halt.

Worse yet, this speaker gesticulated often; and every time he brought his right hand into the air the slide changed on him, disconcerting him very much. Gradually this aversive event actually "trained" the speaker to keep his right hand in his pocket, though it jumped around in there now and then; and gradually the projectionist figured out when the person was asking him for a new slide, and when he was not.

I was the next and final speaker. I had thirty or forty slides to cram into twenty minutes. It took me three slides, using positive reinforcement (eye contact and a smile and nod), to re-establish Darlene's right-hand flick as the projectionist's slide-change cue. Things went briskly then. The projectionist and I congratulated each other when it was over. And Darlene Ketten and I became friends for life.

Dolphin training: one more time...

One day Ken Norris called me from California . "Karen, I've got a dolphin training problem. Can you come down for a day and fix it?"

I said no. I said it would take four days. I said I'd need my airfare. Ken was aghast, but he agreed to find some travel money. Finally, I pointed out, I was still waiting for his final essay for *Dolphin Societies*. If he'd write the essay, I'd look at his problem. So a deal was struck. Jon and I went to Santa Cruz to spend a few days with Ken and Phyllis, while I looked at the dolphins.

Ken was engaged in a dolphin sonar research program at the Long Marine Laboratory, in Santa Cruz. He was using two large, old female dolphins that had been given to him by the Navy. Both had been captured many years earlier from the coast of Florida.

In the wild, by this age both of these dolphins would probably have been alpha animals, the matriarchs of their own female-calf band of sisters, daughters, nieces, granddaughters, and calves. They would be making decisions, keeping the peace, and driving off nosy boyfriends; they would not be taking tests and obeying commands day after day for some researcher.

Teenage dolphins love a puzzle, and enjoy being trained to do new things. Dominant mature dolphins do not. So there was part of the problem. Ken had the wrong dolphins. In my opinion this was not the first time the Navy had foisted crabby old lady dolphins off on innocent scientists.

When I got to Santa Cruz I also learned that Ken had encouraged some volunteers to participate in his research.

Gregarious and ever the teacher, Ken responds strongly to student and public interest in his projects. He had said, "Come get involved," to fourteen people, all of whom were coming and going and getting involved as they pleased. While the staff tried get the animals to do what was needed for the research tasks, the volunteers were throwing fish, trying to train, asking questions, and trying to pet the animals. Meanwhile Ken himself interrupted training and fed the dolphins, or let his guests do so, at his pleasure.

Ken's trainer, Michelle Wells, was thoroughly competent, but taxed not only by difficult animals and constant interruptions but by dismal working conditions. The dolphin tanks were what I call frog ponds. Good training tanks are set waist-high above ground level so a human being can stand beside the tank and conveniently touch or feed the dolphins. These tanks were sunk into a concrete deck, like a swimming pool, so to reach the dolphin you had to kneel, sit on the tank edge with your legs in the water, or lie flat on your stomach with your arms out over the tank. Try doing any of these things for five or six hours a day, month in, month out; not biologically appropriate for humans.

In addition there was no underwater viewing, so you couldn't watch the animals as you worked except through the surface, and the holding tank gate could not be shut by one person, so it was impossible to separate the animals for individual training sessions. Finally, and this to me was a sacrilege, the food Michelle had. prepared for the dolphins was sometimes expropriated by sea lion researchers at the same lab, so that meals were delayed and dolphins disappointed for an hour or more while Michelle thawed out more fish. The wonder was not that the training wasn't progressing but that Michelle was caring for her charges as well as she was, under the circumstances.

I felt sure I couldn't solve Ken's training problems in two days or four days, if ever. What I could do, I thought, was to pinpoint some problems and to make suggestions and recommendations. I furthermore did not intend to do any training myself; but then Michelle generously gave me permission to try working her animals. What resulted was, to me, a superb example of how operant conditioning, in experienced hands (and fins), can enable one to have real two-way communication with a member of another species.

Chapter Nineteen

The Dreadful Dowager Dolphin

by Karen Pryor

When we got to the lab Ken showed me the way to the dolphin tanks. Ken's post-doc, Randy, and some assistants were draining one tank in order to strand the two dolphins on the bottom to medicate and force-feed them. They seemed to be sick; they certainly were not eating, another little detail Ken had not told me about. I peered down into the tank. The dominant animal, Josephine, was FURIOUS, thrashing the last bit of water with her tail and flinging her head and jaws about at the handlers. She didn't look all that sick to me.

I took Michelle out to lunch and got to know her. Then we called a meeting of the volunteers the next day. About half of them showed up. Michelle and I played several rounds of the training game with them. Shaping behavior is a process, and interrupting the process usually means starting over; it is also distressing for the animal. Playing the role of the trainee, volunteers quickly learned how a dolphin feels when the training is interrupted or inconsistent.

At the end of the second day, when the volunteers and the other lab staff had all left, Michelle was planning to try a last feeding, though neither animal was eating very well. I asked Michelle if she'd like to do a little training together; she said she'd love to.

The first session

We stationed ourselves in separate places on the tank edge. I suggested we start by calling the animals back and forth and having them carry toys between us, behavior which was certainly well within their repertoire. Each animal had a small soundmaker which was supposed to be their "name-cue:" a little bell for Jo and a cricket or clicker for Arrow. You put the toy in the water and operate it; the sound is not heard in the air but is very clear, below.

It was quickly obvious that we weren't going to get anything in the way of organized response right away. Both animals swam by a couple of times, eyeing us. Then Arrow came to me twice, so I got a clicker (her name-sound), and began using it, which led to both of us calling her at once. Michelle suggested she stop and I work Arrow alone.

Fine. I called Arrow over again, using the clicker underwater, and tried to get her to touch a little hoop, neck-ring size, which I was holding in my hand underwater. I gave her whistle and fish each time she came near, though she did not eat the fish. Jo began exhibiting aggression to Arrow. You could hear her making burst-pulse sounds along with the bubbles and threatening movements. In fact I have never heard worse dolphin language; I was shocked. Michelle shrugged; "She does that all the time." Tsk tsk.

As I had hoped and expected, the dominant animal wanted to have all the attention. Jo barged in and did the behavior I was asking Arrow to do: she touched the hoop. I gave her a whistle (the signal that you did the right thing) and a fish which she ignored. It fell to the bottom of the tank. Nevertheless, she touched the hoop again; and then she drove Arrow away from me to the far side of the tank. Fine. I was beginning to suspect Arrow was not going to be able to work anyway unless Jo was occupied; and now I had Jo mad enough to want to work, herself.

Since I had Arrow's clicker in my hand I then called Jo with that sound, making it clear that I meant *her* by starting to click when she happened to come toward me, and stopping the sound when she turned away. She finally came over to me on purpose, which I reinforced by stopping the clicker and presenting the hoop in the water. She touched the hoop and got the whistle and the fish (which she let fall to the bottom unnoticed). We repeated this sequence a couple of times.

To make it easier to reach the water I finally lay down on the concrete with my arms over the edge, a damnable position to work in but less wearing on the whole than crouching or kneeling. Josephine immediately swished by briskly enough to send a wash of water over the concrete, effectively soaking my front side; if there's one thing dolphins are good at, it's making waves.

"She got you wet!" Michelle exclaimed. So what, I thought; it wasn't a cold day. Part of the job. If I had recoiled, or objected, or went away to change my clothes, Josephine would Win, and we can't have that. Josephine also apparently recognized this as a draw; she didn't do that again, though I continued to work lying prone on the concrete.

Then she tried touching my hand very gently with her rostrum, instead of the hoop. This is a dolphin game that might be described as "Let's pretend I don't know what you want;" also called "Maybe you'd like it better if I did it upside down?" I was big about it; I reinforced Jo for touching my hand. She then touched the clicker. I did *not* reinforce that (two can play at being unpredictable, can they not?)

Jo immediately quit on me; she left the training station and went and sulked in the middle of the tank: "If you won't play my way I won't play."

"If you won't play with me, fine, I'll play with the *other* dolphin." I got up and tossed a toy toward Arrow, and from another location started reinforcing Arrow for going anywhere near the toy. This caused Jo to be very aggressive to Arrow, until Arrow was hanging motionless in the middle of the pool, afraid to move. Poor bullied Arrow. I'm sure she didn't ask to live in the same tank with Josephine.

I went back to the spot I'd chosen as Jo's training station, lay down, and went back to work with the hoop. Jo came over more briskly, and touched the hoop promptly when asked, and now was sometimes mouthing her reward fish.

Then she tried another famous dolphin game. She swam briskly up to the hoop and stopped dead about a quarter inch from actual contact. "I can *almost* do it, won't you help me a little?" This is a fine stunt; the trainer is of course tempted to move toward the animal and complete the contact. I have seen a dolphin train a researcher in this manner, over a period of days, to lean so far over the tank, to put on blindfolds, that the scientist eventually actually fell in. (I have had an elephant try this game on me, too; it is a subtle version of keep-away).

"Oh, you're going to do that?" I thought. "Well I know a version of that game too." The next time Josephine swam up and didn't *quite* touch the hoop, instead of being lured into reaching toward her, I moved the hoop briskly six inches further away from her, toward me. She let out a bucket-sized bubble (an indication of surprise) and sank backwards two feet or more (sinking tail-first is a dolphin sign of annoyance).

I called her again with the clicker. This time she came briskly and touched the hoop firmly, and got a whistle and a fish— which she didn't eat.

Twice more, during the session, she quit on me, and when she did, I just got the pool broom and started netting out the fish she hadn't eaten. Not exactly a time-out, but not letting her keep me hanging around coaxing and waiting, either. I made eye contact with her from time to time, too, so she knew I was not through with her.

At the end of one of these pool-tidying periods I came back to the training station, lay down, called Jo over, held a large herring in the middle of the hoop, and asked her (by positioning the clicker right next the fish) to touch *that*, instead of the hoop. Asking a dolphin who won't eat to touch a fish on command? What a dirty trick! Josephine echolocated on the herring, swinging her head around in wild disbelief. When she had to believe her senses, that I was *training* her to touch a fish, she barged by me and rapped the hoop sharply with her rostrum as she passed, hard enough to make my hand sting a little — just as clear a statement of opinion as you could possibly wish.

The session ended somewhere in here. She had eaten nothing, although she had been surprised once when I reinforced her with two fish, and looked them over very carefully.

Michelle then gave Jo a hand signal, asking her to jump, which she did, very nicely. Her final, and usual evening reinforcement was a highly preferred mackerel, which was also her "pill fish:" essential daily medications were tucked in the body cavity of the fish. Jo wolfed two mackerel down, the first vigorous eating she had done in days.

Second session

The next day Michelle was eager for me to have another go, so, with her permission, I did. Jo stood half out of the water on her tail when I came into the training area. She followed me around with evident excitement, and stood up again at the training station, making the most penetrating eye contact with me. She was looking at me not with one eye, as dolphins usually do, but belly-forward with both eyes meeting mine, looking around her jaws, a startling sight (dolphins have binocular vision straight down, but I had never seen one use it to make social eye contact with me before).

I talked to her, which I usually don't do. The hand signals and acoustic commands we give dolphins are very clear in their meaning, and both sides agree to what that meaning is. Conversation, on the other hand, and in my opinion, is a jumble; you may think you are encouraging the animal or pleasing it, when what you are doing is quite meaningless in fact. But here, with this unusual eye contact, I felt Josephine deserved some sort of social greeting. She wasn't permitting me to touch her, so chat was all I had to offer.

Then we started where we left off. Carol, a volunteer, was observing, behind me, and still as a stone the whole time; the animal's eyes never flicked to her once. I praised Carol for that.

Again we started with the recall behavior — come when I click the clicker underwater — and the touch on the hoop. Once I gave her the whistle and then the arm-wave "jump" cue instead of a fish, and she jumped, and got a whistle and fish.

Then I asked her to jump two times for one fish, and she balked. Let's work Arrow, I said to Michelle, but it was difficult to work Arrow from my station, since Jo could interfere by driving her away, which she did, often. So I asked Michelle to reinforce

Arrow for any natural behavior, reasoning that Arrow could earn a fish in any part of the tank.

By this means Arrow was able to do a few little flops and get rewarded for them though she did not eat her fish. As I had hoped, because it is a tried and true way to get an inappetant dolphin to eat, Jo got so mad at Arrow for earning fish that she did begin to eat — she stole fish Arrow had earned and defiantly swallowed them. (One of the volunteers asked me later how much of this improvement was from the training situation rather than from medication for an illness, and thus a gradually returning appetite. Who could tell? I said anything from 100% to zero.)

After stealing Arrow's fish, Jo came back to work with me and at last began eating the fish I gave her, just gulping them down to get them out of the way, I felt, so she could hurry back and see what I had up my sleeve next. And these were herring and capelin, not her favorite mackerel.

I uncovered a couple of other behaviors she already knew, which could be executed right in front of me; I wanted her attention on me, not on Arrow. Josephine knew a "pec wave," a standard behavior: the animal flaps a pectoral fin in the air, often signaled by the trainer waving bye-bye. Josephine responded very nicely to that cue. She knew how to station with her chin on my cupped hand —another standard behavior—when I asked her to. I seldom stationed her; it was more important to keep her thinking and doing. She also volunteered to vocalize.

Except for vocalizing—which we needed no more of, thank you—each behavior earned both whistle and fish. Once I reinforced her with three little capelin. She positively *counted* them, aiming her rostrum at one, the next, the other, back and forth, as if truly astonished. No one ever gave her three fish! I don't think she ate those, but later when I gave her two capelin, she certainly ate both. Once, on purpose to surprise her, I gave her just one especially small fish. She mangled it, and then went by at speed and spat it at me. "Here's what I think of your fish; I spit on your gifts! Take it back!"

Whenever Josephine quit on me, I just cleaned the pool, but I only needed to do that twice, this second day. She was much more "present," active and attentive. One time, after I had won, so to speak, some training exchange, she breezed past me, a yard away, and just lifted her large tail from the water and sailed it past my nose. I assumed she was going to tailslap right in front of me and get me wet, but she just glided by with her tail in the air as if to say "See what I could do if I wanted to?"

I expect she had been given time-outs in the past for wetting people will a big tail slap, which will get you even if you are *not* lying on the deck as I was. So she didn't quite dare actually slap, since she didn't want to stop the fun.

Once, I gave Josephine the jump cue and she "took off" but then didn't actually jump, just went through all the motions. Of course I am too old for that trick, and told her so. In this case, I reasoned that talking aloud to her with laughter and eye contact would be useful, since it would constitute a definite response but neither a positive or negative reinforcement.

I asked for and reinforced a pec wave, and then asked her to jump again. This time she did jump; but she "took off" with a speed-building rush right in front of us, and accidentally-on-purpose made such a big splash, in doing so, that she got all three of us, Carol, Michelle and me, soaking wet. Then she did a fine big jump. Then she bounced up with her head out of water and cocked an eye at us: "Oh, what a shame, you're all wet! But I was doing what you told me to, lady, wasn't I?" You bet. I wouldn't dream of punishing such a nice jump by withholding reinforcement. She'd gotten her whistle in mid-air, and now I tossed her a fish while I wiped the water out of my eyes, laughing.

Until now, to reduce the personal conflict, and also to make the fish more tempting, I had consistently been tossing the fish into Jo's path rather than expecting her to eat them from my hand; but at about this point in the session Jo started bolting her fish. And she also began taking and eating fish directly from my hand. Meanwhile I switched to calling her with the bell, which was Jo's name-cue, instead of Arrow's clicker. Of *course* Jo had initially responded more vigorously to Arrow's cue than her own, just being obnoxious to Arrow and trainer both; but I couldn't let her go on doing so forever, now could I!

Now that we seemed to be getting on working terms, to add variety and keep things moving I decided to ask Jo to retrieve the hoop back to me. I called her over, and let the hoop float away a foot or so, and ran the clicker when she stuck her nose in it. She knew what I meant, all right, but wouldn't fetch.

The hoop floated quite far away, beyond my reach even with the pool brush. Jo went over to it several times, but she tried to bring me Arrow's floating bat, instead. I stopped the sound cue when she did that. (The bat was in the pool because during a hiatus I had tried getting Arrow to bang on it while it was in my hand, in order to "get her going" as well as to provoke Jo out of her sulk.)

After the second bout of Josephine sulking and me netting scorned food from the bottom of the pool, with the hoop floating unretrieved in the middle, I got another little hoop from the toy box and invited Jo to retrieve it to me from just a few inches, which she did, as nice as you please. This let her save face, I thought (and me, too). We did that twice. Jo was docile, almost purring. She even let me touch her on the forehead.

I thought that was a great time to end the session. I got to my feet. Jo thought it was a nice time to stop too, presumably, since she went over and floated peaceably next to Arrow, having a lot to think about, and a slightly full stomach.

Carol and Michelle and I sat down together and talked over what had happened. Most of it had gone by so fast, it was hard for even Michelle to see, and of course they couldn't hear my underwater cues, so the crucial starts and stops, the timing of cues, had been hard to perceive. But they had certainly witnessed Jo's change of attitude. We finished our discussion and put the toys away. To say goodbye I called Jo with her name-bell and gave her a jump signal. She jumped, I whistled, and then tossed in the last four fish in the bucket with a dramatic sweep, a nice little jackpot.

Carol was stunned; she'd never seen anyone give that many fish. I told her it's a question of individual style, which is true. But also an occasional or final jackpot is good technique; it keeps the animals excited and slightly off-balance, and ends work on a high note so the next session begins with happy expectations.

I was touched that Jo had so obviously remembered me when I arrived that morning, and I felt sorry for her now. She's going to feel as if the circus left town, I thought. We left the tank area. Ken came up as Michelle was throwing her arms around me and saying "Thank you!"

"What happened?" Ken said. Michelle said the animals were working again. I was by no means sure that would last (it didn't). Ken wanted details. I was still particularly amused by Jo's angry response when I ordered her to touch a fish for a fish reward, so I told Ken about that. Ken was not amused; he said, "God, you're tough. God, you're mean!"

But I knew that Jo thought I was a friend, and more than a friend: an opponent worthy of her steel. I felt much the same about her.

Retiring lives...

That evening at a small get-together at his house Dr. Norris, at the request of the volunteers who now understood a bit more about training, put Michelle in charge of the volunteers. Also he exercised his might to make sure the sea lion caretakers no longer helped themselves to the dolphins' fish!

The main problem here, however, was that Josephine and Arrow had a long history of being handled by many, many trainers and researchers. They were, really, too sophisticated. They were also too old. My feeling was that Josephine and probably Arrow too naturally belonged as senior females in a female-calf band, where dominance would be appropriate and useful. They should be either retired or released.

I'm happy to say that that is what happened. They were shipped to Florida. Arrow was marked with an identifying sign on her dorsal fin, and then released in her natal waters, where she has successfully taken up life with other female dolphins. Jo proved to have a chronic kidney ailment requiring lifelong medication. That precluded release under the provisions of the Marine Mammal Protection Act. However, she was established in a breeding female band in a research facility in Florida. She is reported as being in charge of the other dolphins but not too bossy—and is happy.

Ken did finish his essay, by writing it at night during the time we were there. The room Jon and I stayed in adjoined Ken's office. He was writing on his new and unfamiliar computer. I slept the sleep of the just, having thrown fish all day, but Jon was amused to hear Ken, through the walls, going "Clickety clickety click ... Damn! Click click click ... God damn!" far into the night.

Ken Norris and his team concluded their research with young dolphins. Ken is now professor emeritus at Santa Cruz, but hardly retired. He is in the Arctic with the *National Geographic,* in China saving river dolphins, in Japan on government business, in Chicago at the ballet, in the desert with returning students. He has two more books out, on spinner dolphins, and another in press. I'm glad we got our joint tasks finished while he was still teaching full-time and had some leisure!

A curious sight...

At last *Dolphin Societies* was finished, proofread, and out of my hands. Jon and I took a trip in Brazil with his brother Scott, a biologist who lives in Brazil, and Scott's wife Raquel, also a biologist. The men were looking at the Brazilian crab fishery. For Jon, it was a business trip. For me it was a holiday. A holiday from dolphins.

We drove from Rio Grande, in the south of Brazil, up the Atlantic coast, not through jungle as I had innocently imagined, but through smoky, industrialized cities, on highways thick with heavy truck traffic. We stopped at fishing ports and harbors along the coast, talking to fishermen and scientists, looking at fishing boats and processing plants.

One night we arrived after dark in a beach resort town called Laguna, on the edge of a huge lagoon, dotted with the lamps of shrimp fishermen. We checked into a hotel and found a restaurant. The restaurant served shrimp: fried, boiled, curried, cold, in sauces; just shrimp. While we were drinking cachaça and debating how we wanted our shrimp, Raquel talked to the waiter. I caught the word "delphines," but paid no attention. Suddenly Scott lit up and exclaimed, "The waiter says we should go tomorrow to see the dolphins here that help the fishermen. Let's rent a boat and go watch."

There have been occasional eye-witness accounts, throughout history, of schools of dolphins and aboriginal tribes jointly hunting mullet; but I said immediately that if such a thing occurred here, which I doubted, it would be a sporadic, chance event, and we shouldn't waste any time looking for it. Besides, hadn't I just finished putting together a Tome on dolphin research? If anything of the sort were happening, I would know about it. And I didn't.

The next morning we drove to the middle of town, where the fishing boats docked at the public wharves, so the men could investigate the crab fishery. The passage from the ocean into the huge Lagoa San Antonio was flanked by a long breakwater with a lighthouse at the far end. Nearby, along the beach inside the breakwater, we saw a curious sight: about forty men in yellow raincoats were standing hip deep in the water in a line paralleling the shore.

"What is going on?" Scott wondered, parking the car on the grass. Mystified, we all got out. There were other cars, and quite a crowd on the beach, although it was a chilly day. There was a person with a pushcart selling sandwiches. Each man in the water, we noticed, had a circular throw-net over one shoulder. A few feet past the line of men, I suddenly saw something very familiar—a dolphin dorsal fin. *Tursiops truncatus*, the bottlenose dolphin, good old Flipper.

There were, at first, two dolphins. I could see that they were indeed helping the fishermen. They appeared to be rounding up schools of fish that swam into the harbor entrance, driving the fish into the line of men, and signaling the fishermen, with a splash, when to cast their nets. Then the dolphins were helping themselves to the fish the nets missed.

As we watched, a third dolphin rolled in the distance, and a roar went up from the beach: "Bate-Cabeça!" The men had recognized "Head-banger," a specially good fish-finder. Bate-Cabeça swam up to the line and began swinging his head around in a personal fishing style (later copied by his younger brother, we were to learn.)

We watched all morning. Scott and Raquel interviewed fishermen. We hired a boat after all, and learned more. This remarkable business was not sporadic by any means; it had been going on all day every day, year in, year out, for nearly a hundred years. And it was, technically at least, unknown to science.

A curious sight: a long line of throw-net fishermen, standing hip deep in the water, wait for a dolphin to drive fish into net range.

CHAPTER TWENTY

A Dolphin-Human Fishing Cooperative in Brazil

by Karen Pryor, Jon Lindbergh, Scott Lindbergh, and Raquel Milano[1]

In the town of Laguna, in the state of Santa Catarina near the southern tip of Brazil, a cooperative fishing method has arisen between local fishermen and members of an apparently resident population of bottlenose dolphins, *Tursiops truncatus*. Laguna is on the Atlantic coast at the entrance to the Lagoa Santo Antonio, one of three large connected brackish lagoons totaling over 30 km in length. The cooperative fishing occurs primarily on the shores of the inlet from the ocean to the lagoon, near the center of town. The authors observed this fishing during 3–6 April 1988, and 15–18 February 1989. During our visits typically 30–40 fishermen and one to four dolphins were present in the principal fishing location throughout the daylight hours.

Fishermen and townspeople report that the fishing takes place all day every day except during bad weather, and all year except in the winter months of July and August. Town records state that the cooperative fishing began in 1847. Some fishermen report that their fathers and grandfathers fished before them,

[1]Reprinted by permission from *Marine Mammal Science* 6(1):11-82, January, 1990. Copyright by the Society for Marine Mammalogy.

sometimes with the same individual dolphins. Currently at least three generations of dolphins are involved (as evidenced by a female, "Chinela," with at least two known adult offspring, one with a calf, active in the fishery).

The primary prey fish is the mullet, *Mugil cephalus:* juveniles are caught in November through March, as we observed in February, and breeding adults in April (as we observed) and May and June. Fishing with dolphins largely ceases in July and August; in September and October other species are reported to be exploited, including the Brazilian croaker, *Micropogonias furnieri,* and the black drum, *Pogonias chromis.* While some people fish with the dolphins for sport, for most participants this is a commercial rather than a subsistence fishery. The catch is sold in nearby metropolitan markets. The dolphin-associated fishery is said to be the primary source of income for about one hundred families.

On both visits we observed and photographed the fishing from shore and by boat, either traveling in the lagoon or anchored among the fishermen or among the dolphins. The fishing is highly ritualized, and appears to involve learned behavior in both men and dolphins. The fishermen, each with a circular nylon throw-net rimmed with weights, position themselves in a single line, a net's diameter apart, standing in approximately 1 m of water parallel to the shore. One or two dolphins station themselves several meters outside the line of men, facing seaward, floating or moving slowly at the surface. From time to time a dolphin submerges, usually moving seaward; the men then brace themselves. The dolphin reappears, usually in a few seconds, travelling toward the line of men. It comes to an abrupt halt and dives just out of net range, 5–7 m from the line, thus making a surging roll at the surface, a movement markedly different from normal respiratory surfacings. Men who are in front of the dolphin as it rolls then cast their nets. Fish are caught under the nets and become entangled in the meshes. Successful fishermen return to the beach to harvest their catch, and others replace them in the line.

The water is extremely turbid; visibility is less than 1 m. The men cannot see the fish, and must depend on the dolphin's behavior to know when to cast the nets. They state that the dolphins detect fish, round them up, and deliver them to the line; the fishing depends on this behavior. Occasionally we observed and photographed mullet jumping just ahead of a dolphin returning to the line; but even when we could not see the fish until they were netted, the dolphins certainly appeared to us to be detecting and herding fish. We never saw a dolphin perform the roll toward the line without exhibiting the submerge-depart-and-return behavior sequence first. The men rarely cast without a dolphin's cue (refolding the net takes time, and one might thereby miss a better opportunity); and nets were not cast behind a dolphin, or in its general vicinity, or in front of dolphins that had not signaled, but only in front of dolphins performing the correct behavioral sequence indicating the arrival of fish.

The cue is quite informative: the timing of the dolphin's roll indicates that fish are present; the direction of the dolphin's movement indicates the location of the fish, and the vigor of the movement appears to indicate whether the school is large or small: the dolphin may show the head, back and dorsal fin, or just the head or blowhole. A spectator can quickly learn to predict whether one fishermen or several will respond to a particular signal.

The dolphins apparently take advantage of the confusion which the falling nets cause among the fish schools to catch fish for themselves. Episodes which are successful for the fishermen are often followed by bouts of dolphin feeding behavior, including rapid changes of direction underwater, waving the flukes in the air, and heads in the air with fish in the jaws. We have seen individual dolphins working at the line for a single pass or for two hours or more, before moving away, often to be replaced by newcomers.

The method is efficient. In one half-hour period in April we observed a single dolphin bringing fish to the line of fishermen six times. In four of these episodes one or more fishermen caught fish, typically 10 or more adult mullet weighing up to an estimated 2 kg each. On February 17 we observed one man, working from a small boat with a single dolphin, who took over 100 kg of juvenile mullet in approximately two hours. The system is probably efficient for the dolphins as well. Based on captive studies, 10-12 kg of mullet would be an ample daily ration for an average-sized adult bottlenose dolphin (Defran and Pryor 1980). Bel'kovich reported dolphins in the Black Sea hunting mullet in groups, using a variety of cooperative strategies; search time could be long, and individual pursuit was often unsuccessful (Bel'kovich *et al.,* 1991). Others have described strenuous pursuit of mullet in shallow waters by individual dolphins (Hamilton and Nishimoto 1977, Shane 1987). The Laguna fishing method provides a reliable, easily located resource, and allows successful fish capture by individuals, including females with calves, with minimal effort.

The fishing appears to be initiated and controlled by the dolphins, not by the men. On four occasions we have seen a dolphin leave the line of men and move to another section of the beach; immediately some or all of the men ran through the water to reform a line in the new site selected by the dolphin. In other parts of the lagoon on several occasions we have seen one or more men waiting on shore in the hope of a dolphin's arrival. Fishing does not begin until a dolphin initiates it.

While wild bottlenose dolphins in other parts of the world have been known to play or socialize with swimmers and boaters, notably at Monkey Mia in Australia (Connor and Smolker 1985), such informal interaction apparently does not occur at Laguna. At no time did we observe a fisherman call out, signal to, or in any way attempt to affect the behavior of a dolphin. The fishermen do not consider that they train the dolphins. They never give them fish. They do not attempt to touch them. Several fishermen said that it is important not to distract the dolphins from their work.

The local population of bottlenose dolphins is estimated by experienced fishermen at about 200. Of these an estimated 25-30, referred to as "good" dolphins, are said to be participants in the cooperative fishery. On 17 February from a boat in the inlet we saw six separate groups (varying in size from 1-3 dolphins and 4-40 men) engaged in cooperative fishing in different locations simultaneously. We were able to see a maximum of 10 adult dolphins working at the same time. Including juveniles and calves at least 10 more dolphins, which may or may not have been associated, were also present in the inlet.

The participating dolphins are named and recognized by many fishermen. Animals which we ourselves could recognize by marks and scars were correctly identified by several fishermen at a distance of 50 m or more, sometimes before the identifying marks could be seen. The men have deliberately marked some dolphins with dorsal fin notches or cuts for identification purposes (the opportunity typically arises when a calf rushes ahead of its mother and is accidentally caught under a net). In February in the lagoon inlet we saw and photographed five such individuals, including one we had photographed in the same location the previous April.

Dolphins which do not work with the fishermen are called "bad" dolphins *(ruim* in Portuguese). The *ruim* may occasionally interfere with the fishing, typically by dispersing fish and by damaging nets and netted fish. "Good" dolphins are said to defend their resource by displaying aggression toward the *ruim;* we did not witness any encounters between the two (we have seen several groups of 2–7 dolphins, identified by the fishermen as *ruim,* offshore and in central parts of the lagoon). The fishermen consider that the "good" dolphins are largely resident in the lagoon. Some believe that there are at least two separate populations of *ruim,* one in the lagoon and one coastal or offshore. Confirmation of the distribution and range of these groups awaits future investigation.

We interviewed eight experienced dolphin fishermen, as well as some townspeople and family members. We have collected 22 names of individual dolphins so far, some with preliminary identification sketches or photographs, and some with life history information. The age of an animal is sometimes known, especially if it has distinguishing marks or if it shares a birthdate with a person in the fishing community. Matrilineal relationships are recognized for some animals. Laurenci Zeferino, a Laguna fisherman locally considered to be an expert on working with the dolphins, provided extensive information on dolphin associations and kinship. However disparities exist in reports from different informants (for example some animals may have two names) which will require further investigation and clarification.

The "good" dolphins appear to constitute an interactive social group consisting of several females, their calves, some but not all of their previous offspring and their descendants, and a mixed-age group of males. Calves are said to remain with the mother for about three years. They then join juvenile bands which do not participate in the fishing. Animals begin participating in the fishery as young adults; the calf of a fishing female may or may not rejoin the "good" dolphins, but at this stage in our investigations all recruitment appears to be from such calves. This picture, if accurate, is consonant with the social structure of female-calf bands and associated male bands described by Wells and others in the resident bottlenose dolphin population in Sarasota Bay on the west coast of Florida (Wells *et al.*, 1980, 1987).

Several historical accounts exist of dolphin-human interaction in the catching of mullet (Pliny the Elder, A.D. 23—79, Longman 1926, Busnel 1973, Ascherson 1982). Ranging from the Mediterranean to North Africa to Australia, these accounts are strikingly similar. Men on shore observe mullet travelling along the coast, too far out to reach from land. Then, if bottlenose dolphins happen to be passing simultaneously, the men shout, whistle, or slap the water to attract the dolphins. If the dolphins then move inshore, the mullet are trapped against the beach, and a great melee follows, with men scooping or spearing mullet in the shallows and fish and dolphins leaping in every direction.

The similarity of these accounts, centuries and continents apart, suggests that they are basically accurate. These previous accounts, however, do not resemble the complex choreography of the Brazilian dolphin-human fishery, in which dolphins work individually, and in which the fishing is initiated and controlled by the dolphins. Furthermore these earlier episodes of joint predation, while surely involving some learned behavior, appear to have been sporadic, opportunistic, and seasonal, related to the inshore movement of adult breeding mullet. The Laguna dolphins in contrast have developed techniques which can be adapted to juvenile mullet or other prey and which provide the dolphins and the humans with a reliable and almost year-round resource.

Shane (1987) has shown that bottlenose dolphins in the Gulf of Mexico fish in varied ways. Dolphins may fish in deep water or in shallow; some have learned to take fish discarded by shrimp boats. Shane postulates that individual dolphins may specialize in particular feeding behaviors, as has been shown for humpback whales (Weinrich 1982) and for killer whale pods (Felleman *et al.*, 1991). Since dolphins learn by observation (Herman 1980) feeding specializations might be transmitted culturally within long-term associations of related individuals. Laguna's "good" dolphins may represent an example of a culturally transmitted fishing specialization.

We thank Sam Liberman, Buenos Aires, Argentina, and Floramerica, Inc., Miami, Florida, for the research opportunities so generously accommodated during consulting duties in Laguna and elsewhere in Brazil. S. Lindbergh, R. Milano and L. Lloyd-Clare provided translations for our interviews with fishermen and townspeople. We are grateful to F. G. Woods and Victor Scheffer for much-appreciated editorial suggestions, and to William Schevill and Bernd Würsig for their advice and their assistance in tracking down references.

References

Ascherson, P. 1892. Note in *Sitzungsberichte der Gesellschaft naturforschender Freunde zu Berlin* 8:145-148.

Bel'kovich, V.M., E. E. Ivanova, O. V. Yefremenkova, L. B. Kozarovitsky and S. P. Kharitonov. 1991. Searching and hunting behavior in the bottlenose dolphin *(Tursiops truncatus)* in the Black Sea.. In *Dolphin Societies: Discoveries and Puzzles,* K. Pryor and K. S. Norris, Eds., University of California Press, Berkeley, CA.

Busnel, R.G., 1973. Symbiotic relationship between man and dolphins. *Transactions of the New York Academy of Sciences* 35:112-131.

Conner, R.S., and R.S. Smolker, 1985. Habituated dolphins *(Tursiops* sp.) in western Australia. *Journal of Mammalogy* 66:398-400.

Defran, R.H., and K. Pryor, 1980. Social behavior and training of eleven species of cetaceans in captivity. In: *Cetacean Behavior: Mechanisms and Functions.* L. M. Herman, Ed., John Wiley and Sons, New York.

Felleman, F.L., J.R. Heimlich-Boran and R.W. Osborne. 1991. The feeding ecology of killer whales *(Orcinus orca)* in the Pacific Northwest. In *Dolphin Societies: Discoveries and Puzzles*, K. Pryor and K. S. Norris, Eds. University of California Press, Berkeley, CA.

Hamilton P.V., and Nishimoto, R.T., 1977. Dolphin predation on mullet. *Florida Science* 40:251-252.

Herman, L.M., 1980. Cognitive characteristics of cetaceans. In *Cetacean Behavior: Mechanisms and Functions,* L. M. Herman, ed. John Wiley and Sons, New York.

Longman, H.A., 1926. New records of Cetacea, with a list of Queensland species. *Memoirs of the Queensland Museum* 8:266-278.

Pliny the Elder, A.D. 23—79. *Natural History, Vol. III, Libri VIII-XI;* H. Rackham, translator, 1940. Loeb Classical Library, Harvard University Press.

Shane, S., 1987. The behavioral ecology of the bottlenose dolphin. Ph.D. thesis,University of California at Santa Cruz. 147 pp.

Weinrich, M., 1982. The humpback whales of Stellwagen Bank. *Whalewatcher* 16(4):12-15.

Wells, R.S., A.B. Irvine, and M.D. Scott, 1980. The social ecology of inshore odontocetes. In: *Cetacean Behavior: Mechanisms and Functions,* L. M. Herman, Ed. John Wiley and Sons, New York.

Wells, R.S., M.D. Scott and A.B. Irvine, 1987. The social structure of free-ranging bottlenose dolphins. *Current Mammalogy, Vol. I.,* H. H. Genoways, Ed. Plenum Press, New York.

Part Five

New Worlds
1992 to...

Karen Pryor and Gary Wilkes teaching operant conditioning to 250 dog trainers, veterinarians, and other professionals, in a two-day "Don't Shoot the Dog" training seminar; this one is at the University of Guelph Veterinary College, near Toronto, in 1994

Going to the dogs...

Don't Shoot the Dog! was about changing behavior with positive reinforcement, using the principles of operant conditioning. It was *not* about dogs, per se, in spite of the title. Oh, there are a few dogs in there as examples, but really the book is about people. Nevertheless, dog trainers began buying it. And there were a lot of them out there.

When I was competing with my Weimaraner in the 1950's, obedience training was a rather esoteric sport. Now it has become enormously popular, with regional and national competitions all year long, and tens, perhaps hundreds, of thousands of people striving to train their household pets to competition level.

One day Sue Cone, the president of NADOI, the National Association of Dog Obedience Instructors, phoned me and asked me if I'd like to give a few hundred dog training instructors an all-day workshop based on my book.

No, I would not. I knew how to write about operant conditioning, but talking about it would be an unfamiliar task. I didn't even know if I *could* talk all day long; and finally, I was not a dog handler and did not want to deal with strange dogs and maybe get bitten. I named a prohibitive fee. "Fine," she said.

That was the beginning of a delightful acquaintance with Sue and with many other dog training enthusiasts of all sorts. The first workshop was hard, but the next year I did another, and then a couple more, lured into it partly by the respectable fees, and partly by my increasing fascination with what these ardently enthusiastic trainers did *not* know.

They knew a fair amount about ethology, the biological aspects of behavior; but they knew next to nothing about the science underlying learning. Operant conditioning and reinforcement theory had been in development for thirty years; but these people had no access to that information. They had no idea how it related to their work and interests. Furthermore, they were beset with problems in their work that could have been avoided through better theoretical understanding.

The problem most obvious to the trainers themselves was that many popular "systems" of training relied heavily on physical punishment, from yanking and yelling to pronged collars, ear pinching, and electric shock. My book opened the door to training successfully, and perhaps competing and winning, without having to do any of those horrid things to your nice dog.

The problem most obvious to me, as I talked to and with dog trainers, was that the obedience trainers did not understand the use of the conditioned reinforcer. The dog trainers used praise and thought they were telling the dog something; but often they used it in ways that did not work as reinforcement. Furthermore, without understanding conditioned reinforcers and how to use them, these trainers couldn't really understand behavior chains, shaping, extinction, stimulus control and all of the other phenomena which they needed, and used, and were at the mercy of, whether they knew it or not.

We got to know a few trainers in the North Bend area. People brought me problems, stopped by with questions, brought out-of-town experts over to chat. Jon and I and our border terrier sometimes went to watch search-and-rescue dogs practice. While I studied breakdowns in the training, Jon developed a popular sideline as the Escaped Criminal. He remains much in demand for his ability to lay fiendishly hard trails across water and from tree to tree, and for cheerfully staying out in the cold rain for hours while one dog after another tries to find him.

The rising popularity of *Don't Shoot the Dog!* led to the commissioning of this article in Canada's leading dog magazine.

CHAPTER TWENTY-ONE

A Dog and a Dolphin: Training without Punishment

by Karen Pryor[1]

Dogs, dolphins, and training

If you've seen trained dolphin shows at oceanariums or on TV, you will know that dolphins appear to be wonderfully trainable. On command they exhibit all kinds of precision behavior, including splendid acrobatics and interactive behavior with other dolphins or with human swimmers. The audience marvels at how eagerly they respond, and how intelligent they must be; wouldn't it be nice if dogs responded like that?

As we dolphin trainers know well, the truth is that dolphins aren't geniuses, and neither are dolphin trainers. The dolphins' speed, precision, and obvious enjoyment of their work is due *entirely* to the principles dolphin trainers use in training them. And the same techniques can be used on dogs.

Omitting punishment from the start

The first thing to understand about dolphin training is that we are working with animals you *can't* punish. No matter how mad you get — even if the animal makes you mad on purpose,

[1]Reprinted with permission from *Dogs in Canada* Annual, 1992.

by splashing you from head to foot, say — you can't retaliate.

Maybe you're thinking "I bet I could think up a way to punish a dolphin...." and I bet you could; but it doesn't matter, because dolphin trainers don't need it. Trainers can get whatever they want from a dolphin, using positive reinforcement only: mostly just a chirp or two from a training whistle, and a bucket of fish. We "shape" every behavior by positive reinforcement. We use positive reinforcement to elicit prompt and correct response to commands—to achieve obedience. We can even use positive reinforcement to discipline an animal—to control misbehavior such as attacking a tank mate or refusing to go through a gate. This sophisticated use of positive reinforcement results in an animal that works brilliantly and *loves* to work.

The methods we use to train dogs often include the use of force, both to put the dog through required movements and to correct the dog when it makes mistakes, which it inevitably does. Although we may also use praise and petting, unavoidably the dog experiences some confusion, fear, and maybe even physical pain in the training process. Some dogs tolerate these negative experiences well, but dolphins, being wild animals, would not. If you were to train a dolphin by these techniques, the dolphin might learn, but it would offer a sluggish, sulky, unreliable performance; and it might well begin to exhibit aggression toward people. (Does that sound like any dogs you know?)

On the other hand if you train a dog the way we train dolphins, through positive reinforcement, the dog behaves just like a dolphin: it becomes eager, attentive, precise, cooperative, and capable of fantastic performance. Here's how it's done.

The magic signal: conditioned reinforcers

When I talk to dog trainers a big misconception I run into is that positive reinforcement just means "food." Wrong. The crucial element in getting wonderful behavior out of a dolphin is *not* the food reward. The dolphin is not working for the fish; the dolphin is working for the whistle. The sound of the whistle is the magic signal that brings about that wonderful performance.

The first step in training a dolphin is to teach it that every time it hears a whistle, it's going to get a fish. Once the animal knows that the whistle means "Fish is coming," the trainer can use the whistle to *mark* a behavior she likes, and then, gradually, to shape or develop something more complex, such as a response to a cue.

For example: Suppose, on several occasions, the dolphin heard the whistle (and later got a fish) when it happened to be jumping in the air. Soon it would start jumping every time the trainer showed up. Then it might be allowed to discover that jumping only "works" when the trainer's arm is raised. So a raised arm becomes the green light, as it were, for jumping.

The trainer could gradually impose other conditions — jumping only "works" when the direction of the jump is away from the trainer and toward the audience; when the jump is higher than four feet; when the jump occurs within three seconds after the arm is raised. At the end of a few training sessions the trainer has trained the dolphin to "take a bow," on command and with precision; and the dolphin has trained the trainer too: "All I have to do is make a certain kind of jump when she sticks her hand up, and she immediately gives me a whistle and a fish every time!"

Note that the whistle is *not* used as a command. It does not tell the dolphin to start doing something — the hand signal does that. The *whistle* tells the dolphin, during or at the end of a behavior, that the trainer likes that behavior and the dolphin deserves a fish for it. (You don't have to stick with food, either; you can also associate a conditioned reinforcer with a pat, or a toy, or maybe just another chance to work.)

The whistle has now become a conditioned reinforcer. In the language of psychologists, food, petting, or any other pleasure is an *unconditioned* reinforcer — something the animal would want, even without training; the whistle, a *conditioned* reinforcer, is something the animal has *learned* to want. (Some people use the term "primary reinforcer" for food and "secondary reinforcer" for the signal; I avoid those terms because I find it leads people to think that if the whistle is "secondary" it should occur *after* the food, which of course makes it meaningless to the animal and useless as a training tool).

Why the conditioned reinforcer is crucial

What would happen if you tried to train a dolphin to do a simple jump, away from you, on cue — without the whistle? First, you could not possibly time the fish to arrive when the animal was in mid-jump; so no matter what kind of jump the animal gave, it would either get the fish later, or get no fish at all. It would have no way of telling why you rewarded one jump over another or what you liked about the jump. Was it the height? Or maybe the way the animal took off or landed? To develop a jump of a particular height, timing, and direction you would have to eliminate mistakes by trial and error over many, many repetitions; you would be lucky if the animal didn't get bored (and the trainer too!) before the performance was correct and reliable.

Because of this lack of information, the trainer who uses a food reward without using a conditioned reinforcer first typically produces an animal that works eagerly (as long as it is hungry) but learns slowly. We see this in dogs that have been rewarded with lots of treats without any clear signal as to why; they often seem to be enthusiastic and friendly but they don't know anything.

Also when a trainer uses food without a conditioned reinforcer the animal is apt to look toward the trainer for food all the time. Horses nose your pockets and dogs lick your hands. Dolphins hang around the training station and worship the fish bucket. And with the animal constantly looking at the trainer it would be difficult to train our dolphin to jump facing *away* from the trainer, toward the audience. Once you've established the conditioned reinforcer, however, you can use the whistle to reinforce behavior that occurs at a distance, or with the animal facing away from you, with no trouble at all. And the well-conditioned animal, instead of nosing around for a snack, is going on about its business, but also attentively *listening* for the magic sound, whatever else it may be doing. In horses and dogs as well that attentiveness is a valuable training asset in itself.

Because of the split-second timing that the conditioned reinforcer makes possible, the whistle also communicates just exactly what it is that the trainer is looking for. This allows you to teach the animal what you want, in a very clear way, one detail at a time. For example, let's say that a dolphin has assimilated one rule ("Jump facing this way"), and you know that because the animal almost always jumps with the proper orientation, when you signal it to jump. Now you can add another detail or rule. You decide—"I'll only reinforce the higher jumps." Pretty soon the dolphin has learned one more detail ("I have to jump facing this way *and* jump this high.")

This step by step process may seem elaborate but in practice it is a fantastic short cut to complex trained behavior. Even with a naive dolphin, a trainer can develop an on-cue, spectacular, and very specific behavior, such as the bow I've described, in two or three days—sometimes, if things go well, in a single ten-minute training session. Many times in my dolphin training experience I have "captured" a behavior, shaped it into something special, and put it on cue in a single training session; and so have other dolphin trainers.

How about dogs?

You can easily experience dolphin-training your own dog, using a conditioned reinforcer, in one quick ten-minute experiment. Some dogs are afraid of whistles. A handy conditioned reinforcer for dogs is a clicker, a child's toy that goes click-click when you pinch it; they are available in toy and novelty shops and some import stores [and now from Sunshine Books, Inc., Karen Pryor and Jon Lindbergh, prop., (206) 888-3737. KP]

Get yourself a clicker and a few treats. Make the treats small enough so that you can give the dog fifteen or twenty treats without him filling up. Some dogs will work for kibble, especially just before dinnertime, but you might have to go to something more tempting; in demonstrating this with strange dogs I generally use diced chicken. Teach the dog the meaning of the click by clicking the clicker and giving a treat, four or five times, in different parts of the room or yard (so the dog doesn't get any funny ideas that this only works in one place).

Then click the clicker and delay the treat a few seconds; if you see the dog startle and actively look for the treat, you will know the signal has become a conditioned reinforcer. Now you can establish a behavior —we call this "shaping."

An easy behavior to shape is "chase your tail." There are, of course, as many ways to elicit this behavior as there are trainers to think them up: you could turn the dog around by its collar; you could put bacon grease on its tail tip so the dog circles to lick its tail. Here's one way to shape the behavior "from scratch," without any prompting.

Stop clicking and just wait. Your dog may be intrigued and excited by now; when you do nothing, the dog is likely to move around, and maybe even to whine and bark. The instant the dog happens to move or turn to the right, click your clicker. Give the treat.

Wait again. Ignore everything the dog does, except moving to the right (don't hold out for miracles; one turn of the head or one sideways step with the right front paw is all you need.) If you "catch" the behavior — if your timing is good — in three or four reinforcements you will see your dog turning to the right further and more often.

Now you will find you don't need to reinforce just a single step to the right, but can reinforce right turns that go several steps, perhaps through a quarter of a circle; and, from a quarter turn, a full circle may come very quickly.

That's a good time to stop the first session: quit while you're ahead is the golden rule. Put the clicker away, with lots of hugs and praise, and try again the next day, starting with a single step, then a quarter circle, and then more; it will come much faster the second time.

From one circle, the next step is to get two circles, and the next step — an important one — is to go for a variety, rewarding half a circle sometimes, then two circles, or one, or three full turns, or just one and a quarter; this keeps the dog guessing. The click might come after one turn, or two, the dog doesn't know, so he keeps turning, faster and faster; and thus you begin to develop an amusing whirl after his own tail.

This is a silly trick, of course, and not very dignified; there are other behaviors you could use for practice, such as targeting, in which you shape the animal to touch some object with its nose (sea lion trainers teach their animals to "target" on the trainer's closed fist; then by holding their fist on the ground or in the air or over a stand they can move the sea lion where they want, without using force). The purpose of this experiment is not to teach the dog the trick, but to show *you* how to use a conditioned reinforcer to shape behavior, and how effective this kind of reinforcement can be.

Why do you need to use a clicker? Why couldn't you just use your voice, and the words "Good boy," as the conditioned reinforcer? The main reason is that you can't say a *word*, even "Good boy," with the split-second precision that you can achieve with a click. With the clicker and a little practice you can reinforce very tiny movements—one paw stepping to the right—in the instant that it occurs; a praise word is inevitably rather "fuzzy," because it takes longer.

The second difficulty with using a word is that we also talk near our dogs and even *to* our dogs when we are not reinforcing them. It is hard for the dog to sort the meaningful words out from the stream of noise we make; but the clicker is unlike any other sound in the room, and its meaning is crystal clear. You will in fact see the difference very clearly in the way the conditioned dog responds to the clicker (electric attention, galvanized, thrilled) as compared to the way the dog responds to "Good dog!" (Hunh? Oh. Smile, wag.)

Using a conditioned reinforcer in the real world

"Well," I've heard dog trainers say, "the clicker's good for tricks but not for anything else — you can't, for example, use it in the obedience ring." Of course not, and you don't need to. The clicker's value is in shaping new behavior, or refining details; it's not necessary in exhibiting behavior the animal has already learned. But even in the accomplished champion working dog, the conditioned reinforcer can be a useful training tool. One competitor told me he taught his Doberman to understand the clicker, and then used it to reinforce her for looking into his face, instead of away from him, while she worked. "It's as if she were grateful for the information, really: it cleared up the vagueness, for her," he said. Of course once the dog had come to understand what was wanted, she did it correctly in the ring, without any clicks.

Don't think, however, that people never use a conditioned reinforcer in the ring; all the trainer has to do is establish a signal the dog is aware of that no one else notices. I know a keen obedience trainer who uses a barely audible sniff as a conditioned reinforcer. I have seen a competitor convey "Great job!" (as evinced by the overjoyed expression on the dog's face) just by touching one finger to her dog's head.

One competitor I know has taught her dog, Rex, that treats are called "Billy." Then as the dog performs in the obedience ring, she can reinforce an especially good behavior—a nice recall perhaps—with what appears to be a command: "Billy, heel!" No one questions why she doesn't use the dog's usual name in the ring.

Once a behavior is learned, there's no rule that says you have to give a tidbit for every click; so using a conditioned reinforcer allows you not only to delay the food, without loss to the performance, but to give less food overall; you don't have to worry that your animal will fill up before the job is done. One example: at dog shows I have often noticed handlers repeatedly baiting or feeding a dog to get nice pose or alert look. Whenever I see that food-food-food going down the dog's throat I know at once that the person doesn't understand conditioned reinforcers! How much more effective it would be to "shape" the pose, develop a cue ("Ten-shun!") and then reinforce the dog with a click for assuming and holding the proper posture a respectable length of time—with the actual food following later, outside the ring or when the judge has moved on.

Another virtue of the conditioned reinforcer is that it works—it conveys information, and affects the animal's behavior—in all kinds of situations in which real reinforcement is not merely undesirable but in fact impossible. Think for example of how useful a simple conditioned reinforcer would be in training scent discriminations, tracking, long sits and downs, go-outs, pointing and flushing birds, and all other dog behaviors that require the animal to work away from you.

Controlling misbehavior with positive reinforcement

It might seem unreasonable that you can control bad behavior with positive reinforcement instead of "correction," but dolphin trainers have many ways to do it. Here are three examples:

• Establish a conditioned negative reinforcer: this does not need to be a signal that means "I'm going to beat you" (although you could establish that, too) but a signal that means "Nope, I'm not going to reinforce you." It tells the animal that some particular effort it is making is not going to pay off; the animal swiftly learns that whenever it gets this "red light" or "Wrong" signal it should change what it is doing. You could use such a signal, for example, to help teach a dog not to jump up, in greeting, but to keep its paws on the floor for a patting reinforcement.

• Use positive reinforcement to train an incompatible behavior: in our dolphin shows at Sea Life Park one animal took to harassing the girl swimmer who performed in the show. Rather than give the swimmer a stun gun (or some such punishment) we trained the dolphin to push on an underwater lever, for a whistle and fish, and we asked the animal to do that when the swimmer was in the water. The dolphin could not press its lever and pester the swimmer at the same time; the behaviors are incompatible (and apparently lever-pressing was more reinforcing, because the swimmer harassment ceased). You are using this technique if you teach your dogs to lie in the living room doorway, at mealtimes, so they can't beg at the table.

• The time-out: Sometimes a dolphin does something really bad, such as showing aggression (swinging its head or teeth at the trainer's hand, for example). The instant this happens, you turn your back, snatch up your training props and fish bucket, and leave, for one full minute. That's the end of all the fun. The dolphin is apt to stick its head out of the water looking dismayed — "Hey, what'd I do?" In a few repetitions it learns to mind its manners.

Time-outs are used successfully by oceanarium trainers to eliminate aggression toward human swimmers, even in highly dominant animals such as adult male killer whales, and to control many other sorts of misbehavior; the technique is, however, distressing to the animals and must be used sparingly. (The use of reinforcement to reduce misbehavior is discussed more fully in my books on training.)

Mental attitudes

Using reinforcement is a lot of work for the trainer, because it forces you to think. Oh no, what pain! It's so much easier just to follow someone else's rules: If the dog makes a mess, rub his nose in it; if the dog doesn't heel, jerk the chain. However, in thinking out what you're going to reinforce, you'll be a better trainer. And the focus you will need, in order to perfect the timing of your reinforcements, makes training a thrill instead of a bore.

From the animal's standpoint, this kind of training is not a matter of learning how to stay out of trouble by doing what's required—a chore and nothing more. Instead, this kind of training gives the animal a chance to win, over and over, and also a chance to control at least part of its world. For example, from a dolphin's standpoint, once it has learned the meaning of the whistle, the training is not an exchange of commands and obedience, but a guessing game in which the dolphin tries to "discover" various ways to *make* the trainer blow that whistle. It is a game, with strict rules, but with equality on both sides. No wonder the dolphins enjoy their obedient trainers!

The effect of using the conditioned positive reinforcement is in fact *far more powerful* than merely giving free goodies could ever be. If you stop relying on control of misbehavior and start shaping good behavior with clear-cut conditioned signals for reinforcement, your dog will respect you in a new way; to your dog, you will *finally* be making sense.

A new venture begins...

The more I talked to and with trainers the more I realized that it was not enough to find out what the dog trainers didn't know about reinforcement (and, by extension, what the public in general—parents, teachers, and so on, didn't know) and explain it to them. I also needed to find some new ways to transfer the technology. For many people, a book is not enough.

One of my visitors in North Bend was a dog trainer named Gary Wilkes, who grasped the concept of reinforcement after watching me train our border terrier, Skookum, to spin in circles (using a porpoise whistle and the method described above.) Gary immediately put operant conditioning to use helping his clients with their problem pets. Gary assimilated and applied theoretical concepts with electrifying speed. He also had an knack for creating metaphors that made abstractions real. For example, when a pet owner began to understand that you should not reward every "Sit," just the especially good ones (quicker, or straighter) Gary might tell them, "There. You have just turned yourself from a coke machine into a slot machine." The concept, in my vocabulary, was the power of the variable schedule of reinforcement; Gary's image of the dog working better for an occasional jackpot than for a less interesting sure thing was far more likely to stick with the client.

A Californian training organization invited me to give another all-day program to dog trainers. I asked Gary if he'd like to participate. We were both going to be in San Francisco for a scientific meeting. The fee from the dog trainers would cover expenses, not only for us but for our spouses.

That first attempt at a *Don't Shoot the Dog!* Training Seminar taught us a lot. Team-teaching was a lot more fun than soloing, and much less wearing. Our styles and our experience were different, but complementary. Gary could shape behavior in the most unruly and unlikely dogs, in no time, while I could demonstrate any principle by shaping behavior in humans; and seeing shaping happen was truly informative to the audience. We had to learn to stop interrupting each other and treading on each other's punch lines, but we would pick up better theater techniques with a little practice.

We accepted another seminar invitation, in Toledo, Ohio, setting a higher fee. I brought a couple of boxes of *Lads Before the Wind* and *Don't Shoot the Dog!* and some videos of recent scientific presentations. Gary had designed and made some target sticks in his back room; he brought those, and a hundred extra clickers. Michele Wilkes set up a sales table, and in one day, to our astonishment, sold *thousands* of dollars worth of stuff to the dog trainers. Wow! This could be a business!

Top: Pat Brewington guides her young Percheron, James, toward a log to be hauled from the muddy paddock. Center: James balks, afraid of the mud. On Pat's command, "Pony's choice," he chooses a preferred path on the other side of the log. Below: Socializing after work.

Building bridges...

I had often wished that I could draw the attention of behavioral psychologists to *Don't Shoot the Dog!* Now I did the necessary research and sent off copies of *Don't Shoot the Dog!* and, just in case, *Lads Before the Wind,* to various psychology journals for possible review.

Back came a letter from Phil Hineline, the president of the Association for Behavior Analysis, the professional society for behavioral psychologists. He had been bowled over, really, by both books, which he didn't know existed. We found we had a lot to talk about. Phil sent me sheaves of brain-taxing papers and invited me to give a talk to the next national meeting of the Association for Behavior Analysis, in San Francisco.

I had already talked to two regional meetings of behavior analysts, with the hope of a) finding kindred spirits to discuss training theory with, and b) promoting *Don't Shoot the Dog!* Neither goal had been successful. The psychologists didn't seem to use or to think about operant conditioning the way dolphin trainers do. Most of what I had to say just seemed to bounce off, somehow. I knew we had common ground, but it was hard to locate.

Now I had Phil Hineline to help me find it. I agreed to speak, and also organized a panel of operant conditioning trainers, to help show ABA members what it is we actually do with their science. The panel would consist of myself, Gary Wilkes, Ingrid Kang Shallenberger, and Gary Priest, a killer whale trainer who had become the first Curator of Behavior at the San Diego Zoo.

Phil's plans for my talk gradually escalated from a twenty-minute paper into The President's Invited Scholar's Address, a major speech to all of the 1000 psychologists at the meeting. I had never written out a speech before, but I wrote out parts of this one, and practiced it, too. It felt important to me, and it turned out that it was.

CHAPTER TWENTY-TWO

If I Could Talk to the Animals... Reinforcement Interactions as Communication

by Karen Pryor[1]

Operant conditioning and dolphin training

Humans have been training animals for thousands of years. The model for our training behavior is our social behavior toward subordinates: "You do what I say, or else!" Most domestic animals are genetically adapted to respond with appropriate behavior, that is, moving away from spur, goad, or whip, without exhibiting either fight-or-flight reactions.

A new training system, based upon operant conditioning and positive reinforcers, is now enabling us to train animals unmanageable by traditional methods, and to establish new kinds of interactions and understanding. The sophisticated use of reinforcement began in the dolphin training community in the early 1960s. Two innovative scientists were, in my opinion, responsible for this event: Dr. Kenneth Norris, a biologist and then curator of Marineland of the Pacific, and Dr. William McLean, a civilian scientist working for the U.S. Navy. Both men

[1]Adapted from the President's Invited Scholar's Address, Association for Behavior Analysis Annual Convention, San Francisco, 1992.

wanted to study aspects of dolphin behavior and physiology; both hired students of B.F. Skinner to develop training programs for research. Dr. Norris also recommended behavioral psychologists to several brand-new oceanariums, including Sea World, and Sea Life Park in Hawaii. These behaviorist trainers—Ron Turner, Kent Burgess and Keller Breland, and the corps of trainers they taught, of whom I was one—changed the face of animal training, perhaps forever.

The dolphins we trained were, of course, a contributing factor, not because of their vaunted intelligence, but because they were unusually suitable subjects for the new approach. First, like most domestic animals, they are a social mammal, more given to interaction than to fight-or-flight responses; they are easy to "tame." Second, they are large animals that can ingest a lot of reinforcements before satiating; that gives the trainer room for error. Third, they live in the water; they can't get at us and we can't get at them. Thus one need not fear personal injury (always a possibility in the training of horses, for example), and perhaps more important, the traditional aversive control of harness, leash, and spur is not easily available. Finally, we had no tradition of training dolphins in captivity; there were no established methods, no wise old trainers telling us "You can't do that," or "You have to do it this way." We were free to innovate.

Marine mammal trainers—of whom there are now over 1000—differ from traditional trainers not only in their conscious use of operant conditioning, and their reliance on the conditioned positive reinforcer, but also in their aims: they do not aim at producing a finished product—a Seeing Eye dog, a race horse—but at developing a process through which the animal can keep on learning any behavior that it is physically and mentally capable of doing.

Social signaling

This kind of training is, in effect, a system of communication. First, operant conditioning allows the trainer to communicate to the animal, by means of the conditioned reinforcer, the specifics of any desired behavior. I can "tell" a dolphin not just the command, "Jump!" but how high, what shape of arc to make in the air, in what direction, how often, with what tail and head posture in the air. I can add cues for the jump, and a time limit; I can require that the jump be made in the company of specific other animals, and in synchrony. And I can establish that and many more criteria in perhaps fifteen or twenty ten-minute training sessions.

The experience can arouse states of affect in the animal, ranging from elation to frustration and distress. Trainers quickly learn to read the signals given inadvertently, such as increased respiration rates, to gauge the internal state of the animal. Meanwhile, the conditioned reinforcer becomes not just a signal that food is coming, but what Ogden Lindsley calls an "event marker," a source of information to the animal. That is reinforcing in itself. The animal seeks information. Since the trainer is the source of information, a new kind of communication soon arises: the animal begins to direct at the trainer the social signals it would direct toward a member of its own species, expressing its state of affect.

In dolphins this may range from a social greeting gesture, such as rolling partly on one side, to attempts to strike the trainer with the rostrum. Training with reinforcement leads to social signaling in other species, as well. At the National Zoo, I was watching a keeper shape the behavior, in a tiger, of getting into the moat and retrieving a floating toy to the shore. The wind came up, and blew the toy across the moat, near the place where the trainer was standing. The tiger looked up at its keeper with big yellow eyes and said, perfectly clearly, "Meow?" meaning, "Help," or "You get it for me!"

This interspecific social signaling is especially useful if one is working with a species in which the social signaling is not well understood. Ethologists learn about social behavior by observing animals interacting in the natural environment. The operant setting gives one a short cut. There is, for example, much speculation in the scientific literature about the role of aerial acrobatics in dolphins. Jumping and flipping about has been attributed to everything from sexual display to parasite removal. However, if I am bringing a dolphin's behavior under stimulus control, we may enter a period where the signal is absent and the behavior must be allowed to extinguish. Extinction breeds frustration; if, during this period, the animal leaps into the air and comes down sideways in such a way as to soak me from head to foot, I can say, based on a single event, that in some cases, at least, jumping has to do with aggression.

The transformation of the sea lions

This kind of social exchange does not constitute real socialization, of course. The polar bear that gives its keeper a play invitation through the bars would probably be glad to eat the keeper, were the bars not there. The reinforcement training system, however, can lead to genuine socialization, communication on an even richer level. A case I have witnessed myself is the transformation of the sea lions.

When I began working as a trainer in the 1960s, sea lions had been kept in captivity and trained, far longer than dolphins; even the Romans had a trained sea lion act. But they had a reputation. They were unfriendly; they bit; they did not like to be touched. They worked for food, but not willingly. One old circus trainer gave me this advice about sea lions: "They're bad-tempered; they're not too bright; they bite like hell. Keep 'em hungry and carry a two-by-four." Keeping them hungry, in order to force compliance, meant that most of the sea lions one saw in captivity in my childhood were small, compared to wild sea lions, and a bit thin. Also they were known as one of the commonly kept animals that apparently could not reproduce in captivity.

Then oceanariums began, for convenience usually, assigning the care of the sea lions to the dolphin trainers. Dolphin trainers, inevitably, and for convenience, began managing sea lions as they did dolphins: with conditioned reinforcers, conditioned stimuli, and shaped behavior. First, they stopped food depriving; with a conditioned reinforcer food deprivation is not needed. An immediate result was that the dispositions of the sea lions improved. Another result was that sea lions began to grow. An adult male in the wild may weigh over a thousand pounds, and stand much higher than a person; oceanaria began developing fully mature males.

Trainers began using shaping to reinforce what oceanariums call "husbandry" behavior—behavior that facilitates physical care and medication of the animal. This includes shaping the behavior of sitting still while being touched. Soon trainers discovered that they could use touch itself as a reinforcer. Indeed, in the wild, sea lions touch each other all the time, and lie around in congenial heaps on rocks. They in fact enjoy being touched, but only by human beings they like; those fellows with the two-by-fours were not popular.

Now, in less than three decades, sea lions have become incredibly trustworthy. I have seen trainers take huge male sea lions swimming in the ocean, without losing them to the wild; or out amongst the public, where children are allowed to touch them. Backstage at one oceanarium I was amused to see a group of sea lions basking in the sun, while their trainers, on their lunch break, lay around among them; one trainer had his back against a large, plump sea lion and his feet up on a smaller one, while reading a book and eating an apple. They are not pets—behavioral control is maintained carefully—but they are definitely social companions.

Furthermore, now that males are allowed to grow to full size, and females are well-nourished, sea lions reproduce abundantly in captivity. Sea lion pups are a glut on the market, and some institutions have resorted to IUDs.

Musical cats and dogs

Reinforcement training allows the trainer to communicate some rather sophisticated concepts; for example, by giving a jackpot, an unusually large reinforcement, one can signal that the behavior that has just been offered is especially wonderful. On the other hand, by giving a much smaller-than-normal amount one can signal that what the animal is doing is not quite right, or not quite up to par, very useful when an animal begins minimizing its effort deliberately. As trainer Ingrid Shallenberger puts it, with a "mini-reinforcement" you can indicate, "You know what you are doing wrong, and now you know that I know what you're up to, as well." Social signaling such as eye-contact can also be used or avoided deliberately, to convey information.

A corollary to this is that animals too can begin to use the behavior learned in reinforcement interactions to convey information outside the training situation. For example: I was having dinner with my cousin and his family, and after dinner, to amuse the children, I trained the cat to play the piano. That is, I used a word, and bits of ham, to shape the behavior of sitting on the piano bench and plinking at the keys with one paw.

After that one evening, no one ever asked the cat to do this again, nor did the cat offer the behavior. Two years later, my cousin called to say that the previous night, after they had gone to bed, they were wakened by sounds from the piano downstairs in the living room. The livingroom door had been shut to conserve heat. On investigation, my cousin found the cat sitting on the piano bench. Normally the cat slept upstairs in the bedroom. It had accidentally been left behind in the livingroom. When, one presumes, the normal responses of meowing and perhaps scratching at the door didn't work, the cat offered a learned behavior to ask, not for food, this time, but for its preferred sleeping place; and the effort was a success.

My colleague, Gary Wilkes, was coaching a family with several dogs, including a dachshund. While training the larger dogs he noticed the dachshund moving backwards in a comical way reminiscent of Michael Jackson's "moonwalk" dance step; so he reinforced the behavior. On a subsequent visit, one of the larger dogs had a bone. The dachshund, wanting the bone, "moonwalked" at the other dog. This, of course, did not work.

What we have here, however, is neither the world's smartest cat nor the world's dumbest dachshund, but two examples of animals using the learned behavior they have been given, as a communicative tool.

Pony's choice

The reinforcement exchange can proceed easily to the abstract level; one example is my own work, and that of others, in teaching creativity, that is, innovative behavior. Other fascinating outcomes of this rich learning circumstance include the ape-language experiments, Irene Pepperberg's remarkable parrot experiments, Louis Herman's work with artificial languages with dolphins, and Ron Schusterman's studies of abstract learning in sea lions. However, it doesn't require a phenomenally intelligent species to carry the game to an abstract level. Here is an example involving a horse.

My neighbor and fellow trainer Pat Brewington bought a Percheron colt. Pat weighs about 100 pounds, and Percherons are enormous. There was no way Pat could train this horse by whips, chains, and force, the traditional method. She trained the horse, James, with a clicker and carrots, and was able in this way to shape him to carry a rider, wear a harness, and so on: the traditional tasks. Pat also plays games with her horses: for example, there is a place in our woods where one of the trails forks; both ways lead home, and they are of equal length. Sometimes Pat asks her horse to go left, sometimes right; and sometimes she loosens the reins and says "Pony's choice," and lets the horse decide. Sometimes they go left, and sometimes right. The same game can be played with a log in the trail; they can go around it, they can jump over it, or Pat can say "Pony's choice" and let the horse decide; again, sometimes her horses decide one way and sometimes the other.

I was invited to watch James having his first lesson of actually hauling logs, sections of cut-down trees, the ultimate work for which he had been purchased. Having trained horses myself, I knew that the first experience of something new is especially important. Horses learn fast. If something goes wrong, they never forget it; I have personally built behaviors into young horses, by accident, that created problems for years.

Now, in James' paddock, a big tree had been felled and cut up into ten-foot-long logs. Pat walked behind the horse, guiding him with long reins and voice commands. James would be driven alongside the log until he was in front of it, so that the attachment point on his harness, the singletree, could be hooked onto a chain on the log. Then he would be urged forward, to drag the heavy log to the log pile outside the paddock.

The first log went fine. At the second log, James walked quietly beside the log and actually parked himself in the proper place to be hooked up. The third log, however, was further back in the paddock, toward the base of the tree, in a muddy spot. Pat tried to drive James alongside the log, and he balked, ears laid back: "I don't want to go there."

This was a dangerous moment. Were the young horse to learn, now, that balking "works," he might well balk forever. A traditional trainer would instantly have laid into him with voice and whip to force him forward. Pat doesn't own a whip. What was she going to do?

What she did was slacken the reins and say "Pony's choice." James looked at the mud, ears forward, and then he carefully stepped *over* the log and came forward along the other side. He thought the ground looked safer on the far side of the log. Pat had developed a cue, in a very young horse, that meant, "Use your own judgment." Horses do have some judgment, particularly about where to put their feet; the folk expression, "horse sense," is not wrong. Now, for the rest of James' life, Pat has a horse of whom she can say, "I'm not sure what's the best way to pull this log, left or right—let's ask James."

Applications and implications

Are these just anecdotes about animals? I think not; these are descriptions of observations. And unfashionable as it may be at present, observation and description are as much a part of science as hypothesis and experiment. Every one of these examples was elicited by an operant conditioning exchange. Therefore, they are replicable, and thus available to hypothesis and experimentation. Some of these interchanges, even those that have become standard training devices, are not represented in the behavioral literature, and should be fruitful sources for investigation.

What if one works with people, not animals? Are these trainerly interactions irrelevant? I think not. The sophistication and richness of communication that reinforcement training develops in animals can apply in human situations as well. Suppose, for example, that you are working with someone who can't communicate verbally: who is too old, or too young, or too damaged. Would it not be useful to be able to shape the behavior of confident cooperation in, say, necessary medical procedures, even without words?

Or, suppose you would like to communicate with somebody who doesn't take instructions from you, and whose behavior is not governed by your rules—such as your boss. The operant trainer looks at these problems in a fresh way. Recently I heard behavior analysts talking about a wonderful program in the hospital where they worked. The patients were responding beautifully; the psychologists wished to expand the program. For that they needed more money. The hospital administrator, however, was not interested; one staff member commented ruefully, "All he cares about is clean halls." Of course the administrator may have reasons of his own for needing clean halls, such as Congressional inspection tours coming up; but the behaviorists were discouraged.

A dolphin trainer, however, would respond differently: "He wants clean halls? Got him!" That is, if you have something the animal wants, all you have to do is make it contingent on what you want, and you can get the desired behavior.

Gary Priest, head trainer at the San Diego Zoo and Wild Animal Park, told me that he was watching Carl Sagan, the astronomer, on television. Dr. Sagan was speculating about meeting another life form, in space. How would we ever communicate with them, if they were totally alien? Priest, of course, being a reinforcement trainer, saw no problem. If they are alive, they need an energy source. If they need energy sources, you can reinforce them. And reinforcement exchanges rapidly lead to communication. We don't have to struggle to imagine a way to communicate, even with little green extragalactics—we already have one.

Building more bridges...

This speech was well received, and our panel discussion was a success. We made video tapes of both presentations—pretty rough and ready, even though we used professional cameramen, but popular nonetheless, it turned out. We gave clickers to the overflow crowd at our trainers' panel. For the rest of the conference the halls and atrium of the San Francisco Hyatt ricocheted with clicks as people reinforced each others' behavior.

In the next two years, animal trainers flooded into the Association for Behavior Analysis. Faculty members and clinical psychologists reached out to the trainers, and a new, merged set of information began to grow. We operant practitioners wanted access to the theoreticians; now we had it.

The trainers and psychologists formed a Special Interest Group, the Trainers Forum, within ABA. Some immediate results included: using dolphin-training techniques for gentler medical care of institutionalized, developmentally disabled children; joint research programs between zoos and universities; dog trainers going after their Ph.D.s; new Ph.D.s becoming pet counselors instead of professors; and a good deal more.

I began, at last, to have some feeling for what it might be that these erudite folks did *not* know. It was the other side of the coin from the dog trainers. Applied operant conditioning, and particularly the rich possibilities of the conditioned reinforcer, have been in development by us trainers for thirty years; but the academic community had no access to that information. They had no idea how it related to their work and interests; and they were beset with problems in their work that could have been avoided through better *applied* understanding. Indeed, the conditioned reinforcer, to me the key concept in applied operant technology, had fallen so far into disrepute that it is actually missing from some current textbooks. Now we are bridging that gap.

It is still true, in my opinion, that the discipline of behavioral psychology tends to ignore useful behavioral information from the biologists (and vice versa, of course.) But I no longer see the gap as being just between ethology and behaviorism. The laws Skinner and his colleagues identified are real laws, not statistical trends or opinions but real, like the laws of gravity; and worthy of continued research as pure science. But from my viewpoint there seems to be a gap between understanding the laws, and finding out what to do with them.

The circumstances seem similar, to me, to the early decades of the computer explosion. Behavior analysts are comparable to the folks who figured out how to build computers. Those scientists thought the computers were for doing math (hence the name); they never envisioned spreadsheets and word processing and Tetris and Myst and Reader Rabbit and whatever else lies in store for us. In operant conditioning, the scientists have developed theories and techniques for analyzing behavior; but they were not entirely aware that they had also provided fantastic new tools, not really for "controlling" behavior as so many people have feared, but for creating behavior including wonderful new things such as communicating horses and sociable fish. The trainers, you might say, are inventing the software and finding fantastic and splendid things to do with it.

Transforming the universe...

At the request of ABA, I had arranged for professional video taping of our panel and my speech, to be made available by ABA members for classroom instruction. Jon and I went home and edited videos, designed labels, and arranged for duplication. It was these videos which the dog trainers had snapped up in Toledo. We didn't realize it right away but thanks to ABA, we were now a video production company.

I used to joke that lecturing was a form of theater— "a low form, like juggling in the streets." The *Don't Shoot the Dog!* Training Seminars that Gary Wilkes and I were doing now turned into two days of real theater. We charged a big fee. We required experienced sponsoring groups and a theater-type setting, with a stage and major audio-visual support. We used color, sound, movement, stories, jokes, games, live animals, video clips, interactive groups, anything we could think up to make our information accessible. Our aim was to transfer the technology of operant conditioning, in two days, in such a way that people could truly go home and use it.

Jon took over the direction and principal camera work, and videotaped the seminars. From 100 hours of tape we created two one-hour videos on shaping and stimulus control. The videos turned out to be good teaching tools, as well as fun. Especially popular was the ultra-closeup footage of our trained fish, a cichlid I trained, in a tank on our kitchen counter, to swim through a hoop on command.

An ABA member, James Kopp, Ph.D., wrote a delightful Study Guide to *Don't Shoot the Dog,* which we published. Gary wrote a book. I put this book together. As we developed more videos and products, the seminars became lucrative. We limited ourselves to four or five a year; by 1994 we were booked into 1997.

As a dolphin trainer I had taught no more than a few individuals to be good trainers. Now we were transferring the technology to thousands of people at a clip. It wasn't just me, anymore, or my book, or a few dolphin trainers, or the occasional gifted individual, who was learning and teaching operant conditioning: it was a community.

Nowhere was this community more accessible, and more visible, than on the Internet. Everything that happens on Internet is communal, in a sense. The following is a post I made in late 1994 to a group consisting of about six hundred obedience trainers, some of whom were graduates of our seminars. The post was paired with an analysis by a behavioral professor whom I knew only from the Internet.

This communal Post is not an essay, and makes perhaps dull reading for a non-trainer; but it clarified operant conditioning for a huge number of people. Anything you post becomes public property; this pair of Posts have been reprinted in seven publications that I know of, and probably many more.

Fourteen-year-old Sarah Klapstein and one of her well-trained llamas, Dasha, an adult female.

CHAPTER TWENTY-THREE

The Llama Post

Hi, everyone: this is a posting from Karen Pryor.

Friday I participated in such a delightful training session that I'd like to share it with you. Perhaps the events described here will clear up some confusion or answer some of the questions I see floating by on the List, about training with a clicker and treats instead of correction.

The animal in question is not an "obedience breed" and the behaviors are not strictly speaking obedience behaviors, although they are the equivalent. If you can accept that, you will see that the events described here are the same as in any training task, be it a go out or broad jump or whatever, and be the animal a border collie or a basenji.

We were visiting 14-year-old Sarah Klapstein, who raises llamas, in order to videotape her targeting, clicker-trained two-year-old female, for our upcoming Click&Treat™ Basics video. (This sweet animal trusts her target — a manila envelope—so much that last month they took her to a nursing home to visit Alzheimer's patients, and actually got her in and out of the elevator without a problem.) We set up an obstacle course: a 3x6 piece of carpeting, laid on the lawn; a one-foot-high jump; and a plank raised two inches off the ground to be a "bridge." Dasha obediently negotiated all these obstacles, both for a target, click, and treat, and also on the lead line with no target or treats.

After Dasha, Sarah decided to show me her six-month-old female, Dakota: she had trained this baby to lead by the traditional method—tug on halter till animal moves, then release and praise: but she "loves to go forward, loves the obstacles." So she haltered Dakota and led her out of the pasture: an unusually pretty baby, cocoa colored with a black and white face (this baby is presently about the size of a deer.)

Jon (cameraman, my husband) asked us to stay by the gate for a little while, so to pass the time I asked if Dakota had any experience of the clicker. None. "We don't really know that she eats grain yet, she isn't weaned."

I had the clicker and feed bowl, so I clicked. The baby jumped, scared. I held out the feed bowl. She was shy of that, too. Now is when the trainer feels, "this isn't going to work." But you push that thought away, and continue. I gave Sarah a little feed in her hand, and she offered it to the baby. Dakota took a taste. Hmm. She took another taste, bigger. I asked Sarah to shut her hand, and then open it and give the baby just one taste, each time I clicked. I clicked, the hand opened, the baby ate. I clicked, the baby nosed her person's hand, the hand opened, the baby ate vigorously.

Now the baby seemed to be enthusiastic about this; she crowded into Sarah. This is definitely not behavior to be encouraged in hoofed stock. Sarah said "back!" and pushed on the leadline, physically moving the baby back a step. I asked her to do that again, first making sure she had more feed in her free hand. "Back!" Push on halter rope. Baby resists, then moves front feet, then left hind. Click! Feed. We did this again. One hind step, click. Then again, only this time the baby started moving backward when Sarah leaned toward her, before the rope was taut. Click, stop, feed. Twice more—lean, step, click treat. Now the baby's tail end was about at the fence corner, so we tried Forward (pull on halter) one step, C&T then back one step, C&T. Then Jon asked us to move to the lawn, so Sarah led the baby forward, having to tug on the halter to get her started. I clicked on the fourth step (clicking front feet for forward motion.) After eating her treat the baby moved forward on a loose line the instant Sarah stepped forward, and so I clicked the first step.

That was the first part of the training. Sarah led the baby to the lawn, brushed her, played with her a little (chatting, petting) and then led her across the obstacles.

Dakota did this: as she saw each obstacle, she went into full protest-position, front legs dug in, llama leaning backward, long neck stretched out, head on ground, total resistance to the lead line. Very funny to see. Sarah stood her ground, maintained pressure on the leadline, and by and by the llama capitulated, and accompanied the person over the obstacle. Three obstacles, three balks, three finally-give-ins.

Obviously, if you keep this up day after day, eventually the balking will cease and the llama will go anywhere with you including over weird things, right? The pressure on the halter is negative reinforcement, capitulation puts an end to the neg. thing, and the llama becomes habituated to carpeting, jumps, and bridges—that is, the fear wears off by getting used to the stimulus. Of course, introduce a *tunnel*, say, and it's back to negative reinforcement and habituation. By this means it would take not weeks, but months, even years, to get a llama to go trustingly through ANY and ALL new places with you. Most people don't bother, right?

I wanted to show Sarah a faster way. So, again, she handled the llama and the feed, I handled the clicker. Walk toward the carpet. I clicked *before* Dakota balked, while she was still moving. Now she eats with gusto, by the way—suddenly this food has become prized.....

Go around, line up again facing carpet, walk toward the carpet, and again I clicked before she balked. Stop right there, click and treat.

Now Sarah continues, and the baby doesn't balk but walks right onto the carpet.. I click when front feet are on the carpet, and Sarah stops instantly and feeds her right there . They circle around, and I held my breath but Dakota moved right onto the carpet without balking and got her next click for stepping onto the carpet and got her treat on the carpet. The next one, I withheld until she'd crossed the carpet and was clear of it on the other side. Then we did that twice more. By now she is going around the carpet, up to it, and across it, on a loose line, "heeling," as it were, right next to Sarah's right side (the correct side for horses and llamas.) Then I let a pass go "unclicked," and the llama stops on the far side of the carpet, not balking, just "Hey! I thought I got clicked here!" and then goes nicely one more time, gets her click on the carpet.

Now we decided to reverse direction; crossing the carpet north to south is not the same as crossing the carpet south to north, and this is true of dogs, too, by the way. (In fact it's not a bad idea to throw in some east and west, with retrieves, go outs, etc. Thank you, Mark Lipsitt.)

I give the clicker to Sarah. She circles Dakota the other way, clicks her once on the carpet. On the second circle, the llama throws a balk while going around the end of the carpet, resisting the new direction? Who knows. Sarah waits her out, and then lines her up and leads her across the carpet, clicks her on the carpet. Once more; the llama makes a good, quick, confident circle and cross, and Sarah clicks her on the far side of the carpet. Fantastic.

We decided to move on to the jump. Has this llama now got the picture? I guess so. She approaches the jump with no hesitation, jumps over tidily, gets her click in mid-air, treat on the ground, turns around and does it the other way, click in mid air, treat after.

We decided that was so easy we might try the bridge. Here we ran into trouble. The bridge wobbles, and the behavior is really a chain—i.e. one must get on the plank, take several steps down its length without letting any foot step off onto the grass, and then get off the end of the plank. Not a good task to end a session with; we try a little—then we level the bridge so it doesn't wobble, and try again—four clicks are spent on various configurations of legs on and off the plank. We can see the baby is getting tired, and no wonder. Probably full, too.

We decide to save planks for another day; we've done a lot. Still, it is always advisable to end on a high note, with something that can be reinforced, so we agree to try one more jump. The llama seems to say "Yay, this is SO easy, I KNOW how to get a click this way!" our baby's ears go up and she and Sarah almost trot, and the llama BOUNDS over the jump with room to spare, gets a click in mid-air, stops on the far side and collects her treat. Sarah turns Dakota back out to pasture with her Mom, after praising and petting and snuggling her.

The whole training session took a bit over ten minutes and used up approximately 30 clicks. (Probably more feed than that baby ever ate before at one time, by the way; and we have almost all of it on video so I went over it before writing this for you). Almost every click was useful and moved us forward. Look what this baby learned:

Click means treat. I guess I like this treat pretty well. Lots, in fact. Moving makes the click happen. Moving backwards makes the click. Moving forward. Moving where my Person moves. Moving on a loose line gets clicked.

Moving over rugs gets clicked. Sometimes you have to go further. Sometimes you have to go twice. It doesn't matter which direction you are going in, moving over rugs works, gets clicks to happen.

Moving over jumps gets clicked too. Either direction.

There are various ways to make this person click.

I like this. I want to do it again.

Look, also, at what a forgiving system this is; the fact that we had some unproductive and confusing clicks on the bridge did not mean that we can expect trouble with the bridge tomorrow. We just don't have bridge behavior yet; period. We quit on that one while still retaining all the learning listed above, plus the beginnings of a motivated, trusting, and confident subject. Take note, however: had we started muscling the llama over the bridge, we might have undone all this enjoyment.

Now, without analyzing this further, I leave you with it as an example. It was a good, fast, smooth training session, even though the subject is a) very immature, b) fearful by nature, c) surely no brighter than the average dog? My guess, anyway. I hope that shows you a little about what the conditioned reinforcer can do for you.

See, the point is NOT that *no* force was used; the llama was on a halter, after all. In fact once, when Sarah and I were figuring out what to do next, the llama, feeling itself at liberty, headed right for Sarah's mother's perennial border at the edge of the lawn, (which must look to a llama like a splendid buffet table loaded with delicacies—phlox, dahlias, roses, yum!) Sarah said "No!" and jerked twice on the halter, and the llama confined herself to long looks at the flowers after that.

The point also is *not* that we were nice to the llama and praised it and loved it and that it trusts and loves Sarah. That and fifty cents will get you on the subway, as we used to say in New York.

The point is not that the clicker in itself is special. The clicker is just a signal—useful in that it is different from other sounds (which human words are not) and useful in that it conveys NO EMOTION, only the honest, simple message, "Bingo: you win." (Actually, with llamas I would prefer to use a whistle, which frees up your hands. Sarah had a time of it, with both hands full of lead rope plus feed plus clicker. Somehow, though, people have associations with whistles, but the clicker is something new, and so everyone wants a clicker—llama people too)

The point is that using real reinforcement—food in this case— and a conditioned signal to tell the animal what activity or movement has just paid off for it—allows you to shape behavior incredibly fast, in spite of fear, previous conditioning, or whatever, provided you get the information to the animal in a timely way, and keep raising your goals steadily, but by small steps.

Since food is your "message," you have to stop before the animal gets full, and it is wise to schedule sessions when the animal is hungry, i.e. before meal time, not after. Also the food should be in as small a portion as feasible; Sarah at first held out whole handfuls, which take a long time to eat and fill a baby up fast; we cut to "just one mouthful and the hand closes again."

Once the behavior is accomplished, you don't have to click and treat every time; on the next lesson, I would plan to use most of my reinforcements for the bridge, and give a cursory click or two for rugs and jumps, and then expect to braid jumping and rug crossing into sequences before and after bridges. But that is up to Sarah. She knows how to do this now.

The Parsing of the Llama Post

Hi, folks. Karen Pryor here. If you are interested in this kind of stuff, read on. If not, now is the time to hit the Delete button!

After I posted the description of a training session, now known as the "llama post," I asked Jon Krueger if he would be willing to "parse" the session, in terms of operant conditioning: that is, to explain the various events in terms of the principles those events illustrate.

Jon Krueger quotes the "llama post:"

> I had the clicker and feed bowl, so I clicked. The baby jumped, scared. I held out the feed bowl. She was shy of that, too. Now is when the trainer feels, "this isn't going to work." But you push that thought away, and continue. [The >marks indicate that the following is a quote from a previous post. KP]

Right—your intuition is that the animal is going to avoid the whole situation! But intuitions about behavior sometimes are accurate, sometimes not, and sometimes miss critical distinctions. Here, you don't yet know what is aversive to this animal in this situation yet. So you find out. You try a different reinforcer delivery:

> I gave Sarah a little feed in her hand, and she offered it to the baby. Dakota took a taste. Hmm. She took another taste, bigger.

And you discover: the feed bowl is aversive, but not the food itself. Which is surprising (why should the feed bowl be aversive?)—but no problem; you have a reinforcer now. So now you have everything you need to set up the conditioned reinforcer:

—a primary reinforcer
—a (more or less) neutral stimulus that's easy to deliver and precise in time (the clicker)
—control over timing of delivery of each

> I asked Sarah to shut her hand, and then open it and give the baby just one taste, each time I clicked. I clicked, the hand opened, the baby ate. I clicked, the baby nosed her person's hand, the hand opened, the baby ate vigorously.

You arrange it so the click sets the occasion for food delivery. Food is available only following the click. The click becomes a positive discriminative stimulus for arrival of food itself. Over repetitions, the click acquires the power to reinforce; the click becomes a conditioned reinforcer.

Which of course is a good thing. "More immediate consequences can be provided for the response than is possible with the food itself.... this kind of immediate reinforcement...is essential to produce rapid operant conditioning" (Millenson and Leslie, 1979).

> *Now the baby seemed to be enthusiastic about this; she crowded into Sarah. This is definitely not behavior to be encouraged in hoofed stock. Sarah said "Back!" and pushed on the leadline, physically moving the baby back a step.*

Which shows both a behavior that we want to reduce, and how we sometimes try to reduce it: physical restraint and/or aversive consequences. But there is another way, bringing it under stimulus control using nonaversive contingencies:

> *I asked her to do that again, first making sure she had more feed in her free hand. "Back!" Push on halter rope. Baby resists, then moves front feet, then left hind. Click! Feed. We did this again. One hind step, click. Then again, only this time the baby started moving backward when Sarah leaned toward her, before the rope was taut.*

Already, on the third trial, behavior changes. Rapid operant conditioning. Here as elsewhere, probably impossible without use of the conditioned reinforcer.

But we don't stop there:

> *Click, stop, feed. Twice more—lean, step, click treat. Now the baby's tail end was about at the fence corner, so we tried Forward (pull on halter) 1 step, C&T then back one step, C&T.*

So six trials "back", then one trial "forward", then a seventh trial "back." We want reliability, so we practice it.

> *Then Jon [my husband, who was videotaping the session—KP] asked us to move to the lawn, so Sarah led the baby forward, having to tug on the halter to get her started. I clicked on the fourth step (clicking front feet for forward motion.) After eating her treat the baby moved forward on a loose line the instant Sarah stepped forward, and so I clicked the first step.*

Again, rapid operant conditioning: first or second trial.

> *That was the first part of the training. Sarah led the baby to the lawn, brushed her, played with her a little (chatting, petting) and then led her across the obstacles.*

Socialization; truly outside the scope of the present examples.

> *Dakota did this: as she saw each obstacle, she went into full protest-position, front legs dug in, llama leaning backward, long neck stretched out, head on ground, total resistance to the lead line. Very funny to see. Sarah stood her ground, maintained pressure on the leadline, and by and by the llama capitulated.*

Classic avoidance. Dakota avoids both the obstacles and the pressure on the leadline. Her behavior is the result of which she avoids more at any given moment. These methods can be used to control behavior. The animal learns to avoid getting pushed and pulled on the leadline. But there is a cost:

> *Obviously, if you keep this up day after day, eventually the balking will cease and the llama will go anywhere with you including over weird things, right? The pressure on the halter is negative reinforcement*

Yes.

> *capitulation puts an end to the neg. thing*

Yes. Withdrawal of the stimulus (pressure on the leadline) is made contingent on the behavior (going over the obstacle); behavior increases.

> *and the llama becomes habituated to carpeting, jumps, and bridges — that is, the fear wears off by getting used to the stimulus. Of course, introduce a *tunnel*, say, and it's back to negative reinforcement and habituation.*

Habituation is a phenomenon in respondent behavior, not operant: reflex strength decreases after repeated elicitations. Novel stimuli elicit an orienting response, and other responses which interfere with the desired behavior. Over repeated exposure, carpeting, jumps, and bridges lose their novelty.

However, this merely reduces task difficulty. It doesn't do much for getting a particular result. It doesn't generalize well; the tunnel etc. will be novel again. Progress will be slow. One of the problems is the aversive methods we're using.

What we're doing is, we give the llama a choice of two aversive outcomes, getting pulled or crossing carpeting etc. We jack up the aversiveness of one of them; the llama comes to choose the less aversive one. What has the llama learned? To avoid the more aversive one. Not the same as to choose the indicated one. This difference applies when we introduce a new outcome; the llama will choose it only after we make all other outcomes more aversive, and/or their novelty wears off. Neither efficient, nor generalizable, nor fun.

> *By this means it would take not weeks, but months, even years, to get a llama to go trustingly through ANY and ALL new places with you. Most people don't bother, right?*

Yep. The trainer's own behavior extinguishes.

> *I wanted to show Sarah a faster way. So, again, she handled the llama and the feed, I handled the clicker. Walk toward the carpet. I clicked *before* Dakota balked, while she was still moving.*

Reinforce the desired behavior. Set up the contingency: do this, get reinforcer. Reinforce the available behavior, what she already emits. Don't wait until another behavior (balking) has been emitted! Timing is critical; reinforce the desired behavior, not the next behavior.

> *Now she eats with gusto, by the way—suddenly this food has become prized.....*

A relationship between the primary and conditioned reinforcer has developed. However, characterizing each feature of the relationship isn't of interest here. It's relevant that the conditioned reinforcer hasn't taken away from the usual consumption of the primary reinforcer.

> *Go around, line up again facing carpet, walk toward the carpet, and again I clicked before she balked. Stop right there, click and treat.*

Reinforcing the behavior closest to the final outcome.

> *Now Sara continues, and the baby doesn't balk but walks right onto the carpet. I click when front feet are on the carpet, and Sarah stops instantly and feeds her right there. They circle around, and I held my breath but Dakota moved right onto the carpet without balking and got her next click for stepping onto the carpet and got her treat on the carpet. The next one, I withheld until she'd crossed the carpet and was clear of it on the other side.*

Shaping. Plain and simple. We shift the population of responses toward the final outcome.

> Then we did that twice more.

Then I let a pass go "unclicked," and the llama stops on the far side of the carpet, not balking, just "Hey! I thought I got clicked here!" and then goes nicely one more time, gets her click on the carpet.

Gradual shift of criterion. Note that we did three trials at the lower criterion of approaching and moving into the carpet, before increasing criterion to crossing the carpet.

> Now we decided to reverse direction;

Generalization. We want the spoken command to control the behavior, not the particular situation and incidental cues. So we make the spoken command the only thing in common to all reinforced trials. This requires that we vary the other things: location, orientation, order of presentation, and so on.

> I give the clicker to Sarah. She circles Dakota the other way, clicks her once on the carpet. On the second circle, the llama throws a balk while going around the end of the carpet, resisting the new direction? Who knows.

We get random variation from trial to trial. Over the session, however, we see measurable progress.

> Sarah waits her out, and then lines her up and leads her across the carpet, clicks her on the carpet. Once more; the llama makes a good, quick, confident circle and cross, and Sarah clicks her on the far side of the carpet. Fantastic.

Sometimes very gratifying progress :-) Imagine instead blaming the animal, saying it "knows what to do but refuses to do it", thereby giving ourselves permission to punish ("correct") non-compliance. We'd risk less rapid training, poorer generalization, and extinction of behavior. Probably wouldn't get:

> We decided to move on to the jump. Has this llama now got the picture? I guess so. She approaches the jump with no hesitation, jumps over tidily, gets her click in mid-air, treat on the ground, turns around and does it the other way, click in mid air, treat after.

Nice generalization, speed of acquisition, reliability.

> We decided that was so easy we might try the bridge. Here we ran into trouble. The bridge wobbles

And there may be "hardwired" aversion to stepping on unstable surfaces, which may also be species specific. We could overcome this, but it's not efficient to start that way. Better to establish the desired behavior first, and later work up to getting it on unstable surfaces if desired.

> *and the behavior is really a chain—i.e. one must get on the plank, take several steps down its length without letting any foot step off onto the grass, and then get off the end of the plank.*

Right, and we're likely to lose the whole chain if we lose the first step.

> *Not a good task to end a session with; we try a little—then we level the bridge so it doesn't wobble, and try again—four clicks are spent on various configurations of legs on and off the plank. We can see the baby is getting tired, and no wonder. Probably full, too.*

Keeping food treats small only goes so far toward extending session length! Beyond satiation there's just fatigue. The animal's tired.

> *We decide to save planks for another day; we've done a lot. Still, it is always advisable to end on a high note, with something that can be reinforced*

Right; we don't want to establish the pattern that sessions get worse the longer they last. That would be a good way to train the animal to attempt to terminate the session early!

> *so we agree to try one more jump. The llama seems to say "yay, this is so easy, I know how to get a click this way!"*

Beautiful demonstration of why and how nonaversive methods do better. We could have gotten the jump with aversive methods; they do work. It would probably have taken longer, generalized less well, and been less fun for animal and trainer. And when it was done, we probably wouldn't have had this active cooperation, easy and fun, and useful to develop further, fine tune, use in other situations and tasks.

Useful to consider what would have been learned if we'd used leash pulling and aversive methods.

I get pulled. I don't like that. I can avoid that. Guess I'll avoid it. But there are so many things to avoid. I don't know what to avoid all the time. Maybe sometimes I just can avoid the bad stuff. Better give up. Until once again there's something bad enough and clearly avoidable enough. Then I'll avoid that. Not much else to do.

Another set of terms to express it is, it's easier to pull behavior than to push it. That way the animal learns to perform, not to avoid.

And the technical terms have their merits too. Aversive stimuli give us avoidance and escape behavior. Setting up aversive contingencies lets us arrange it so the only way to avoid or escape from the stimulus is to emit a certain behavior. We can maintain that behavior and put it under stimulus control (the voice commands) by designing the right contingencies. It's not that this doesn't work; it does. But the cost is high: slower acquisition, poorer generalization, less fine control, less resistance to extinction. Nonaversive contingencies get the results we want without those costs. They're also more fun. They're also more robust, more resistant to extinction:

> *Look, also, at what a forgiving system this is; the fact that we had some unproductive and confusing clicks on the bridge did not mean that we can expect trouble with the bridge tomorrow. Take note, however: had we started muscling the llama over the bridge, we might have undone all this enjoyment.*

If everything becomes aversive, or "seems" that way, we might say the animal has become confused. In fact we've set up a confusing situation. However, no trainer is perfect; we'll all set up unintended variation in the situation from time to time. If we're using aversive methods, we risk extinction; the animal just "shuts down". If we're using nonaversive methods, the risk is lower; the animal's behavior may get some unintended variability, which we can deal with in the next session.

I hope that shows you a little about what the conditioned reinforcer can do for you.

I think so.

> *See, the point is not that *no* force was used; the llama was on a halter, after all.*

> *The point also is *not* that we were nice to the llama and praised it and loved it and that it trusts and loves Sarah. That and fifty cents will get you on the subway, as we used to say in New York.*

Right—it's great, but no substitute for results. But the good news is you can have both, by using the right contingencies, secondary reinforcers, getting criteria right, shaping, setting the situation right, getting stimulus control, and so on.

> *The point is that using real reinforcement—food in this case— and a conditioned signal to tell the animal what activity or movement has just paid off for it—allows you to shape behavior incredibly fast, in spite of fear, previous conditioning, or whatever, provided you get the information to the animal in a timely way, and keep raising your goals steadily, but by small steps.*

Yep. Criterion shift is one of the toughest things for the trainer to learn. (I suspect that good timing is what separates a poor trainer from a good trainer, but good criterion shift may be what separates an excellent trainer from a good trainer.)

> *Since food is your "message," you have to stop before the animal gets full, and it is wise to schedule sessions when the animal is hungry, i.e. before meal time, not after. Also the food should be in as small a portion as feasible; Sarah at first held out whole handfuls, which take a long time to eat and fill a baby up fast; we cut to "just one mouthful and the hand closes again."*

Right. Most people's intuition—mine anyway—is that that bigger treats train better. Turns out it's not so. It's incredible how small a treat makes a perfectly good reinforcer, and of course gives you more trials before it satiates.

(In fact, you can push up the ratio of an FR schedule until the animal spends more calories working to get the reinforcer than it gets back from the food value of the reinforcer! The animal actually loses weight over the session. Which provides an example of how "reinforcer" is more accurate than "reward." In most senses of "reward", that animal isn't getting rewarded, it's losing! But its behavior has been shaped, is being reinforced, and we find that's sufficient to maintain the behavior at a high level.)

> *Once the behavior is accomplished, you don't have to click and treat every time; on the next lesson, I would plan to use most of my reinforcements for the bridge, and give a cursory click or two for rugs and jumps, and then expect to braid jumping and rug crossing into sequences before and after bridges.*

We raise each criterion gently and steadily. When I'm training, what I'm thinking of almost all the time is, what's the next criterion shift?

> *But that is up to Sarah. She knows how to do this now.*

— Jon

Communal creativity...

By 1994, many psychology professors had adopted *Don't Shoot the Dog!* as a textbook. The sales figures tripled. Gary Wilkes was writing a syndicated newspaper column and a magazine column on pet behavior, both of which won national awards. Our company, Sunshine Books, which came into being to reprint *Lads Before the Wind*, now published several titles, including this one. We were a corporation now too, with a 1-800 number, a mail order catalog, rapidly increasing sales, and half a dozen videos in the pipeline.

The big developments in training, however, were coming not from us, but from the new training community. The people who came to our seminars tended to be pretty smart. They might be there because they loved training or competing with dogs, but in their day jobs they were airplane pilots, trial lawyers, teachers, stockbrokers, veterinarians, computer experts (lots of those) or cops. As we got better at transferring the technology, more and more of these people began going home and using it. We got the phone calls and letters and e-mail, not, as in the beginning, consisting of pleas for help and descriptions of things "not working" but, now, full of excited stories of near-magical breakthroughs. The dog trainers spoke of it, jokingly, in religious terms: they came to a seminar and "had an epiphany." They were "born-again" trainers.

Bright minds with new tools: it was exciting. And they were not just training dogs. Practicing on dogs, they were then carrying their insights into their highschool "incorrigible" classes; to their offices, to their staffs, to their families. They were teaching the applications to dozens and in some cases hundreds of other people. And telling us about it. The development of practical applications of reinforcement theory had become a group enterprise.

I think the culture and times arrived at a point where these concepts were ripe for acceptance. Ten years ago, when *Don't Shoot the Dog!* first came out, the ideas in it contradicted conventional wisdom. Many people who read it gave up on it in confusion. Last week, in contrast, I heard from a veterinarian who gives *Don't Shoot the Dog!* to each new client. I thought three quarters of them would put it away unread; but not at all. She reports that they read it at a gulp, stay up all night reading it, and come back to her with discussions of how it applies to their whole lives. The Zeitgeist has changed; this information, with or without us, is going mainstream.

B.F. Skinner put the tools in our hands. We dolphin trainers worked out how to use them; now, a widening circle of creative trainers are thinking up what to do with them. They are not solely the educators, the academics, the researchers. They are cops, customs officers, dog show exhibitors, trainers of dogs for the deaf, hunters, hobbyists, physical therapists, coaches, teachers, parents—people who have a real need for *establishing behavior:* not talking about it, not analyzing it, but getting the behavior they want.

Like any new technology, where we are going with it cannot yet be foreseen, nor is it up to any one person to say. But we are definitely off and running!

Bibliography

The following is a chronological, annotated list of publications by Karen Pryor. Entries republished in whole or in part in On Behavior *are indicated by a bullet.*

Pryor, Karen W., 1963. *Nursing Your Baby,* Harper & Row, New York. Revised edition, 1973, Pocket Books, New York. Portuguese translation, 1974, Summus Editoriale, Ltda., Sao Paulo, Brazil.
    A guide for mothers, on breastfeeding. Physiology, behavior, nature of human milk, month-by-month guidelines.

———1963. They teach the joys of breast feeding. *Readers Digest,* June. Abridged chapter of *Nursing your Baby,* on La Leche League, a nursing mothers' organization.

Pryor, T.A., K.W. Pryor and K.S. Norris, 1965. Observations of a pygmy killer whale (*Feresa attenuata* Gray) from Hawaii. *J. Mammal.* 465:450.

Pryor, K.W., 1967. Sea Life Park and the Oceanic Institute. *Curator,* Vol. III, American Museum of Natural History, N.Y.
    Problems and benefits of running a public attraction and a research facility interactively.

Pryor, K.W., R. Haag, and J. O'Reilly, 1967. Deutero-learning in a rough-toothed porpoise (*Steno bredanensis*). Naval Ordinance Test Station *Technical Paper* #42370, NOTS China Lake.
    Initial government report on the "creative porpoise" experiment (Pryor *et al.,* 1969); emphasis is on higher-order learning.

Lang, T.G., and K. W. Pryor, 1967. Hydrodynamic performance of porpoises (*Stenella attenuata*). *Science* 152:531-533.
    Spotted dolphins pacing a mechanical lure reached maximum speeds of 21.5 kts.

•Pryor, K.W., R. Haag, and J. O'Reilly, 1969. The creative porpoise: training for novel behavior. *J. Exper. Anal. Behavior* 12:653. *Ibid.*, 1971, in *An Introduction to Experimental Design in Psychology: A Case Approach*, H.H. Johnson and R. L. Solso, Eds., Harper & Row, New York. *Ibid.*, 1984. In: *Research and Issues in Psychology*, P.W. Kennedy, Ed., Kendall Hunt, Toronto.

   Shaping response to the criterion, "Only new responses will be reinforced."

Pryor, K., 1969. Behavior modification: the porpoise caper. *Psychology Today*, Dec.

   Informal article based on Pryor, Haag and O'Reilly 1967.

Pryor, K., and I. Kang, 1969. The red-footed booby colony (*Sula sula rubripes*) at Sea Life Park. *International Zoo Yearbook*, Zoological Society, London.

   Seabird husbandry; breeding of free-flying birds; genesis of nest-site specificity in males.

Pryor, K., 1970. Wild things in the wild sea. In: *Alive in the Wild*, V.H. Catalane, Ed., Prentice-Hall, NJ.

   Description of the behavior of rough-toothed dolphins (*Steno bredanensis*).

Norris, K.S., and K.W. Pryor, 1970. A tagging method for small cetaceans. *J. Mammalogy* 51:609.

   Marking a dolphin with a deer ear tag through the dorsal fin. It proved temporary.

Pryor, K., 1971. The puzzling porpoise. *Friends*, Sept.
   Chat about dolphins.

•——1974. Learning and behavior in whales and porpoises. *Die Naturwissenschaften* 6):412.

   A survey of behavior and training of several species of cetaceans at Sea Life Park. .

——1975a. *Lads Before the Wind: Adventures in Porpoise Training.* Introduction by Konrad Lorenz, Harper & Row, New York. German translation, 1977, Albert Miller Verlag. Russian translation, 1981, MAP, Moscow. Republished 1989 as *Lads Before the Wind: Diary of a Dolphin Trainer*, Sunshine Books, North Bend, WA.

   First-hand account of developing an oceanarium, Sea Life Park, in Hawaii, and of learning applied operant conditioning while training dolphins (also otters, birds, other animals) for public shows and research. Includes vignettes of Konrad Lorenz, B.F. Skinner, and Gregory Bateson.

——1975b. The oculostatic machine. *Honolulu*, Aug.
   Phil Wylie plays a joke on nosy small town neighbors.

• ———1976. Symphony conductors would make good porpoise trainers. *Psychology Today*, Nov.
Conductors' rehearsal techniques follow the principles of operant conditioning.

• ———1978. The wicked winds of New York. *New York*, April.
Buildings generate wind effects that influence our behavior.

Pryor, K., and K.S. Norris, 1978. The tuna-porpoise problem: behavioral aspects. *Oceanus*, May. *Ibid.*, 1980. In: *Wildlife: The Science Supplement, Grolier's Encyclopedia*, Grolier's, Inc.
Behavior of tuna and dolphins in associated schools and implications for the tuna fishery.

• Pryor, K., 1979. Phil Wylie, dancin' man. *Prime Time*, Sept.
Shaping the behavior of ballroom dancing.

Pryor, K., and I. Kang, 1979. (Abstract). Social behavior and school structure in spotter porpoise (*Stenella attenuata*) during purse seining for tuna. In: *Proceedings*, Third Conference on the Biology of Marine Mammals.
See Pryor and Shallenberger, 1991.

Bratten, D., W. Ikehara, K. Pryor, P. Vergne, and J. DeBeer, 1979. The tuna-porpoise problem: Dedicated Vessel Research Program. Summary of research results from the second leg of the third cruise of the dedicated vessel. *Southwest Fisheries Center Administrative Report* #LJ-79-13.

Pryor, K., 1980.Abstract. A methodology for ethological study of marine mammals. In: *Proceedings*, 60th Annual Meeting, Am. Soc. Mammal.
Modifications of Altmann's Focal Animal Sampling system, for underwater work.

Pryor, K, and I. Kang, 1980. Social behavior and school structure in spinner and spotter porpoises (*Stenella attenuata* and *S. longirostris*) during purse seining for tuna. *Southwest Fisheries Center Administrative Report* #LJ-80-11C.
Preliminary report; includes behavioral dictionary. *See* Pryor and Shallenberger 1991.

Defran, R.H., and K. Pryor, 1980. Social behavior and training of eleven species of cetaceans in captivity. In: *Cetacean Behavior: Mechanisms and Functions*, L. Herman, Ed., Wiley-Interscience, New York.
Statistical analysis of a survey of experienced trainers reveals behavioral differences and similarities across dolphin and small whale species. "Trainability" is also assessed.

• Pryor, K., 1981a. The rhino likes violets. *Psychology Today*, April.
Operant conditioning as a zoo management tool.

• ———1981b. Why porpoise trainers are not dolphin lovers: real and false communication in the operant setting. *Annals of the New York Academy of Science,* 304:137-143.

  1) Common misconceptions about dolphin behavior. 2) Social and learned communication in operant conditioning interactions.

———1982. The marine mammals and birds of Georges Bank. In: *Georges Bank: Past, Present, and Future of a Marine Environment.* G. McLeod and J.H. Prescott, Eds., Westview Press, Boulder, CO.

  The principal species of sea birds and marine mammals that live in or pass through the Georges Bank fishing grounds off New England; possible effects of oil spills on these populations.

———1984a. *Don't Shoot the Dog! How to Improve Yourself and Others through Behavioral Training,* Simon and Schuster, New York. Republished in 1985 as *Don't Shoot the Dog! The New Art of Teaching and Training.* Bantam Books, New York.

  An introduction to the practical applications of positive reinforcement, in the home, school, and workplace; with pets and children; and in learning sports and skills.

• ———1984b. My favorite joke. *The Sun,* Summer.

• ———1984c. The power of praise. *Readers Digest,* July.

  Abridged from and based on *Don't Shoot the Dog!* (Pryor, 1984a).

Lindbergh, J.M., and K. Pryor, 1984. Six ways to lose money in aquaculture. *Aquaculture,* May/June.

Pryor, K., 1985. *How to Teach Your Dog to Play Frisbee.* Simon & Schuster, New York.

  Behavioral approach to the sport. Does not include teaching yourself to play Frisbee.

• ———1986a. Why punishment doesn't work. *Mothering,* Summer. Alternatives to punishment for managing the behavior of children.

———1986b. Non-acoustic communicative behavior of the great whales: origins, comparisons, and implications for management. In *The Behavior of Whales,* Report of the International Whaling Commission, Special Issue 8: 84.

  Contribution to a symposium on whale behavior, based on personal observation and a survey of whale field researchers.

———1987a. Behavioral conditioning. In: *Acoustical Deterrents in Marine Mammal Conflicts with Fisheries,* B.R. Mate and J.T. Harvey, Eds. Oregon Sea Grant Publication No. ORSU-W-86-001.

Uncorrected transcript of oral presentation on effects of conditioning associated with the use of noisemakers intended to protect fish from sea lions.

• ———1987b. Reinforcement training as a method of interspecies communication. In: *Dolphin Behavior and Cognition: A Comparative Approach,* R. Schusterman, J.A. Thomas, and F.G. Wood, Eds. Erlbaum Associates, Hillsdale, New Jersey.

Using operant conditioning to investigate animal behavior, intelligence, and communication. A contribution to an Office of Naval Research symposium on dolphin cognition.

———1990a. Fishermen take cues from dolphins in rare partnership. *Los Angeles Times,* September 14.

Account of Laguna dolphins based on Pryor *et al.,* 1990.

———1990b. Abstract: A family business: three generations of related wild dolphins (*Tursiops truncatus*) in a dolphin-human cooperative mullet fishery in Brazil. *Proceedings,* Fifth International Theriological Congress, Rome, Italy.

Relatedness of Laguna dolphins. See Pryor *et al.,* 1990.

———1990c. Abstract: Traditional methods of identifying individuals in a dolphin-human fishing cooperative in Laguna, Brazil. *Proceedings,* 8th Biennial Conference, Society for Marine Mammalogy.

Fishermen recognize individual dolphins by natural marks, man-made marks, and behavior.

• Pryor, K., J.M. Lindbergh, S. Lindbergh and R. Milano, 1990. A dolphin-human fishing cooperative in Brazil. *Marine Mammal Science* 6:1.

Observations of long-standing daily cooperative fishing for mullet, involving resident fishermen and a resident group of dolphins.

Pryor, K., Ed., 1990. *Crunch and Des: Classic Stories of Salt Water Fishing,* by Philip Wylie. Introduction by Karen Wylie Pryor. Lyons & Burford, NY.

A selection of 25 short stories by Pryor's father, mostly published in the *Saturday Evening Post* between 1935 and 1950.

• Pryor, K., 1991a. The domestic dolphin. In: *Dolphin Societies: Discoveries and Puzzles,* K. Pryor and K.S. Norris, Eds., University of California Press, Berkeley.

The dolphin as the newest candidate in the history of domestication of large mammals.

• ———1991b. Mortal remains. looking at dead animals. In: *Dolphin Societies: Discoveries and Puzzles,* K. Pryor and K.S. Norris, Eds., University of California Press, Berkeley.

Value of museum collections to future cetacean researchers.

• ———1991c. Non-acoustic communication in small cetaceans: glance, touch, position, gesture and bubbling. In: *Sensory Abilities of Cetaceans*, J.A. Thomas and R.A. Kastelein, Eds., Plenum Press, NY.

———1991d. Report of the workshop on cetacean sensory systems. In: *Sensory Abilities of Cetaceans*, J.A. Thomas and R.A. Kastelein, Eds., Plenum Press, NY.

> Summary by Pryor, chairman, of working group presentations and discussions by Louis Herman, Paul Nachtigall, Vladimir Kuznetzov, and others, with emphasis on new findings, especially in the areas of cetacean vision and chemoreception.

• Pryor, K., and K.S. Norris, 1991. Some thoughts on grandmothers. Introduction. Afterword. In: *Dolphin Societies: Discoveries and Puzzles*, K. Pryor and K.S. Norris, Eds., University of California Press, Berkeley.

> Discussion of possible roles of post-reproductive female pilot whales; comments on marine mammal science and politics.

• Pryor, K., and Gale Pryor, 1991. *Nursing Your Baby: Updated for the 90s.* Pocket Books, New York.

> A joint revision of Pryor 1963. Includes a new chapter on working and nursing, and new sections on lactation consultants, neonatal jaundice, pollutants, good and bad research, milk cytology, milk banks, nutrition, innate behavior in parents and infants, learning and reinforcement, and more.

• Pryor, K., and I. Shallenberger, 1991. School structure in spotted dolphins (*Stenella attenuata)* in the tuna purse seine fishery in the Eastern tropical Pacific. In *Dolphin Societies: Discoveries and Puzzles*, K. Pryor and K.S. Norris, Eds., University of California Press, Berkeley.

> Final report on observations made during dives in the net of a tuna purse seiner while surrounding schools of tuna and dolphins.

Pryor, K., and K. S. Norris, Eds. 1991. *Dolphin Societies: Discoveries and Puzzles.* University of California Press, Berkeley.

> Thirteen original field, captive and laboratory studies by various authors, giving insights into cetacean social organization and behavior; with essays and comment by the editors. Emphasis on wide variety of research approaches to a single problem, and on interdependence of captive and wild studies.

• Pryor, K., 1992a. If I could talk to the animals: Reinforcement interactions as communication. President's Invited Scholar's Address, Association for Behavior Analysis. In: Pryor, 1995.

How principles and techniques of both behavior analysis and ethology can contribute to training and social interactions and communication between species.

• ———1992b. A dog and a dolphin. *Dogs in Canada Annual.*

How operant conditioning, as used to train dolphins, can apply to the training of dogs.

———1992c. Indexing: a new burden for authors. *Authors Guild Bulletin,* Winter.

On finding and working with an indexer.

———1992d. Photographing nursing mothers. *Journal of Human Lactation,* March.

On getting attractive and natural photographs of mothers and nursing babies.

Pryor, K., 1993. Abstract. The dolphin-human fishing cooperative in Laguna, Brazil: cognitive aspects. *Proceedings,* 10th Biennial Conference, Society for Marine Mammalogy.

Learned behavior and possible reinforcement-based origins of this example of cooperative fishing.

• Pryor, K., 1994. A gathering of birds. In: *The Nature of Nature,* William Shore, Ed. Harcourt Brace, NY.

Investigative behavior in multi-species bird communities on two continents.

• Pryor, K., and J. Krueger, 1994. The Llama Post and the Parsing of the Llama Post. *The Clicker Journal,* Nov./Dec.

Account of a training session using a conditioned reinforcer, followed by technical interpretation of the conditioning taking place.

Pryor, K., 1995. *On Behavior: Essays and Research.* Sunshine Books, North Bend, WA.

Twenty-three chapters on behavior, with comments by the author. Introduction by Ellen P. Reese.

• ———1995. The dreadful dowager dolphin. In: *On Behavior: Essays and Research.* Sunshine Books, North Bend, WA.

Operant conditioning interactions during training sessions with a sophisticated dolphin.

• ———1995. When the President Appointed Me. In: *On Behavior: Essays and Research.* Sunshine Books, North Bend, WA.

Bureaucratic misadventures upon being appointed to the federal Marine Mammal Commission.

Videos

Pryor, K., 1992. *If I Could Talk to the Animals: Reinforcement interactions as communication*. President's Invited Scholar's Address, Association for Behavior Analysis. Video, 60 minutes. Sunshine Books, North Bend, WA.

How principles and techniques of both behavior analysis and ethology can contribute to training and social interactions and communication between species.

Pryor, K., and G. Wilkes, 1992. *Click! Using the conditioned reinforcer*. VHS or PAL. 55 min. Sunshine Books, North Bend, WA.

Highlights of a one-day seminar on operant conditioning for dog trainers, Toledo, Ohio, 1992.

Pryor, K., G. Priest, I. Kang Shallenberger, and G. Wilkes, 1992. *Supertraining: how modern animal trainers are using operant conditioning*. 120 min. video. Sunshine Books, North Bend, WA.

A panel presentation to the annual conference of the Association for Behavior Analysis, San Francisco, 1992, by four operant conditioning trainers.

Pryor, K., J.M. Lindbergh, and G. Wilkes, 1993. *Shaping, building behavior with positive reinforcement*. 55 min. video. Sunshine Books, North Bend, WA.

Highlights of three two-day *Don't Shoot the Dog!* seminars for dog trainers: Part I.

Pryor, K., J.M. Lindbergh, and G. Wilkes, 1994. *Sit! Clap! Furbish! Bringing behavior under stimulus control*. 55 min. video. Sunshine Books, North Bend, WA.

Highlights of three two-day *Don't Shoot the Dog!* seminars for dog trainers: Part II.

Index

Note: Illustration locations are listed in **bold** type

395